A PRAYER FOR THE NATION

*A*lmighty God, You have given us this good land for our heritage.

We humbly ask You that we may always prove ourselves a people mindful of Your favor and glad to do Your will. Bless our land with honorable endeavor, sound learning and pure manners.

Save us from violence, discord, and confusion, from pride and arrogance, and from every evil way. Defend our liberties and fashion into one united people the multitude brought here out of many nations and tongues.

Endow with the Spirit of Wisdom those to whom in Your Name we entrust the authority of Government that there may be justice and peace at home, and that through obedience to Your law we may show forth Your praise among the nations on earth.

In time of prosperity fill our hearts with thankfulness, and in the days of trouble do not allow our trust in You to fail. Amen.

—President Thomas Jefferson
Washington, DC
March 4, 1801

DEDICATION

I want to dedicate this book to my husband, Bud, for his incredible patience and encouragement through the whole process of rewriting; to my daughter, Linda, for her input, editing, and encouragement; to my granddaughter Summer, for editing and taking her precious time to care; to my sons, Joe and Ron, and to my brothers, Glover and Gail, who recently departed from us; to the encouragement of my friends; to the memory of my dad, who did much writing about his life when younger, but could never get his stories published. And to my great friend Julie Parmeter, who is writing her book, *The Forgotten Men and Women*, giving me encouragement to finish mine.

ACKNOWLEDGMENTS

I wish to acknowledge the person who inspired me to write this book, Kevin McGary, with the Frederick Douglass Foundation, who is the author of the book, *Instanity*. Mr. McGary helped me to decide that I had to do something to encourage more people to vote, to help people to realize that each of us can make a difference. To my husband, Bud, who is so supportive and patient; to my daughter, Linda, for her help in editing suggestions and highlights; to my granddaughter, Summer, for her support and editing skills; to all of those who write blogs, books, and op-ed columns that enlighten us. A special thank-you to my late brother, Glover Shipp, who had published over forty books, for his help in general book-writing procedures; and to our kitty, CC, whose lap she sits on has been replaced by the laptop computer. Below is a photo of my kitty helping me write my book.

Most of all, I want to thank all of those to whom we owe our eternal freedom, from our founders, to those who have fought in our wars and given their lives so that we have the freedom to write, speak up, and to vote. And to our Heavenly Father who gives us the ability to think, form words, and understanding in order to write.

About the Author:

Twila Le Page Hughes has written this book, partly as history as she lived it, during the Depression and WWII as it happened, taking us from the early 1900s and from the Great Depression in the '30s, World War II, Korea, and the Vietnam Wars, being very interested in what was happening around her. She feels that our country has been going downhill with the leftist movement dragging us more and more to the left, with the PC and socialist movements, and as she is a capitalist, so she feels strongly that capitalism is far superior to that of socialism. She will write on the differences.

Twila Le Page-Hughes is an author of *Don't Hit the Iceberg, Vote!* And this current book is partly a rewrite of the history section of that book, plus the first *Your Vote Matters* that was never completely published due to that publisher going under.

She feels very strongly about voting as an honor and privilege and that everyone should vote. She has served in several precincts working with elections.

Twila has been active in politics, being an officer and program chair in the Republican Women

Federated in South Bay, Los Angeles, area. She helps promote local candidates and works on their campaigns. She is a bona fide conservative.

She is a writer of articles and columns, having written for two newspapers in Northern Arizona and the state newspaper, with articles in the *Arizona Magazine*. She served on the Governor's Advisory Board for Energy Regulations for the State of Arizona. She promoted solar energy in the '70s. She started her own magazine, which was called at first *Solar Energy Greenhouse*, then later *Solar Living*. She was later editor and publisher of a national RV travel magazine, *The SMART Traveler*. She has been a contributor to westernjournalism.com and to *Citizens Journal*, an online newspaper, and writes articles for newsletters. She is an artist and painted the cover of her last book and paints acrylic landscapes for her grandkids as her legacy. She is active in her church, playing prelude music on Sundays and hymns and teaching senior Bible classes.

Twila has a big family—with three grown children and one adopted daughter, twelve grandchildren and one adopted grandson, twenty-two great-grandkids, and three adopted greats. She keeps accumulating those to love. She is now married to her present husband, Bud, and lives in Southern California with him and her kitty, CC.

CONTENTS

PROLOGUE

Why Does Your Vote Matter?

Freedom is never more than one generation away.
—President Ronald Reagan

S o many people say "I don't vote" as if that is a great thing to boast about, a sort of smug mantle. If you do not vote, it is automatically a vote for the other side that you may not really want. If you do not vote, the consequences of who gets into office may make a 360-degree turn of how your life will become, economically, freedom-wise, and enjoying personal liberties. I am not just talking about presidential elections, but voting at the local level for decent people to run our cities, counties, and states and who represents us in Congress.

Ninety-three million Americans, or 40 percent, did not vote in the last general election. What a sad thought. How can they not remember the hundreds of thousands who have given their lives in the wars for peace for our country and not honor that by becoming an informed voter who understands what a privilege it is to vote. But to become educated so that the vote matters.

Some elections have hung by a thread with only a few hundred votes difference. Some have had to have a recount, as they were so close. When George W. Bush and Al Gore, former vice president under Clinton, were running in 2000, Al Gore, when he learned Bush was slightly ahead, insisted on a recount of two of the most Democratic counties in Florida. It ended up with what many considered a dishonest recount. Ballots that had been discarded, because of incompletely punched holes in the ballots, with hanging chads, were taken out and reexamined, with the Democrats deciding what they believed the intention of that voter was. In the end, when the questionable votes were added in, Bush still won by 537 out of 6 million ballots. (See why each vote counts.)

Many liberals say George W. Bush stole the election or that the Supreme Court gave it to him. Gore and his supporters asked the counts to be redone because of what they said were the many voting problems. This counting of hanging chads (to try to determine the voter's intent if the chad was pushed out enough or not) had never been done in other precincts or even in the precincts in question, and the Democratic officials had never complained before. The Florida Supreme Court ordered another recount of the disputed ballots. The Bush team asked the Supreme Court for their opinion, and they said that Florida law did not explain how officials should judge the ballot. They found in a 7–2 vote that the situation in Florida was unconstitutional because there were different standards in the state, and only two counties' votes, which just happened to be predominantly Democrats, were being counted.

If you are NOT concerned about the direction of our country and think it is going just fine, then stop reading right here. If you are feeling scared about the direction of this country and yet feeling helpless or thinking there is nothing you or we can do, then read on. There is something we _can_ do.

The US was founded on the principles of government _of the people_, _by the people_, and _for the people._

At first, it worked pretty well, but as we moved from farms to villages, to cities, things began to break down. We started depending on government bureaucracies to solve problems for us. We stopped taking responsibility for fixing these problems for ourselves. Churches used to help the poor. But few do now.

We will have to take part in government once again, teach our children, through example, to take part in government at all levels. We are responsible for what does happens or does not happen. It starts at home and goes all the way up to Washington. We no longer can count on government to fix it all.

Voting is the most powerful thing that we can do in order to affect change in our country. That, along with personal involvement, in many different areas, such as taking the time to work toward creating a better community or working in local or national government, is what gives us a government of the people and by the people. We shouldn't wait around for the government to help us. We can become creative and help ourselves, by getting involved, by working to fix problems locally, such as potholes in the roads or roadside cleaning in our small towns. Volunteers and churches used to help the poor and hungry. Now, we expect the government to take care of them. One of the candidates for president said it well, "The government welfare programs should be a trampoline, not a hammock."

The liberals are very generous with government money, or other people's money, to help the poor and redistribute the wealth, but their actual personal giving is far less than Republicans.

How can we help? We can register people to vote outside our churches after services. Or at local fairs or festivals. At universities. We can walk precincts, contribute to campaigns, help in campaign headquarters, help at the party headquarters, organize fund-raisers, and to help get good people in office at all levels of government, and then we can do all in our power to remind our elected officials that they are there to represent the people and not themselves.

This book goes into the history of our country from the early 1900s, when the socialist movement started and grew, through the wars, court decisions, major laws, and presidents. It is written for those who have not experienced much history, especially the young, so that they can better understand the not-so-subtle march toward progressive, liberal, non-Christian control of our country.

I have also chosen to write this in a possible last attempt to get the Great Silent Majority—those 65 million persons of faith that did not vote in the last general election—to just vote. We can no longer afford to be silent or not be involved. "Speak *up now or forever hold your peace!*"

Believe it or not, we are on the tipping edge right now so that there may be only one last chance to rescue our Ship of State and turn it around by voting in November 2020, for a continuation of our course that President Trump has commenced, to make America Great Again. He was on his way with it with the economy growing and well, until the worldwide coronavirus hitting here in late February, with a few cases at first, then by March, the orders to quarantine and lockdown stopped everything in its track and the country has been locked down for months, with many not working and stores and businesses closed.

It will take strong leadership to make changes or to continue the great course that Trump was doing until the virus took hold and everyone who cares about our country to be involved in some form. Unfortunately, too many are either ill-informed or not aware of the great danger our country has been in, heading on a course, full speed ahead, toward the "sinking" of our "ship." No one thought the *Titanic* could sink, yet one iceberg and man's pride was all it took to send it to the bottom to Davy Jones' locker. What can each of us do to restore our country, to keep it from sinking into history's pile of other mighty countries, who all fell from within?

We are hearing and/or reading the news, but too often it is biased or slanted and we are not getting what is really happening. We are the most uninformed generation in the history of our country and yet we have access to information and news 24/7. In researching this book, as I learned more and more of what is really going on, I gained an understanding of why it is so imperative for everyone to become informed and vote. There have been plans in place for many years, regarding the demise of our country. World treaties from the UN have been underway with Obama's reign to take over our country and our sovereignty. All it would have taken was to be ratified by the Senate, and <u>it is not reversible from then on</u>. The possible result is the UN will own our country, our military, our land, our seas, our property, our energy, our bodies, and take away all small arms. We were just this close to losing all to the UN control. All we need is a Democrat Senate and president to sign a treaty, and this all could happen.

Right now, by executive order, our last president could have shut down the electrical grid in the country and the internet, and all he had to do is to declare an emergency to do this. This has been quietly maneuvered during Obama's last seven years. There are worldwide, very wealthy entities since the early 1900s that have been actively working to destroy our country, which is not known by many. They, which include the leftist socialist liberals, the elite rich in the world, the statists, the new world order advocates, are getting real close now and do not want to give up the power and control they have worked so hard to achieve.

This next election will be possibly the most fraudulent, the most chaotic, the most controversial, and the most important one in our history. The desire is to turn our country into a socialist state, like the European state, which is in bad straits now. We have an avowed Socialist running for president and gaining in the polls and primaries, something no one would have ever thought could take place in our country. Socialism, communism, fascism have never worked, yet the progressive liberal socialists think they can do it differently and will obtain the individual power and control they want by the elimination of religion; by the elimination of the elderly, the elimination of the family, the elimination of those not yet born; by seducing the young to think <u>their</u> way; by invoking national single payer health care and its control by the government; by dishonoring our Constitution; by developing their own police to arrest all dissidents and eliminating it by the use of Sharia law or laws invoked by the United Nations. The Progressive Socialist movement in America seeks to bring America to its knees, so the benevolent Progressive leaders can take control of our government.

And our presumptive nominee for the Democratic Party is also a socialist. He takes money from Wall Street yet denounces it. He wants world government. He will continue in the same path as Obama has done, and that is why Obama wants him in, to continue his legacy.

Socialism is far closer than most realize and could happen very soon. Think dictator control, as in Russia, as in Cuba, as in China, as was in Nazi Germany. It all starts with gradual takeover of power and control by the government, to include you owning any private property or any rights as an individual.

Do you realize just how close we are to socialism? Witness this coronavirus thing where governors can mandate that we have to stay in our homes, can't go to work, a complete economy shutdown. That is sheer pure socialism at its best. Government control, folks. And this was just the appetizer, folks. Watch for the next crisis with the main course that is to come. There will be another man-made emergency, climate crisis, or whatever, and they will declare another shutdown or goodness knows what, and we will be in complete socialism mode again, only for longer and far worse. They got a taste of control and just how easily we could be controlled. Should President Trump not win, we would have pure socialism, as Biden will be using socialist methods. Should Trump win, and I believe he will, then we have four more years with his building up the economy through capitalism values, then after that in 2024, the liberals, leftists will be frothing at the mouth to have a socialist, probably a woman, to be president, so then they can evoke pure socialism. And immediately undo all the good in eight years that Trump will have accomplished.

With the millennials and Generation X raised in the schools under brainwashing that socialism is good, they will vote whomever in. That's when we will probably lose our country as it will all be downhill after that. We will lose our property rights, they will raid our bank accounts and our IRAs, and we will be locked in for sure. The only jobs will be working for the government in factories, etc. All controlled by the government, even our food. Sure, there will be socialized medicine for all for free, but to get anything done that's needed, forget it.

This country was built on capitalism and freedom, making it the most successful and richest country ever to be in the world. Do we really want to lose this? Then vote for freedom, vote for capitalism. Not only for president, but for Congress, state governments, and local governments. It's crucial, folks! Socialism or (Communism) has never worked anywhere it's been tried. In fact, it makes any country go backward. Think Venezuela, China, Russia, Cuba. Are they any better off? How many millions have been killed under communism and fascism, such as dissidents, etc.?

And this past Obama regime wanted Sharia Law invoked here. Indeed, many schools are teaching the Koran as the only accepted religion and won't allow the Bible in the schools. The liberals want Sharia Law. Women lost all rights under Sharia Law. Little do the young, especially, know they will lose all rights under Sharia Law. Under Sharia, women own nothing, must go out only with a male family member, and can be raped, and no abortions, no property owned. Their husbands can beat them all they want. And the men can have more than one wife. Yet our dumb elite and the mainstream press seem to want this kind of rule? A speaker that spoke before my Republican women's club is a pastor who was a former Muslim. He preaches to Muslims and converts many to Christianity. He said our biggest worry is that the Muslims plan to take over the evil America.

We can only hope and pray that we can still turn our Ship of State around so that this election will help continue it in an even better direction, away from the dangerous shoals of socialism, control, and corruption that has been creeping upon us for decades.

DEFINITION OF
A VETERAN

A veteran—whether active duty, retired, National Guard, or reserve—is someone who, at one point in his or her life, wrote a blank check made payable to the United States of America for an amount of "up to and including his life."

Introduction

Why vote? We hear people say, "I didn't vote as didn't know who to vote for" or proudly announce, "I've never voted." *Every single vote counts.* Many close races are only won by a few votes. So therefore, *your vote counts*. Besides, it is a privilege to vote in this country. In some countries, they are told for whom they have to vote and are made to vote. Voting is your personal statement of your wishes. It is the most important task we can do now, not only for us, but for our children and their children. You can't complain if you don't vote. I have never missed voting in an election.

We are living in dangerous times, folks—especially for conservatives and Christians. Not only here in the US, but the freedom of the Western Hemisphere is at stake now, with liberal socialists (communists) movements trying to take over each country. Venezuela, to name one.

This next election of November 2020 is probably one of the most critical elections of our time, not only to choose to re-elect our president and to choose Congress, as we need a Republican Congress, both houses, but also to decide which direction our country is going in now.

The Socialist route, where the government controls all, or the more conservative free route, with a free economy. Capitalism versus socialism. Ensuing chapters will point out the pitfalls of a socialist agenda and explain the benefits of a capitalist country. I will explain the differences between the Democratic Socialists and the Conservative Republicans.

Generally, the party in power loses control of Congress in the midterms, and we did lose control of the House in 2018. The Senate remained in control of the Republicans. However, as we see in the sham of impeachment hearings going on now for three years, that the control of the House has been very harmful to our freedom and way of government. They simply want to undo the 2016 election that was voted in constitutionally. Thankfully, President Trump was recently acquitted of pending impeachment by the Senate, so we can hopefully get back to the business of running the government. It will be important to have a Republican House of Representatives in 2020, in order to better balance the economy and aid President Trump who will be re-elected.

We will talk about the meaning of life and why that is so important to our well-being. And like President Trump—personally or not, he has kept many of his promises—the economy was booming as (well, it was until that manufactured coronavirus stopped everything in its track) and we are all the better for it. It also affects the economy of the world as the way the United States goes, so goes the rest of the world. Since the economy was so good going into this lockdown, then it will probably come roaring back fairly soon. With Trump, the businessman, who understands investments and finances and business growth, it will go good again. My bet is on him. A businessman understands the economy far better than a politician.

In this book, which is a rewrite somewhat of my first book published in 2012: *Our Ship of State, Don't Hit the Iceberg! VOTE!* (out of print), I will go into some history of our country from the early 1900s, and how I lived through some of it, to now and also how the Socialists gained ground in our country as well as all over the world. But mainly to inform you on what is happening now. I have been personally interested in politics since I was about age eleven, during World War II, when I heard President Roosevelt's speeches on the radio (for the younger, that was before TV) and saw the news on *Movietone* news at the Saturday matinee movies. I also read the newspapers of the time and the magazines, such as *Time* and *Saturday Evening Post* magazines. I remember Roosevelt on the radio saying right after the Japanese bombed Pearl Harbor on December 7, 1941. "This will be a day that will go down in infamy!"

I will attempt to go into the history of politics—some from my own experience living in some of that era and remembering the events, and in part, the general history of the times, leading up to the present, and how politics and certain persons have made a real difference.

Many of the reasons for people not voting or even worse, voting completely but were simply not informed, and don't understand the importance of voting or the issues and candidates.

Timeline (1)

World War I
Woodrow Wilson
Federal Reserve Board War Ends 1919
Progressive Party 1912 Taft Appoints 1913
INDUSTRIAL AGE Theodore Roosevelt
1885 TO 1919

Timeline (2)

World War II
FDR New Deal Depression Ends
Women's Suffrage 1932 Atom Bomb Japan
Prohibition '20s Depression War Ends 1945

<u>1929 Market Crash</u> Voting Rights 1919
Great Depression Starts

Timeline (3)

<u>Supreme Court Decisions</u>
Prayer in Schools
Our Ship of State

<u>Peaceful '50s</u>
Super Highways
<u>Post–WWII</u> TV
GI home, GI Bill
GI Loans Schools
Demographic Changes

<u>United Nations Formed</u>
1945
<u>End WWII 1945</u>
Roosevelt Dies

Timeline (4)

<u>'90s Clinton Challenges</u>
GOP Takes Over Congress
<u>'80s Age of Peace</u>
Lewinsky Scandal
Welfare Reform
<u>Vietnam War</u> '70s Pres. Reagan Economy/Surplus
Protests, Civil Rights Prosperity
MLK, RFK Killed

Ends Cold War
Bible Reading-Schools
<u>'60s Cold War</u>
Unrest, Vietnam War
NASA, JFK Killed, Cuba Missiles
Sup Ct. - *Roe vs. Wade*/Prayer in Schools

Timeline (5)

<u>2000s George W. Bush</u>
9/11 Changed All
Wars on Terrorism
Katrina
'08 Demos Run Congress
Start of Housing Meltdown
Supreme Court Change
Obama, 2008–2016 Election of 2012 Romney vs. Obama
Stimulus, Economy Melts Republicans Control Congress 2014–2016
Differences between Rise of the Tea Party
EPA, Obamacare Jobless Economy Slightly Better
Supreme Court Decisions Obama Uses Executive Power Too Much
Too Many Regulations. More Regulations
Executive Power Abused Global Warming Agreements
Demos control 1st 4 years Iran Nuclear Agreement
The Tea Party-2010 House. Liberal judges Appointed to Circuit Courts
Occupy Wall Street. 2 Supreme Court Liberal Judges Appointed.

2016 Elections 2020 Elections
Hillary Clinton the Democrat. Trump, Republican
Bernie Sanders Lost vs. Socialist Joe Biden
Democrat
Trump, GOP Nominee. The Economy Going Good
Won
Jobless Rate Low, Lots of Jobs
Republicans Control Senate Only
Impeachment Failed
Trump Kept All Promises
Foreign Policy in Our Favor Now
2 Supreme Court Judges Appointed, Both
    Conservative
2020 In the Early Spring. The Coronavirus Upsets
    the
Economy. Lockdowns Prevail. Becomes Political.
    May/June of 2020 The Racist Protest
From Some Police Brutality, In Minneapolis.
Protests and Some Rioting and
Burning in the Streets of Major Cities.
Curfews are Evoked and National Guard Called In
The Rioters Calling for Police Defunding

CHAPTER 1

The Angry Voter

Evil prevails when good men do nothing.
            —Edmund Burke
        (famous statesman from the 1700s)

People think their vote doesn't count, so they stay home. (Ninety-three million people did not vote or 40 percent in 2012). 57.5 percent voted in 2012, according to the Bi-Partisan Policy Center, down from 65 percent in 2008. This is by far a lower percentage than in other democracies. NBC News says, "The US ranks 120th of the 169 countries for which data exists on voter turnout." We do have many more elections than most other democratic countries. Could we possibly take our freedom here for granted?

According to an *LA Times* opinion page, January 31, 2016, there are two divisive opinions on the widespread perception about American decline. The outspoken Trump and the softer-spoken Bernie Sanders identify different culprits.

For Trump, it was the Mexican immigrants, political correctness, and US negotiators who are suckered in by the Chinese and Iranians and the decline of the military. His experience in economics and financing leads him to be concerned about our lack of economic understanding or action. His outrage at terrorism in Paris and in San Bernardino and even in Orlando had him asking for a temporary ban on immigrants coming from Islamic states. Now more recently, the terrorist attack in Orlando, Florida, only reinforced Trump's call to slow down the Muslim immigration until these people can be checked out. Trump has had part of the wall built so that hundreds of miles have walls now on the southern border, slowing down the free fall of immigrants from Mexico, Central and South America. There's still too many coming, climbing over the wall by Tijuana.

For Sanders, it was the parasitic billionaire class of which he is one that has profited and is the cause of the decline. A special on *60 Minutes* showed many billionaires giving their money away. One was Warren Buffett, one of our richest billionaires, giving his money to Steve Jobs and wife to give it away to those in need. He started a club for other billionaires to give theirs away too. Without the rich, there would be few jobs. If you took all the money away from the rich and gave it to the poor, some would work harder or take advantage of opportunities and become rich, while many of the poor who were given money from the rich would most likely end up poor again. "The cream always rises to the top" is an old saying. If you pour whole milk from a cow into a milk bottle, the heavier cream will rise to the top. There will always be rich and poor. In America, where we have the largest middle class of any country, the opportunities are greater for individuals to rise to the top.

The stated goal of socialism is to level the playing field, to spread the wealth, but in the end, the government and rich elitists control everything. Socialism has never worked, no matter how many times it has been tried around the world. Communism, socialism, fascism, are all similar, where the government is run by a dictator and he and his appointed government body control everything. The younger generation, due to the brainwashing of the socialist professors in the universities, think socialism is cool and is what we need here. And many teachers at all levels, having been educated in the universities, teach socialism is great. Look at Cuba and how they have fared under communism and total government control. They are still about the same, very poor economically, and many still wanting to come to America for freedom. Many residents of countries under these types of control have eventually rebelled and risen up and taken back their country. The Russian bloc of satellite countries eventually took their countries back. But there are still some under totalitarian rule, such as Russia, China, Venezuela, and Cuba.

Ted Cruz, running for president in 2015, outraged by Obama's inability to neutralize the Islamic State, said he would carpet-bomb the entire group.

Well, something has to be done about terrorism. Marco Rubio, when running for president in 2015, said he would cancel the Iranian Nuclear Agreement first thing and put sanctions back on. He recognizes that Iran is one of our worst enemies and should be dealt with.

Anger is nothing new to American politics. Anger can be a powerful motivator. The initial anger was when we fought the Revolutionary War in 1776, to free ourselves from British rule and high taxation, and to be our own country. There was anger during each of the wars, from the Civil War, to the World Wars, especially after the attack on Pearl Harbor, and the Vietnam War. There was anger during the Great Depression, there was anger because of the attack in New York on 9/11. There is anger at Congress and at the presidents. The Tea Party started because of anger at the Republican Establishment and Congress. It may be an appropriate response to injustice and government run amok. The Occupy Wall Street marches and riots started with anger at Wall Street's perceived riches and possible unscrupulous actions.

To appease this anger and to get elected, many of the candidates make promises that they may not be able to keep. Once in office, a new president may find that it is not easy to jail unscrupulous Wall Streeters, tear up international agreements or treaties, give free health insurance to all, give free college to all, build a wall to stop illegal immigration, or get rid of terrorism.

Over-promising might inflame rather than lessen the anger. Obama, when running for president, promised a new future and hope. Many, especially the young, bought into that dream. Yet the economy still suffered after his stay and unemployment, if counted accurately, including those who have given up looking for work, still remained high. Obamacare has not done that well. Are we really better off than in 2012? Or than in 2008? What had he really done? Racism is worse. The economy was not rebounding very well. We were no longer feared in the world as the world leader and were blatantly disrespected. Since World War I, the United States has been considered the number one power in the world. Where would Europe and the rest of the world be if the US had not entered both World War I and II and won it for them? Then helped to reconstruct each country.

As far as the candidates fighting among each other, that is not new. Thomas Jefferson and John Adams fought bitterly and accused each other of lying and of not being capable of the office of president. Many races were bitterly fought.

How our ship looked in the early 1900s, sort of old-fashioned.
But the state we had been in since 1776, so steady.
Flowing with the wind, gracefully to and fro, but
Always steady as she goes!

CHAPTER 2

Our Ship of Fate

When we celebrated the hundredth anniversary of the sailing of the ill-fated ocean liner HMS *Titanic* in 2011, almost everyone knew the story. The *Titanic*, on its maiden voyage from England in 1911, to the United States, raced full speed ahead through an ocean full of icebergs, struck one, and ended with the loss of 1,500 lives as it sunk. It was billed as totally unsinkable, so no alarm was raised when they knew icebergs were in the area.

The arrogance of Obama, the Party of Unreason, and even some of the Republicans in Washington, was not only breathtaking, but was reminiscent of the builders of the *Titanic*. One of the builders said, "God himself could not sink this ship!" Many in Washington even act as if God himself could not bring down our country.

America, Our Ship of State

We had an administration for eight years that apparently wanted to drive America full speed ahead into the iceberg, sinking our Ship of State. Our president then, as captain of our ship, actually seemed to want to hit the iceberg. Would he, like the captain of the Italian ship, *Costa Concordia*, who tried at the last minute to keep from hitting rocks, but did not plan in time? His cruise ship hit the rocks in the Mediterranean and his ship started sinking. He reportedly did not stay with his ship, but took the coward's way out and stated that he accidentally fell into a lifeboat. Maritime rule has always been that the captain stays with his ship and sees that as many as possible can be saved. Where would Captain Obama have been if our ship sank?

So what is our fate now? What can we do about it? Reclaim our ship and make it stronger, with double hull, more steel, more reinforcement, and a captain and crew with experience in business and economics, and make it invulnerable to icebergs, or do we just keep quiet and let it hit the iceberg and sink into the bottom of the sea?

We were at that point where our ship could have gone either way. It was up to us to decide.

Do we want to continue on our course with Trump again or go full steam ahead with the socialist/liberals and crash? Which will it be?

If we don't want to crash and be buried under the sea, then we have to change course drastically as we are so close to the iceberg now, that it will not take much to hit it. To not hit it, we have to back our captain and crew, we have to reinforce and change our ship, and we have to do everything possible to turn it around, especially after the storm of the coronavirus and shutdown, thus hurting the economy bad.

Trump has almost singlehandedly turned our ship around, but has not had smooth sailing for him.

He did not have to do this job as he was enjoying his wealth and privacy.

We ask ourselves what led up to us being so close to hitting the iceberg. What forces or factors made this possible? We will examine what happened from the 1900s on to see how the course of our ship, since our Great Nation began and had cruised right along for decades until the early 1900s.

When America was young, people of faith, who loved America, worked hard to make this the greatest country in history of the world. Immigrants were standing in lines to come to this great country, as they knew they could do anything, make anything of themselves, and had hope of bettering their lives and that of their children. Those who were born here also had hope to better their lives and that of their children to come. Since 1919, we have been the leader of the world. That status has been slipping and sinking in the eight years under Obama. Now we've had a chance to reclaim our course of our country under Trump. We can steer our ship now. So we need another four years to focus more on pushing our ship ahead faster toward a more and greater country than ever.

What on earth has happened? Why did we start losing our status as leader, with many jobs and businesses going to other countries? Why was our economy so bad? How could this happen?

> "We the People, do ordain and establish this Constitution for the United States, in Order to form a more perfect

Union, establish Justice, insure domestic Tranquility, provide for the common defense, promote the general Welfare, and secure the Blessings of Liberty to ourselves and our Posterity, do ordain and establish this Constitution of the United States of America."

—The Preamble of the
United States Constitution

We are on a long voyage with our Ship of State. Entering the *Perfect Storm*, we find that ships do not have brakes; they do not change direction fast and often have to stop first before going in any different direction. Ships might even have to go backward to correct course. How can we handle this ship through possibly the biggest storm of all time?

Ships cannot wait until the last minute and then change course suddenly as they are about to hit the iceberg. Our Ship of State must plan ahead to avoid serious collisions. We must stop and alter our course before it is too late, as we did in 2016.

We voters are the rudder that is steering our Ship of State by our votes. We must plan ahead our course in order to navigate to smoother waters and to avoid crashing our ship. In 2016, we did just that. We elected a new Captain. Captain Trump is hell bent on righting our ship and sending it smooth sailing in a far different direction. With easing burdensome regulations, many of which Obama put in place that were job-killing and sent many businesses overseas, there are far less regulations now, and it is a much more business-friendly country. In spite of all kinds of interference from the leftists to try to remove him from office.

Are you aware that in the general election of 2016 that at least 65 million people of faith (estimated to be 70 to 75 percent of our country) did NOT vote? For too long now, the Silent Majority has stayed silent and many have not voted or made their voices heard. We can make a difference if we vote, especially if we vote our values, to head America in the right course once again. By changing course and righting our ship once again, we can see a much healthier economy, with unemployment being lower than in many, many years, and new jobs growing every day.

This is called capitalism, folks! And it works, believe it or not, capitalism works. We have as a captain, a CEO who understands business. The United States is the biggest corporation in the world. The head is like the most important CEO of any corporation so we need a businessman to run it.

This book will reflect the importance of voting and why voting has changed our course many times. This book is a layman's look through history since the early 1900s, as it relates to the course of our nation. Our presidents are the captains of our ship. We, the voters, are the owners of this ship, who can move the rudder and change the direction, by changing the captains and crew (Congress) through our vote.

In the following timeline, we will outline the most significant and profound course where our votes have decided our journey, either directly or indirectly. Directly, by voting for our elected representatives at all levels, and indirectly, by whom we vote for and who they may appoint to carry out their ideologies or by presidents appointing Supreme Court Justices, whose votes can create a profound change for many years.

Silence is NOT acceptable.

Not voting usually becomes a vote for the other direction and alters our course just as much, if not more, and it may not be in the direction that is good for our Ship of State. I have heard far too many people say, "I think they are all corrupt, so I don't vote!" or "I don't think Christians should be involved in politics." There are many examples in the Bible of Christians involved in politics or God-loving prophets advising kings. After all, Jesus threw the money changers out of the temple. A very political act.

The duties of American citizenship are few, but they include voting, jury duty, and paying taxes. <u>Political participation is a civic duty</u>. Although duties of citizenship appear in our Constitution, everyday American citizens seek to avoid this, forgetting the importance of an active citizenry in a republic.

Each chapter will be devoted to some significant landmark changes, elections, and decisions, along with judicial decisions that affected our course and decided our voyage, from the early 1900s to now. Several chapters will deal with some candidates and their politics and beliefs and a solution to save America. Some of this book is based on my own observations and knowledge gained since I became interested in politics, at the age of eleven and history as I lived it. The rest is from diligent research.

CHAPTER 3

Voting Rights Are Honored

The will of the people is the only legitimate foundation of any government, and to protect its free expression should be our first object.
—Thomas Jefferson, 1801

A recent ruling from the Supreme Court in North Carolina's voter ID law mandate is coming down soon. The outcome is likely to affect their upcoming elections. Thirty states have adopted voter ID laws, and some have been thrown out by the liberal court or the government. Why is this wanted by the states? Because voter fraud has become so rampant. There is no desire by the Republicans to stop anyone from voting that is eligible and a citizen. The liberal Democrats claim there is no or little voter fraud, yet poll watchers and election integrity watchers at the county clerk's offices report much voter fraud.

From the *LA Times*, Sunday, February 7, 2016, ninety-four-year old poster child of the NAACP,

Rosanell Eaton was recently witnessing a trial in North Carolina challenging North Carolina's new voter identification law. She is African-American and grew up in the south. She has been voting for seventy years. With North Carolina's new strict voter ID law, she said that the name on her driver's license and voter registration card did not match. Eaton says she had to make eleven trips, to different state agencies in 2015, totaling more than two hundred miles and twenty hours to try to get her paperwork in order. The name on her driver's license is Rosanell Eaton, and on her voter registration card is Rosanell Johnson Eaton. According to instructions posted recently on the website of the State Board of Elections, the name appearing on the photo ID must be the same or substantially equivalent to the name on the voter's registration record.

Acceptable differences include omission of one or more parts of the name, ordering of names, and use of a former name, including maiden name. Now that sounds a little extreme, even if she lived in the rural areas. All she had to do was go to her county registrar's office and show them her driver's license was different than her voter registration card so she needed her name corrected on that card. Or if the voter registration card name was correct, then go to the DMV, taking some form of identification to prove her name, and ask them to change it. That seems much simpler than making eleven different trips.

The reason the liberals don't want these voter ID laws is that they cannot get away with as much voter fraud, which has been rampant. They pretend it is too costly or too difficult for the poor or minorities to obtain a picture ID. Guess what? You have to use your ID to do anything anymore: to open an account at a bank, especially an account for your welfare or social security check to go into; to use any credit card; to go to the doctors or any hospital; to pay with a check; to sign up for Social Security payments. I wouldn't be surprised to learn that that probably 99.9 percent of these so-called disadvantaged or poor citizens already have an ID card.

To vote without an ID, all someone who wants to commit voter fraud has to do is go to the polls and say who they are, even if it is not them. The polls have to post a list on the door or window near the door, of who has voted and who has not, updating it every hour. This is for the parties to see who has not voted from their party, so they can call them to remind them. But anyone can go there and look at who has not voted and say they are that person. Or vote in one polling place and then go to another and vote or across the state line. Without ID, how can the clerks know if you are that person listed on the registered voter lists? Many felons illegally voted in the last two elections.

I have worked in the precincts many times, as a clerk and as an inspector, and so much of the time, people come in with their ID in their hand and offer it to us and are surprised they don't need it. The only time in California that you have to have an ID to vote is the first time you vote in California.

Mail-in ballots are not immune to fraud either. Anyone can sign them. The county clerks supposedly check the signatures of your ballot, but their time is limited and they are not experts in signature forensics. There are people, many that are lawyers, who go to the county clerk's offices to watch the ballots coming in, watch the counting and the mail-in ballots for signature fraud and persons pretending to be another voter or for voting in more than one precinct or even crossing over borders of states to vote again. These watchers challenge many ballots and signatures, according to Catherine Baker, an attorney in Northern California, now on the State Legislature. There are groups called Election Integrity, and Linda Paine, one of their representatives, says that elections need oversight.

Many new voting laws were blocked by the Justice Department and federal courts during the 2012 election, and Republican attempts to restrict the franchise may have led to a backlash among minority voters. In 2012, for the first time in our history, black turnout rates exceeded white turnout rates. Now some of that popularity may have been we had our first black nominee for president.

In 2013, voter suppression efforts got a powerful shot in the arm when the Supreme Court invalidated the centerpiece of the Voting Rights Act, ruling that states with the longest histories of voting discrimination no longer had to approve their election changes with the federal government. As a result, new restrictions were allowed to take place in states such as Alabama, North Carolina, and Mississippi. Liberals say the 2016 election will be the first presidential contest in fifty years where voters cannot rely on the full protections of the Voting Rights Act. However, asking for voter ID is not against any Voting Rights Act. It is for the protection of what is in the Constitution that one must be a citizen to vote, and our state laws say they must register to vote. It is for the protection of the rest who are voting honestly and are registered legally to vote.

North Carolina is one of the sixteen states that have new voting restrictions in place since the last presidential contest, according to the Brennan Center for Justice, accounting for 178 electoral votes, including in crucial swing states such as Ohio, Wisconsin, and Virginia.

You have to have an ID to open a bank account, to collect food stamps, to sign up for welfare, to go on a plane or train, to cash a check, to go to a doctor. So the upshot of it is that everyone already has an ID.

CHAPTER 4

Voter 101
Basics of the Election Process

Many of us, even the informed, are not too sure of the entire election process or if any recent changes in it affect them. The old way of selecting candidates were for each party to have a large convention and elect delegates, and they, party leaders and politicians, would decide there who the nominee would be for their party. There is no provision for the role of political parties in the US Constitution. In the first two presidential elections, the Electoral College handled the nominations and election in 1789 and 1792 that selected George Washington. After that, Congressional party or a state legislature party caucus selected the party's candidates. Before 1829 Democratic-Republican members of Congress would nominate a single candidate from their party. That system collapsed in 1824. Since 1832, the preferred mechanism for nomination has been a national convention.

In the past, the nominees were chosen at the conventions, but now we have the primary voter system of either private votes or caucuses. Then the delegates are given a proportionate vote from whomever wins in their state and it takes a certain number of delegates to win. With each party having a different number. Then the delegates at the convention vote on the first ballot. If they can't agree, then they can vote on a second ballot and be unbound. Not have to vote from whomever won in their state. Delegates are selected mostly from the party elites. So the upshot is that now the citizens have more of a voice, but it still can be taken away at the convention.

The series of presidential primary elections and caucuses held in each US state and territory is part of the nominating process of United States presidential elections. This process was never included in the US Constitution; it was created over time by the political parties. Some states hold only primary elections, some hold only caucuses and others use a combination of both.

These primaries and caucuses are staggered generally between either late January or early February and mid-June before the general election in November. The primary elections are run by state and local governments, while caucuses are private events that are directly run by the political parties themselves. A state's primary election or caucus is usually an indirect election; instead of voters directly selecting a particular person running for president, they determine how many delegates each party's national convention will receive from their respective state. These delegates then in turn select their party's presidential nominee.

Each party determines how many delegates are allocated to each state. Along with those delegates chosen during the primaries and caucuses state delegations to both the Democratic and Republican conventions also include unpledged delegates, usually current and former elected officeholders and party leaders, who can vote for whomever they want. Democrats call them super delegates. Hillary Clinton claimed she would win as she had so many super delegates.

This system of presidential primaries and caucuses is somewhat controversial because of its staggered nature. The major advantage is that candidates can concentrate their resources in each area of the country, one at a time, instead of campaigning in every state simultaneously.

However, the overall results may not be representative of the US electorate as a whole: voters in Iowa, New Hampshire, and other small states, which traditionally hold their primaries and caucuses first, usually have a major impact on the races, while voters in California and other large states, which traditionally hold their primaries last in June, generally end up having no say because the races are usually over by then. By 2020, California moved their primary to early March, so as not to be the last in June.

As a result, more states vie for earlier primaries to claim a greater influence in the process. California and New Jersey, some of the last, moved their primaries to February for the 2008 election, but in 2012, both states ended up moving them back to June. California lawmakers stated that consolidating their presidential and statewide primary election in June saves them about 100 million dollars, and that it is not worth the cost when there is generally no competitive balance between the two political parties within California (in other words, California votes overwhelmingly for Democratic candidates for president).

Super Tuesday was created deliberately to increase the influence of the South. It is held on a Tuesday in February or March of a presidential election year, when the greatest number of states hold primary elections to select delegates to national conventions at which each party's presidential candidates are officially nominated. This has been going on since 1976. More delegates can be won on that day than any other single day of the primary calendar. It represents a presidential candidate's first test of national electability. In 2008, twenty-four states held primaries or caucuses on the date of February 5 with 52 percent pledged Democratic Party delegates and 49 percent of the total Republican Party delegates at stake.

The 2016 Super Tuesday was held on March 1. The participating fourteen states this year were Alabama, Alaska Republican caucuses, Arkansas, Colorado caucuses, Georgia, Massachusetts, Minnesota caucuses, Oklahoma, Tennessee, Texas,

Vermont, Virginia. Republican caucuses: North Dakota and Wyoming. The number of states in Super Tuesday varies from year to year.

Prior to Super Tuesday, there was a primary vote or caucus in Iowa on February 1, Tuesday February 9 New Hampshire, Saturday February 20 South Carolina.

Then in first Tuesday in March 3 Kansas caucus, Kentucky caucus, and Louisiana and Maine caucuses voted; Sunday March 8, Puerto Rico. Tuesday, March 10 Hawaii caucus, Idaho, Michigan, and Mississippi. Thursday March 12, US Virgin Islands. Saturday March 14, District of Columbia and Guam. On Tuesday March 17, Ohio, Florida, Illinois, Missouri, North Carolina, and Northern Mariana Islands. Tuesday March 24, Arizona, Utah Caucus. March 26, Hawaii and Washington. April 7, Wisconsin. April 7, Wyoming. April 21, New York, Connecticut, Delaware. April 27, Maryland, Pennsylvania, Rhode Island. May 5, Indiana. May 7, Guam. May 12, West Virginia, Kentucky. May 19, Kentucky, Oregon. June 4, Virgin Islands. June 2, Puerto Rico. June 2, California, Montana, New Jersey. June 2, New Mexico, North Dakota, South Dakota. June 16, District of Columbia.

The total base number of delegates allocated to each of the fifty states is ten at large delegates, plus three delegates per Congressional district. In addition, fixed numbers of at-large delegates are allocated to Washington, DC, Puerto Rico, American Samoa, Guam, the US Virgin Islands, and Northern Mariana

Islands, under the party's delegate selection rules, eleven states are awarded bonus delegates based on the following factors:

- Bonus delegates to each state that cast a majority of their Electoral College votes for the GOP candidate in the election prior.
- One bonus delegate for each GOP senator.
- One bonus delegate to each state that has a GOP majority in their delegation to the House of Representatives.
- One bonus delegate for each state that has a GOP governor.
- Bonus delegates for majorities in one of all of the chambers in their state legislature.

The two Republican National Committee members from each state and territory and the Chairperson of the State's Republican Party are delegates unless the state is penalized for violating the RNC's scheduling rules. The individual states decide whether these delegates are bound or unbound.

Democrats use a different formula, but with the same result—theirs takes into account the sum of the state's vote for Democratic candidates in the last three presidential elections. Democrats also make many democratic elected officials into unpledged super delegates, which also has the effect of amplifying power of the states that elect the most Democrats. Hillary Clinton had bragged that she would win as she has the most super delegates in her corner. And so she had. But she did not win. She was not a good campaigner and basically had no message except to trash her opponent, Trump, and to call his voters a basket of deplorables, among other names. She is not charismatic like her husband was, so does not attract a lot of voters, except for her base. She has quite a temper and gets mad easily, so actually did not have the temperament for running the country, nor the stamina. She was not really very well. It was said she had a rally, then a week of rest before another one. Whereas, Trump held several rallies a day. She was lucky to get a couple of hundred attendees, while Trump filled large arenas with many thousands and people waiting in line outside.

CHAPTER 5

The Electoral College
How It Works

I t is a process. Not a place. The Founding Fathers established it in the Constitution as a compromise between the election of the president by a vote in Congress and election of the president by a popular vote of qualified citizens. The Electoral College process consists of the selection of the electors, then the meeting of the electors where they vote for president and vice president, and the counting of the electoral votes by Congress.

The Electoral College consist of 538 electors. A majority of 270 electoral votes is required to elect the president. Your state's entitled allotment of electors equals the number of members in its Congressional delegation, one for each member in the House of Representatives, plus two for your Senators. Under the 23rd Amendment of the Constitution, the District of Columbia was allocated 3 electors and treated as a state for the purposes of the Electoral College.

Now we have established how we vote for our presidents and what the Electoral College process is. The Electoral College was created to give a voice to the smaller states, which forces the campaigners to pay much more attention to, and campaign in, the small states. This is why the Founding Fathers chose to not elect our presidents by popular vote. Otherwise, New York and California would decide all of our elections, and the big cities would control the outcomes of national elections. Our Founders were incredibility foresighted. Imagine then with only a handful of colonies how they imagined a huge United States with areas of larger populations.

CHAPTER 6

The Meaning of Life

[E]xcerpted from a speech by Dennis Praeger, Conservative radio personality and speaker, in Jan. 2020, at the Jewish Center in Redondo Beach, CA.]

What would our Founders say if they came back today? Probably—"Take me back."

If you want to understand a human being, or the human condition, what is the single most important question you should ask? Most religious people would ask, "Do you believe in God? The most important question most secular people could imagine asking is probably a policy question, such as like—"Do you support abortion or transgenderism or environmentalism?"

In attempting to understand human beings, especially large groups of human beings—or their society—the most important question to ask is. "What gives you the most meaning?"

On Marxism. Only matter is real Leftists believe we are unequal in economic inequality—socialism never produced any imbedded in inequality. Marxist was a motivator. Freud was saying sex was his motivation

Holocaust survivors had a sense of purpose to survive for those who hadn't died. Many died when not liberated at the time when told they would be liberated. When it did not happen then, they just keeled over and died as lost their purpose.

To have meaning. A happy life distinguishes us from animals The Freudian view says evolutionary view of everything explains what people do has meaning. What evolution means is survival of the species. Why is there goodness in any species.

Meaning is what we most yearn for—good and bad ways. How historically did America find meaning. There is more unhappiness today then every before, more suicides, especially in the young. God, and Religion, country, marriage and family, getting shelter, volunteering in community have meaning.

The reason that we seek this is after food, the greatest human need and human desire is meaning. Even more so than the ability to reason or even to speak--this is the greatest divide between human and animal.

We share all needs with the higher animal species. Like them—we need food, shelter and companionship.

But while human beings seek and need meaning more than anything except food (and companionship—but for human beings companionship usually provides some meaning and sometimes it is enough). No animal needs or seeks meaning.

This may be one of the reasons we can believe in God, the Creator. There is simply no evolutionary explanation for the need for meaning. Meaning is not a biological need.

Given its unique importance that is why what gives us meaning must be deemed the most important question.

[Now back to where most of the serious changes happened to our country on its trek downward and why.]

CHAPTER 7

The Industrial Age
1885 to 1919

The Industrial Age was full of inventions and advancements in fields of science and math. Many inventions took birth in historic eighteenth century that caused development and the foundation for the upcoming generation. By the early 1900s, we were enjoying prosperity for more than just the elite upper classes.

Prominent progress can be noticed in the fields of mathematics and chemistry and finally the evolution that took place. The inventions to save labor spread, with new machines taking the place of people, or making it easier to work, so people had to work less hours. This industrialization caused huge transformation in people's way of living. People were aware that they were in the middle of a social and economic revolution and that their lives were changing dramatically. The advent of steel mills, the cotton gin, and the electricity grid in some rural areas. The steam engine, electric railways, the steam-powered locomotive, the spinning jenny, the electric telegraph, electric telephone, steamboats and steamships, the internal combustion engine, the automobiles, the phonograph, the Wright Brothers' successful first flights, in early 1903, which started the aviation revolution, hydrofoil boats, submarines, and many more.

The Industrial Age transformed our country from mostly an agricultural society into an industrialized society. The working class worked about twelve to thirteen hours a day and six days a week. That had a profound change in the way mankind lived. Through industrial civilization, people moved away from depending on an agricultural society. More people moved into the cities and away from the family farms, now working in factories, even women and children, although they did not get paid as much as men. They often worked shorter days in the factories, than they had on the farms.

Our society changed in many ways. People lived closer together in the city tenements and apartments and were living less with extended families as they had on the farms. This influenced politics and laws tremendously. People began to vote differently and often were not involved in the large communities in the large cities. Those living in the large cities tended to vote more democratic, changing the demographics of the country significantly.

When the liberal socialist movement took off in our country, it was as an incendiary educational thought. It was in 1904 when John Dewey began his career of teaching at Teacher's College at Columbia University, where he was head of the educational department and where he would start to mold twentieth century thought. Funded by Rockefeller and Carnegie, wealthy industrial giants, this Teachers College propelled Deweyism into the public schools through many radical disciples of Dewey's Progressive Education system. A Fabian socialist, Marxist, and Darwinist, Dewey had an agenda that was to infuse socialism into the public schools for ever after. Columbia Teachers College has been the model program for teacher training across the United States, giving advanced degrees to superintendents and heads of colleges.

Landmark Supreme Court decisions during this era that affected society and the vote were segregation of schools, *Curving v. Richmond County Board of Education in* 1899. *Giles v. Harris,* on Voting Rights 11th Amendment in 1902, *Muller and Oregon, Protecting Labor Laws and Protecting Women: Flint v. Stone Tracy Co.* Consolidation of corporate income tax and *Newberry v US* that Congress lacks power to regulate state's primaries. *Standard Oil Co. of New Jersey v United States* in 1911 was the first gasoline company case confirming the dissolution of the Standard Oil Trust because its monopoly position was an unreasonable restraint on trade under the Sherman Antitrust Act.

Theodore Roosevelt, whom we voted in, appointed business-oriented, more conservative Supreme Court Justices who made decisions affecting labor as the industrial age brought in many labor disputes never heard of before. He was brash, bold, and a completely different politician. Very outspoken but right for the times. The working class could relate to him. The CIO and AFL unions were established to protect workers in the factories. Strikes ensued, so work stopped when they were going on, with supervisors and corporate persons manning the assembly lines, during the strikes. The courts were called upon to mediate many labor disputes.

The First Automobiles

Henry Ford developed his inexpensive black Model T Ford cars off the mass production lines in 1908, allowed many more to own their own automobiles, this made transport easier for all, and forever changed the landscape, with new roads accessing rural areas. Soon affordable trucks were manufactured, which began to haul goods and produce to outlying areas. This changed the demographics of our country and voting patterns, too. Women decided they could drive the new-fangled horseless carriages, too, which required a great deal of strength to crank them up to start them. Tires had to be patched often.

Many men did not want the women to drive, thinking they were not mechanical enough or too weak to do it. Remember, the early autos had to be hand-cranked at the front of the car to start them up, which took a lot of strength. But some still did. It gave women more freedom and families transportation to go further and faster. My mother drove one of the earlier cars.

My grandfather, the first in his community to buy a car, bought one of the early cars, which was a used Studebaker, about 1908 model. He had to go from his country store near Eugene, Oregon, to Portland, Oregon, to pick up his car. Grandpa was over thirty, but did not know how to drive, so the car dealership sent someone part of the way with him to show him how to drive the car. When they left him partway to his home, and he was on his own driving the car, with his two daughters aged nine and eleven in the back seat, he ran it over a ditch and up a huge bank, jostling the girls and nearly knocking them out of the car. He made it home with his new car a bit damaged, but all none the worse for wear. In those days, a hammer and a little bailing wire or even a hair pin could repair most things on those simple old cars.

Later, in the early late '20s or early '30s, he purchased a new black Model A, and that one I remember as I used to ride in it with him. He ran a small dairy route each morning after milking ten cows morning and night, and our delight was to get to ride with Grandpa around the countryside to deliver his milk. That was how people obtained fresh milk, eggs, and butter in those days. It was his social time.

Airplanes Flown for the First Time

The age of aviation started with the Wright Brothers (see photo of first plane flown by the Wright Brothers), who owned a bicycle shop, who then flew their first airplane, in 1903, thus ushering in the age of flight. In 1995, we were able to go to Kitty Hawk, North Carolina, and walk along the ground following the route of the first flight, which was a real experience to walk there and imagine man flying for the first time, and though it was a relatively short length in feet, it was a big leap for mankind. Their invention started the airplane revolution, and by the end of WWI, we were using airplanes to our advantage, as a new warfare weapon in dropping bombs on our enemies, which helped end the war.

Large helium-powered blimps were used for surveillance from the air, due to their being able to fly low and silently. People became more mobile, moving around the country more and traveling for pleasure, having more disposable income and taking advantage of these new modes of transportation. During WWII, aviation warfare was primarily the weapon that helped us to win the war. Air travel is now available for all in the world, opening up vast areas to be able to travel to. We were well ahead of the rest of the world in aviation progress.

The Sinking of the Titanic, 1912

On April 10, 1912, the *Titanic*, largest ship afloat, left Southampton, England, on her maiden voyage to New York City. This ship was deemed unsinkable. It was built to not crash. The passengers were among the world's richest, basking in the elegance of first-class accommodations, while packed in steerage were immigrants coming to America to live.

Four days out, this unsinkable ship struck an iceberg. The collision was fatal and the icy water soon poured throughout. Only about half the passengers and crew survived. There were only half as many lifeboats as they felt they would not be needed. (See photo next page.)

Pic 02 The *Titanic* leaving port at Southampton, England, for her maiden voyage

What could happen if we hit the iceberg?

Panama Canal Opens, Opening Shipping to the World

In 1914, the Panama Canal was opened, using industrialized technology to complete its formation, which opened up shipping and travel as a shortcut from the Pacific to the Atlantic Oceans, forever changing the length of time it took to travel around the world, as well as to transport goods faster. Theodore Roosevelt was instrumental in the completion of the canal.

CHAPTER 8

Progressive Party
Formed in 1912

As we continue on our voyage into the ocean's surprising currents. The winds have changed.

Theodore Roosevelt (cousin of Franklin D. Roosevelt) started the progressive movement, as a new type of party with future ideas. Although he had endorsed Taft who had been his vice president to succeed him, he became dissatisfied with the too conservative ways of Taft, so he formed this independent party to run against him and against Woodrow Wilson, a Democrat. Taft alienated Roosevelt when he had used the Sherman Anti-Trust Act to break up US Steel, so Roosevelt, as a result, formed his own party.

However, Roosevelt jumped too late into the campaign, and therefore, he received two setbacks. Not many Republicans joined the new party, and few progressive senators declared support. The

Democrats nominated Woodrow Wilson, their most articulate and prominent progressive.

The Progressive platform called for national health, social insurance for the elderly, the unemployment, and disabled; limited injunction in strikes; minimum wage for women; an eight-hour work day; a federal securities commission; farm relief; worker's compensation for sick or injured on the job; an inheritance act; women's suffrage; direct election for senators; recall elections; referendum for voters to ask for measures that the legislators will not vote for, and the initiative and judicial recall.

The main theme was an attack on the domination of politics by business interests, which controlled both parties, so they called for strict limits and disclosure requirements on political campaign contributions. Other measures were recording and publication of congressional committee proceedings.

All in all, the platform expressed Roosevelt's *New Nationalism*, a strong government to regulate industry, protect the middle and working classes, and carry on great vast national projects. Some voters also felt that Roosevelt was trying for a third term, which had always been implied that presidents should only serve two terms, though not an amendment to the Constitution yet.

Surprisingly, many of these platform measures have since been enacted mostly by Democrats, but some by both parties as time went on.

This platform was voted down and received little support from Republicans, much to Roosevelt's surprise. This split the vote so that Woodrow Wilson, the Democrat won. Some progressives supported Wilson and some came on board with Franklin D. Roosevelt and his New Deal platform in 1932.

Why this is important is that many left-leaning liberals now call themselves progressives, as they are pushing toward a stronger government with more regulation and government control, higher taxes, and national government-mandated health care.

Our voyage took another turn, because of our votes, and changed course.

CHAPTER 9

The Federal Reserve Formed in 1913

Uh-oh! Are we getting off course again?

In spite of the Constitution spelling out that Congress shall handle the money, 1913 saw the forming of the Federal Reserve Act by Congress, also known as the Glass-Owen Bill, this passing forever changed the way our money was handled.

Then President Wilson signed it into law one hour after being passed by Congress. The speed with which this was passed told us that somebody very powerful really wanted this law passed. The Federal Reserve system is an independent central bank, not what our Founders envisioned for our monetary control.

Although the president of the United States, whom we vote for, appoints the Chairman of the Fed, this appointment is approved by the US Senate (whom we vote for). The decisions of the Feds do not have to be ratified by the president or anyone else in the executive branch of the United States government. Strange that our Congress would allow or vote for this to happen.

Buried in the legislation was the granting of total power over the monetary policies of all US banks. A very curious statement is found in the original 1913 law Sec. 30: "The right to amend, alter or repeal this act is hereby expressly reserved." Reserved expressly to whom or what? No definition is provided. This is the entire section 20 statement.

Stock not held by member banks shall not be entitled to voting power. This clause guarantees that no outsider can justify buying shares in the Federal Reserve.

In Section 341 Second: "To have succession for a period of twenty years from its organization unless it is sooner dissolved by an act of Congress, or unless its franchises become forfeited by some violation of law."

The Federal Reserve was only given a corporate life of twenty years! Their time was up in 1933. Who was president at that time? Franklin D. Roosevelt was president then, of course. Somehow the Federal Reserve termination did not occur. There was never any reauthorization of the Federal Reserve Act of 1913, other than tacit approval given by the Sarbanes-Oxley Act of 2002.

No senator or representative in Congress shall be a member of the Federal Reserve Board or an office or a director of a Federal Reserve Bank. No member of Congress is to have access to the inner sanctum!

Twelve USC 3019 Federal Reserve banks, including the capital stock and surplus therein and the income derived therefore, shall be exempt from federal, state, and local taxation, except taxes upon real estate. Then, as a result, Congress no longer has control over our monetary interests and even worse cannot be involved in any form within the Federal Reserve.

The Federal Reserve (called the Feds) claims nobody owns it, that it is an independent entity within the government. The Federal Reserve is subject to the laws such as the Freedom of Information Act and the Private Act, which covers federal agencies but not private corporations, yet Congress gave the Federal Reserve the autonomy to carry out its responsibilities insulated from political pressure.

Each of the Feds' three parts, the Board of Governors of the Regional Reserve Banks, and the Federal Open Market Committee, which operates independently of the Federal Government is to carry out the Feds core responsibilities. As the Nation's Central Bank, the Federal Reserve derives its authority from the US Congress (which we voted for), which periodically reviews its activity and can alter its responsibilities by statute. There is no information provided regarding the ownership of the twelve.

Federal District Banks. A study of corporate and banking influence published in 1976, chart I, reveals the literal connection between the European Rothschild's Bank through the stockholding of bank stock and their subsidiary firms in New York. J. P.

Morgan Co. and Kuhn, Loeb and Co. They were the first which set up the Kekyll Island Conference at which the Federal Reserve Act was drafted and who directed the campaign to have the plan enacted into law by Congress and also who purchased the controlling amounts of stock in the Federal Reserve Bank of New York in 1914.

It is amazing how few grasped the significance of Alan Greenspan being knighted by the Queen of England in September 26, 2002. He was head of the Federal Reserve Board then. Guess what! The British Crown or the British Monarchy, a family of huge wealth, is the owner of our Federal Reserve. And we thought we disengaged ourselves from the British after the Revolutionary War!

Who voted for the Congress that decided they no longer handled the monetary responsibilities but turned it over to other moneyed interests to handle it for our country? There appeared to be no clamor from the public to disallow this. Our Constitution reads that Congress shall be in charge of our monetary responsibilities. Our Founders set this up, thinking that Congress can be replaced by our votes if they are not treating our monetary interests responsibly. Now with the Federal Reserve Board, our votes no longer count where our money is concerned. The Silent Majority slept through that one.

A serious bump against the shoals of our ship's journey! What a change in direction! Now we are swimming with the sharks.

CHAPTER 10

World War I 1914: The War to End All Wars

Oops, there is a sub, better change course now and vote for a new Congress.

The start of World War I began in Europe in August 1914. A decade of increasingly ever-political crisis, combined with military and naval arms races among Europe's major powers, created an incendiary situation. The murder of Austrian Archduke Franz Ferdinand in Sarajevo on June 1914 provided the catalyst. Serbia, Montenegro, Russia, France, Belgium, and Britain (the Allied Powers) found themselves opposed to Austria, Hungary, Germany, and Turkey (the Central Powers). The Central Powers are joined by Bulgaria in 1915, while the Allied Powers gathered Italy by 1915 and Romania in 1917. The US joined the war as an "associate power" on the Allied side, according to World History Atlas.

World War I is one of history's watersheds. Austria-Hungary's attempt to assert its power developed into a protracted struggle that swept up most of Europe and the rest of the world in its wake. This mobilized 65 million troops, of whom nine million died and over one-third were wounded. Civilians also died as a result of military action, starvation, and disease. The war was won by the Allied Powers but at great cost.

The German, Austro-Hungarian, Ottoman, and Russian empires were destroyed; European political and financial supremacy ended, and by 1918, the US had emerged as the greatest power in the world taking over from Britain.

On top of that, the soldiers brought home the Spanish flu which was thought to originate in Spain and was a pandemic happening all over the world. Unlike the coronavirus, the Spanish flu affected the young, mostly the teenagers.

Our ship now has a good tail wind to push it along, as the dominant ship in the whole fleet.

US Joins Europe and Allies in War in 1917

Woodrow Wilson (Democrat) presided as president when World War I was entered into in 1917 when unlimited German submarine warfare caused the US to enter World War I on the Allied side. Congress voted for us to go to war, when it became apparent that acts of aggression by the Axis powers were hurting our allies to such an extent that we had to help them. This war turned out to be the First World War in modern history after the world had expanded beyond Europe, Asia, and Africa.

War Ends in 1917—Johnny Comes Marching Home!

The war lasted until 1919, when on November 11, the armistice was declared by Congress. The world was ready for peace by then. Countries were in ruin, and while our country was not torn apart, our soldiers came home traumatized, having endured the trenches and hand-to-hand fighting, along with disease and serious injuries. Mustard gas was used, affecting thousands. After that, laws were passed that countries would not use this type of weapons of mass destruction anymore.

The dreaded Spanish flu pandemic took many lives in about 2018, brought home from overseas by many of the soldiers. That virus affected the young people. My mother remembered several of her friends who had the flu and some did not survive.

It was assumed that the world problems were settled. Germany was held down and backed down and agreed to the Peace Armistice. Surely they would not, or any of Europe, wish for another war again?

The debt and disillusionment that followed paved the way for the revolutionary forces of the left and right that emerged in the 1930s and in the wake of the Great Depression. Why is this important to the course of our country and our journey now?

One of the landmark elections happened in 1920 when Women Got the Vote, voted in by a new <u>Republican</u> Congress in 1919. The Democratic Congress had vetoed it three times. Republican women marched to protest for the equal rights for women vote. Tennessee voted to ratify this as twenty-six of thirty-six states voted, so it became ratified in 1920. That forever changed the way outcome of issues and elections were decided. Women finally had a voice in government.

Prohibition was voted in by mainly women's protests in the '20s. When the country found out this law just aided the bootleggers while the rich still got their alcohol in speakeasies, people in rural parts of the country were making bathtub gin out of juniper berries and brewing their own beer, with ample moonshine available for parties, so it was voted out. Alcohol is still legal today for adults over the age of twenty-one, with strict regulations and licensing requirements.

CHAPTER 11

The League of Nations Formed for Lasting Peace in 1919

Voted for by Congress and eventually many allied countries, this allowed the formation of this League of Nations as an intergovernmental organization founded after the peace treaties at Versailles, France, thusly ending WWI, whose principal mission was to maintain world peace. Its primary goals, as stated in its Covenant, included preventing wars through collective security and disarmament and settling international disputes through negotiations and arbitration.

This was President Woodrow Wilson's (a Democrat) and international leader's main idea for ever-lasting peace. Other issues in this and related treaties included labor conditions, just treatment of native inhabitants, humans, drug trafficking, arms trade, global health, prisoners of war, and protection of minorities in Europe. Its greatest membership extended from September 29 to February 23, 1935 (during FDRs reign) when it had a fifty-eight-member nation.

The diplomatic philosophy behind the League represented a fundamental shift from the preceding hundred years. For the first time, there was an international body to try to control the world and wars. What have we voted for? The League lacked its own armed forces and depended upon the Great Powers to enforce its resolutions, to keep to its economic sanctions or provide an army when needed. However, the Great Powers were reluctant to comply with them, not wanting to fight in their regional wars.

The course of the World War I affected the social, political, and economic systems of Europe. The causes included arms races, alliances, secret diplomacy, and freedom of sovereign states to enter into war for their own benefit. It was an international organization whose aim was to prevent future wars through disarmament, open diplomacy, and international cooperation with the restriction on the right to wage war and penalties that made war unattractive. What has Congress with their ratification of this course, the Congress that we voted for, done to us now? Are they selling out our sovereignty?

After a number of notable successes and some early failures in the '20s, the League ultimately proved incapable of preventing aggression by the Axis powers from Germany and Italy, Japan and Spain and others in the '30s.

The ones to fight the Second World War showed that the League had failed in its primary purpose, which was to prevent any future world wars. It was abandoned by then, as a failure to enforce its purpose was determined.

We wonder just what did our vote do this time? We voted for a Congress who ratified the treaty to form the League of Nations. We voted for presidents that encouraged its formation. Was there more behind this League than we knew at the time? Could it have been backed by the same moneyed interests that own the Federal Reserve Board? Could it be the first temperature taken to eventually form a One World Government?

Is that going to be the course of our journey into international troubled waters where the sharks are circling our ship?

CHAPTER 12

The Great Depression of the '30s: The New Deal

*C*hoppy waters ahead, with rough sailing, as we find ourselves in the Stock Market Crash of 1929. It was so sudden and unexpected that those that had invested heavily and lost everything even jumped out of windows at the stock market and financial district in New York, as the shame of facing the world with nothing dawned upon them.

According to *World History and Atlas*, the US economic crisis of 1929 hit a snag, with Europe suffering from the aftermath of wartime and dislocation. Industrial output and agricultural production fell sharply across the world, but the industrial nations were hardest hit. Farmers survived by retreating to subsistence production, but the collapse in industrial output brought unemployment on a massive scale. Without proper systems of neither social security nor unemployment compensation to support the unemployed, poverty became widespread.

The economic and social problems of the '30s encouraged the growth of extreme political movements on both Left and Right, especially in Germany and Italy, where fascism under Hitler and Mussolini became the defining political force. So from then on, how the US went, so goes the rest of the world, making our votes even more important than ever before.

Our votes, as our journey progressed, put Franklin D. Roosevelt (Democrat), a very rich powerful man, who had polio and was consigned to a wheelchair for the rest of his life, into the presidency to save our country in 1932. He was charismatic and had been governor of New York and who also came from a political family.

Roosevelt's New Deal progressive program which was to change the economy and bring it back turned out to not be as effective as was thought. He thought that spending would bring us out of the depression. His "make work" jobs programs, called the WPA (we called them the "We Piddle Around," as we often saw them along roads leaning on their shovels (must have been Obama's famous "shovel-ready jobs") and stimulus bills with millions of dollars spent, in relief, etc., still plugged on for years. Unemployment was about 25 percent. There were long bread lines as people sought food for them and their families. There were little or no welfare or food stamps programs then. Many men had to go away from home to find work, as my own father did, sending money home for his growing family.

Many now think that Roosevelt's administration's spending ended the depression, but it was not until World War II had started and going on for a while, with Germany invading countries around Europe that we started the Lend Lease Program, sending goods and equipment to other allied countries, and arms to help them defend themselves. Then later, our entering the war provided goods and jobs for the war effort.

People who lived on farms in the '30s, as my own grandparents did, and there were still many families who did, found they could feed themselves pretty well, as they could grow most of their food needed, but those living in the cities were hit the hardest. It was bleak times for our country. We see pictures of gaunt-looking people then looking very thin and with sad hard looks. It was not a happy voyage we were on then.

FDR Tries to Pack the Supreme Court

The Supreme Court, about evenly divided, took a *laissez-faire* approach and overturned many of Franklin Roosevelt's New Deal Programs, which were designed he hoped to combat the Great Depression. Most notable was the National Industrial Recovery Act, which was overturned in *Schechter Poultry Corp v. United States* and the Agricultural Adjustment Act was struck down in *United States v. Butler* (1936) which resulted in all 5 to 4 decisions. Thus, as a result, President Roosevelt proposed the Judiciary

Reorganization Bill (called the court-packing bill by his opponents), which would have increased the size of the Supreme Court and permitted the appointment of additional (presumably pro-New Deal) justices.

The bill, however, had many opponents, including his own vice president, John Nance Garner, and was defeated in Congress, which we had voted for.

The way it was, President Roosevelt was able to appoint eight Justices, the most of any other president, partly because he was voted in for his fourth term before he died in office in 1945. This had a decided effect on the Supreme Court as he appointed Justices who reflected his political ideology. In 1945, eight of the nine sitting justices had been appointed by President Roosevelt, the sole exception being Owen Roberts. That was said to be the cause of our later voting for an amendment to only allow our presidents two terms. It was considered that too many terms in office accumulated too much power in a president, as happened with Roosevelt. During Roosevelt's reign, we found Democrats ruled both houses of Congress from 1932 to 1945. This had a strong effect as to the direction of our country, as they embraced social programs and entitlements, which may have actually prolonged the end of the depression.

Building of the Golden Gate and San Francisco Bay Bridges for the World's Fair
(The reason this is important is that all were built without government money.)

One bright note coming out of the Depression was that during the late '30s, a group of people in San Francisco, visionary leaders and financiers, had obtained the World's Fair for 1939/40 to be held in San Francisco. However, San Francisco was all city buildings and homes, and they had no area or room for such a large piece of land in which to place a World's Fair, so they got together with builders, engineers, architects, and wealthy donors decided to build two large bridges to cross the San Francisco Bay, for easier access for visitors to the 1939 World's Fair in cars and busses and an island in which to house the Fair.

They had to construct an island in the middle of the Bay Bridge as it was far longer, in which to anchor the two spans. Then attached to that was the man-made island, Yerba Buena, which connected to a larger island they had built out of mud and cement. This island was called Treasure Island. Money was soon raised allowing for these two bridges and the Islands to be built in record time with absolutely no money from the Federal Government. Imagine anything this large being built without government funds today?

The Fair was deemed very successful and brought much money to the city. From then on, San Francisco flourished even more as auto traffic, trucks, and buses could come in and out of the city from the east and north in a short time; therefore, they no longer had to rely upon slow ferries to get them to the city. San Francisco is still one of the most visited cities in the world.

Treasure Island, after the Fair, was turned over to the US Navy for a Naval Base, which was closed down in about 1992, with one of the base closures. From the entrance to Treasure Island was one of the best views of the San Francisco skyline.

The Golden Gate Bridge Just Being Completed in 1937

Can you imagine any major project like that now without most of the funds, if not all, coming from the Federal Government? It is owned by the State and some funds came from there, but most from private investors. The fact that no union workers were used cut the costs considerably, too. The Golden Gate Bridge was built with an ingenious design that allowed it to swing back and forth to allow for the stresses of high winds and in the case of earthquakes. When painting the orange-colored primer paint, the sun glinting on the bridge brought the demand from the people to leave it that color, thus the name Golden Gate Bridge. This bridge is known all over the world as the gateway to the San Francisco Bay and as a symbol of California. At the time, it was the longest single-span cable-suspension bridge in the world.

(During the later Loma Prieta Earthquake in 1989, the portion of the Oakland San Francisco Bay Bridge that had not been constructed as a cable-held swinging span, similar to that of the Golden Gate, did not fall, but a portion of the other more solid design did fall with cars on it. The Golden Gate Bridge held up well, with no damage, even though parts of the marina that had been built on fill near it suffered considerable earthquake damage.)

CHAPTER 13

World War II (1941 to 1945) Forever Changed Our World

Our ship is dodging German ships and using depth charges to blow up hidden ammo in the water as our ship sails the troubled seas of war

After Germany invaded Poland in 1939 and other satellite countries, we became aware that we might have to wade again into another World War. Many protested that they did not want the US to go into another war to save Europe again. But when the Japanese bombed Pearl Harbor and one of our ships were sunk by the Germans, it became apparent that we would have to enter the war.

I well remember hearing President's Roosevelt's famous radio speech on December 7, 1941 (no TV then with breaking news) wherein he told us, "This will be a day that will go down in infamy." Congress and the president then declared war. Later, in one of our darkest hours, in one of his Fireside speeches on the radio, which I remember hearing, when the war was not going very well, President Roosevelt, in order to bolster our concerns about the way the war was going, cited his famous Four Freedoms, which we were fighting for: freedom of speech, freedom of worship, freedom from fear, and freedom from want. It stirred our imagination, and all realized what we were really fighting for. Other than the Civil War, we lost more soldiers in WWII than ever before. Almost everyone had a son or an uncle or father in the war or knew someone. It was not only a sad time, but a time the country really pulled together.

World-famous magazine illustrator of *Saturday Evening Post* covers, Norman Rockwell, picked up on that theme and painted the famous "Four Freedoms" in four separate paintings. They were made into posters and went all around the world. They became the symbol for what we were fighting for and our patriotism.

I had the distinct privilege of meeting Norman Rockwell in person in 1949 when he spoke at Pepperdine University in Southern California, which I had attended. He asked if he could keep the poster I had painted of him, which was of Rockwell portrayed on a Post Cover, and as a result, he sent me an autographed copy of his Four Freedoms. What an honor!

Those copies are still on my wall. I am reminded, when I look at them, of all the hundreds of thousands who have given their lives for our freedoms and how our vote is <u>all that stands between us and those freedoms.</u>

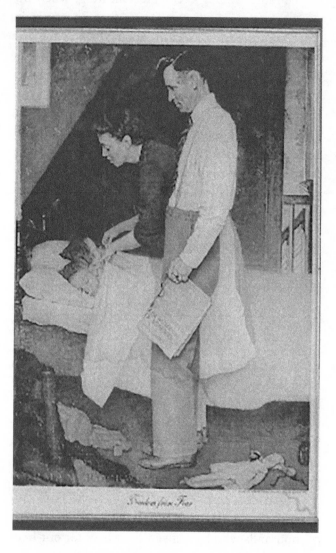

"Freedom from Fear" by Norman Rockwell

"Freedom from Want" by Norman Rockwell

"Freedom of Worship" by Norman Rockwell

"Freedom of Speech" by Norman Rockwell

Left: President Hugh Tiner, president
of Pepperdine University, holding
the author's poster of Rockwell

[Norman Rockwell was one of the most famous artists and persons in the whole world, painting many *Saturday Evening Post* covers, especially after he painted his Four Freedoms posters, based on a speech by President Franklin Roosevelt on our Four Freedoms. The posters of the Freedoms went viral all over the world then. They were so symbolic of what we were fighting for. I was in college at Pepperdine College in Los Angeles, and I had a part-time job painting posters for upcoming events on the campus (no computers then). I was told Norman Rockwell was coming to the campus and to make a poster for that event. They would print several copies and place them around the campus (no computers or printers then).

I decided to make it like a *Saturday Evening Post* cover. I put Rockwell on the cover as he often put himself into his scenes on the covers of that magazine. The evening he spoke, afterward, the art director asked my brother and I if we would like to meet Norman Rockwell. We said we sure would. So just after we walked on the stage, the school photographer came in carrying my poster. He told Rockwell, "Here is the young lady who painted this poster," and asked him to pose with it with the president of the college. Then the great Norman Rockwell very humbly turned to me and asked me if he could have my poster.

I thought, (gulp) *The great Norman Rockwell wanted this lowly little old freshman gal's poster?* Imagine that! Then I piped up. "Well, yes, if you will send me something of yours." I thought even a tiny picture he had painted or even a thumbnail sketch would be a treasure. He said he would. Several months later, I got in the mail, copies of his Four Freedoms, which he autographed. Those are still on my wall to this day. The picture of him holding my poster went into the college yearbook (above) that year. Rockwell was the most famous person I have ever met. [His Four Freedoms paintings as posters went all over the world during World War II and became symbolic for what we were fighting for.]

All we have to fear, is fear itself.
—President Franklin Roosevelt

Getting back to World War II and how it affected me and my family and the nation. I had lived with my family from 1941 through 1943 in Hawthorne, Southern California, in between three large airplane factories. We lived in constant fear that we would be bombed at any time. Indeed, Japanese subs were later reported hovering around the coast. One dreadful night, in about mid-1942, anti-air-craft guns went off, scaring us to death, and kept shooting off and on for about an hour. We were told nothing. But next morning, there was shrapnel all over the ground. We were sure there was something up there they were shooting at. One of the scariest times of my life.

Along with extreme rationing, steel and iron were very scarce. I remember a girlfriend and I, at age eleven, hauled a very heavy steel bedspring to heave on the scrap heap, where it would be sold to be recycled for the war effort. We had little sugar, butter, shoes, tires, coffee, and gasoline, as all were rationed. No new cars were sold. The cost of war was horrendous, so the government sold War US Savings Bonds to help pay for it.

President Roosevelt and Winston Churchill, Prime Minister of England, worked together to win the war. Roosevelt proved to be undoubtedly a better war time leader than a Depression leader. He will always be remembered for his steadfast leadership then and his encouragement in troubled times. He and Churchill both gave us the feeling that they had the courage to lead us out of the war and to win.

It was a very patriotic time, a time of sacrifice and hard work, where the country all pulled together. Churchill believed in strong leadership. He once said, "An appeaser is one who feeds a crocodile, hoping it will eat him last. A man does what he must, in spite of personal consequences, in spite of obstacle, danger and pressures—and that is the basis of all human morality."

The Greatest War in Europe's history was initiated by a series of aggressive annexation and conquests by Hitler's Nazi Germany between 1939 and 1941. When the conflict ceased to be a series of campaigns and became a war, however, Germany was checked and then stripped of the initiative by an Allied Force headed by two nations on the lateral extremes of Europe—Britain and the USSR—and from December 1941, a non-European nation, the US. Each of the latter proved more than Germany's equal in military and economic resources. The eventual Allied victory, following concerted assaults from west, south, east, and the air, saved Europe from the scourge of Nazism but also completed Europe's devastation, bringing to an end four hundred years of European global domination.

President Roosevelt Dies in Office

Soon after we had voted in President Roosevelt to his record fourth term, he died in office in April of 1945 of an embolism. I remember the headlines and hearing about it on the radio. We were all saddened to hear this as he had led us through those dark days of war. Roosevelt, together with Winston Churchill, Prime Minister of Great Britain, had been the real strength and tenacity to bring us through the war and to win. I remember crying when I heard the news on the radio and read the headlines in the paper. After Roosevelt's death, Harry Truman, who had been vice president, automatically became our president. The Japanese kept on fighting in the islands in the Pacific, and it appeared they would never give up. The European war had ended in June of 1945, shortly after that World War II ended in Europe, as our troops and allies marched into Berlin taking over Germany.

Dropping the First Atomic Bomb

Since the atomic bomb had been secretly invented and developed in our country, it was decided in a very difficult decision by President Truman, and agreed to by Congress, that the only way to stop millions more lives from ending, as even if we invaded Japan they would not give up, so we dropped the bomb on two of their cities. That act alone ended the war and Japan's emperor, surrendered to General MacArthur, with the papers of surrender and armistice being signed aboard the battleship the USS *Missouri*, anchored in Tokyo Harbor. By then, it was August 1945, so the war had gone on for over four years.

This was, for sure, the war to end all wars. The Great Depression of the '30s ended with World War II, not with the New Deal or what was done with government spending in the '30s. The production of goods, commerce, uniforms, guns, and equipment needed for the war effort was what ended the depression. Many in our country mistakenly believe that what Franklin Roosevelt did with the economy during the depression and with his New Deal, that it was the reason we were brought out of the depression, but I personally know that was not true, having lived then and observed the course of events happening.

Raising the flag in Iwo Jima, after taking
it over from the Japanese. One of the
hardest fought battles; this was symbolic
and helped end the war in 1945.

CHAPTER 14

Post-WWII: The Late '40s and '50s

We finally cruise into calmer waters on our voyage and can breathe a wind sigh of relief, the calm after the storm—a new direction for our Ship of State.

We voted for war, but we were really glad when it was over. It was a period of great patriotism which brought our country together. We mourned the loss of so many hundreds of thousands in our military and those lives all over the world. Now we needed to pay attention to rebuilding our economy and to accommodating the hordes of military coming home all at one time—to cheers and parades. We wanted to vote for representatives that will honor them and yet pay down our war debt, too.

President Truman, along with Generals Patton and MacArthur, completed the war and settled us into postwar economy and the new growth. The

Democrats controlled both houses of Congress from 1933 to 1945, so it was time to change to a new course by voting for a Republican Congress. This World War II generation has been called the Greatest Generation because of what we survived and that we saved the world. The GIs came home, went to college, or work, raised families, bought homes with the GI Bill, and were most industrious and patriotic. More than any other generation before or since.

The GIs Come Home

Our economy immediately strengthened, even though we had a huge war debt. The returning military came home to the GI college bill that the Congress "we voted for" voted in, affording many the opportunity to go to college that would never have been able to before. They were the best students of all time. They were mature, and many already had families or were planning to get married and have them, so they were highly motivated students. By going to college, they were then able to get higher paying jobs, with many choosing careers in law, medicine, science, or as teachers.

Boomers Born

Along with the GI Bill for college, Congress also passed the GI Home Loan bill. This allowed GIs to borrow at an interest rate of 4 percent, which was a very low rate then, for homes in the suddenly booming subdivisions being built all over the country, especially in the west. Many more were able to buy homes than any young men had ever been able to before. Along with the homes came the kids so that we had the largest generation of kids ever before in the history of any country. This generation was forever after called the Baby Boomers or Boomers. In a few years, more new schools had to be built to accommodate this invasion of children. We had voted for Congress that passed laws to accommodate our returning military and their families. This helped the expansion of our economic recovery from the war.

This was a time of great rebuilding, of industry expanding, of people traversing the country, as many that were stationed in other areas, or when they were being separated out of the service decided to stay in that area or move to a new area. We then saw a huge change of demographics for the country, which affected the vote. Areas that had gone more Democratic were changed to Republican and vice versa.

We had seen much rationing during the war, so suddenly no rationing, with the result that food and gas became plentiful. No new cars were built during the war, as the steel was needed for the war, so in 1946, new cars were once again being sold. Even new tires had become impossible to buy, as the rubber was needed for the war effort, so we had to put patch over patch to keep our old cars going. Now we could again buy a car and tires for used cars and go see the country or take a family vacation. We could use them to get to work, as people started commuting longer to work, to find better-paying jobs. The economy flourished in spite of the huge war debt.

Marshall Plan Saves Europe

According to *World History and Atlas*, after WWII, Europe was divided East and West with Soviet-dominated Communist East Germany, which by 1947 was partitioned along the same lines, it played a pivotal role in the tensions between the two blocs (East and West Germany). From 1945 to 1952, millions of people were forcibly resettled, while many others fled persecution. The US, fearing that Communism would be an attractive alternative to postwar poverty and dislocation, financed the Marshall Plan, an economic recovery program for Europe. By 1948, a pro-Soviet bloc, bound by economic and military agreements, had been established in Eastern Europe. Attempts to challenge Soviet dominance in the Soviet Bloc in the 1950s and 1960 were brutally suppressed.

Between 1942 and 1976, military spending by the Soviets was one-fifth of the budget as a nuclear arsenal to rival that of the US was developed. A return to the modernization program begun in 1928 saw industrial output increase remarkably. Prison camps were used as a labor resource in the Soviet, and by then, Soviet influence had extended into Africa and Asia. The Cold War had begun.

The Marshall Plan granted over 12.5 billion to friendly European countries between 1948 and 1951 to assist postwar economic recovery. The North Atlantic Treaty Organization grew out of this partnership (NATO), committing the US, Canada, and several Western European countries to joining defense against any Soviet aggression. NATO is still going strong today and was involved in the Iraq and Afghanistan wars.

CHAPTER 15

The United Nations Formed in 1945

While our ship is now being steered without a first mate, everything seemed above board, but the powers that be wanted a World Order organization, so our vote steered it in that direction, changing course again.

We had voted for a president for four terms. Could that have been a mistake since we had a stacked Supreme Court and Democrat control for thirteen years in Congress. After the demise of the League of Nations, Franklin Roosevelt did not give up on the concept of a world body to provide peace and work with our allies. He thought of the United Nations, to replace the now defunct League of Nations. After his death, Mrs. Roosevelt carried on with his plans to help develop the UN in New York. But what else was behind this organization's idea?

The charter was ratified by the Congress, which we had voted for with many nations taking part. It would have been a good idea if it were truly for peace, but was it?

In 1941 was the Declaration of St. James Place. During the darkest hours of the war, among London and the Allied government, the people's faith in ultimate victory remained unshaken, as then people were looking beyond military victory to the postwar future. The Atlantic Charter was signed in August 1941. That was the next step to a world organization, the result of a dramatic meeting between Roosevelt and Winston Churchill, Prime Minister of England.

Then by 1943, the Moscow and Teheran Conference was held where all principal allied nations were committed to outright victory.

United Nations Established

In 1945, in San Francisco, forty-five nations including the four sponsors were originally invited to this conference of nations which had declared war on Germany and Japan and had subscribed to the United Nations Declaration. The name "United Nations" was coined by Franklin Roosevelt and was first used in 1942. These delegates deliberated on the basis of proposals worked out by the representatives of China, the Soviet Union, the United Kingdom, and the US. The charter was signed by fifty countries. It was ratified by our Congress (whom we voted for). United Nations Day is celebrated on October 24 each year.

In later chapters, we will discuss where the UN has gone and how it desires to sink our ship before our voyage is completed. (This had started out as a good idea but turned out to have no teeth in their sanctions or declarations and is almost totally supported financially by the US—and yet we have little voting power.)

What has our vote done now? Are we voting for people who have the best interest of preserving our freedoms, who have faith and values and want us to maintain our sovereignty? Or are we voting for an International United Nations that want to control all the countries in the world? One world government is what their aim is. With a world economy, a world bank, a world currency, a world small-arms treaty, a world military, is this organization bent on taking away our individual sovereignty and taking over control of our country, if so, why are we voting for this? Is our ship closer to the iceberg?

CHAPTER 16

Post–World War II: The Plentiful '50s

To continue on our voyage, anchors aweigh again! Smooth sailing for a change.

War hero and leader, former five-star general, Dwight D. Eisenhower, a Supreme Commander during the war (a Republican), was voted in by a majority of us in 1952. Some were concerned he would be a war monger, but it was one of the most peaceful times in our history. By that point, Eisenhower had had enough war. He appointed more conservative types to the Supreme Court, thus balancing it out once more again. During Eisenhower's presidency, in 1952, Republicans controlled both houses of Congress until 1954, but after that, we see a run of control by the Democrats for forty years.

Eisenhower signed the Republican's Party 1957 Civil Rights Act. In 1960, he signed the <u>Republican's Civil Rights Act of 1960</u>.

Advent of the Freeways

The economy by then had picked up and became very good. President Eisenhower, after touring in Germany, right after the war, had driven on the super highway that Hitler had built partly to move troops on, called the Autobahn. Eisenhower, having been a military commander, realized that if we had more wars, and thinking of how military goods and transport could be shipped easier on our highways, realized that we needed better highways. He then, with the vote of the Republican Congress, developed the divided lanes Interstate Highways System, which he is best known for now.

These magnificent, wide, divided highways forever changed our landscape and our world, making it faster to drive cross country, to move goods by trucking, and thus allowing more towns and cities along its route to spring up and prosper. It changed our demographics once more, as people moved around the country more easily and from city to the country and from the country to the city. That changed the vote in many significant ways, as the people in the hugely populated cities tended to vote more liberal or democratic, where the more rural parts of the country voted more conservative.

TV into Every Home

We enjoyed prosperity never seen before with more people owning homes, more of our population working, and families happy. Then TV was invented for home use. Families would sit around together evenings watching mostly wholesome family-oriented programs, first in black and white and then later in color, like *I Love Lucy*, the *Ed Sullivan Talent Show*, where he introduced the Beatles, and Elvis, *Jackie Gleason*, *Ozzie and Harriet*, and westerns, like *Bonanza and The Lone Ranger*, which fairly well reflected the nuclear family of that time. This could have been called the age of innocence, of strong family values, and more disposable income for more people than ever before.

Many of our military bases located around the world in different countries for the war were kept in place and are still there to preserve the peace or possibly strategically placed in the event of aggression.

Soviets Develop Atomic Bomb, and Korean War Starts

The peacetime draft had been instituted by Congress in the late '40s. Soon, we were embroiled in another war in Korea by 1950–53. In the meantime, the Soviet Union had also developed the atomic bomb in 1949. The Communist Chinese drove their nationalists into Taiwan, thus securing control of Mainland China. By 1950, the US had barred trade with Communist China.

From 1945, East Asia was dominated by the conflicting ideologies of communism and capitalism, which brought international war in Korea and Vietnam in 1947 to 1975. In China, Mao Zedong and his successor sought social revolution through centralization, collectivism, and the ruthless elimination of dissent, while attempting to manage phenomenal growth spread around the Pacific Rim. Now China was starting to become a world power, according to *World History and Atlas.*

First Nuclear Sub: The Nautilus Launched

The first nuclear submarine was launched by the US in 1954 named Nautilus. That was the beginning of nuclear being used on ships. The nuclear subs could stay down much longer, including going under the ice of the Arctic Ocean at the North Pole for many days and not having to come up to refuel. This was a decided military advantage. Today, we have the latest in nuclear-powered carriers.

Race for Space Begins

The first US satellite orbits the earth ushering in the age of space for the US, in an attempt to get ahead of Russia which had launched their Sputnik, first spaceship to go into space. Russia going into space first made us realize our schools were lagging behind in science and math. It was a wake-up call for our country, so the teaching of science and math was upgraded in the colleges in order to compete.

NASA was formed for space exploration, with funds being appropriated in answer to the Russians in the race for space exploration. This was a defining moment in the US supremacy in the world.

Our ship was sailing grandly then.

In 1957, the European Economic Community was established to guarantee the economic success of its members and to develop a union of states in an attempt to lessen the risk of another war. This was the precursor of the European Union to come, having an effect on the US and our economy and on our exports and outsourcing.

CHAPTER 17

The '60s: The Boomers Come of Age in the Age of Aquarius

OH! OH! Rocky weather ahead with our ship casting to and fro. What has happened to the sea by then, why is it so bumpy, the waves so high, almost to swamp our ship?

This era turned out to determine the course of our country for a long time. We had some hard years with the assassination of President Kennedy in November of 1963. The early boomers were of age to start to college, by the late sixties, so many mothers had gone to work to pay for their children's college education, while other families saved for that day.

Young parents had vowed that their children's lives would be better than theirs had been, having been raised during the Great Depression and then born the deprivation of World War II. They did not want their kids to have to work through college as they had to do. There were no grants or student loans then.

A few earned scholarships, but the majority had to pay. Mothers working for their kid's college future were leaving kids at home alone after school. They were called the latchkey kids. That turned out to be a big mistake.

Their parents gave this generation more than any other generation had ever given material goods to their kids, therefore bearing essentially a rather spoiled generation as the result.

Boomers Go to College

Suddenly, we had a generation of kids raised fairly strict, not being chaperoned for the first time, let loose with nothing to do but play, drink, and party, because they did not have to work, so had a lot of leisure time. And plenty of money for pot. They went to college and started smoking marijuana (pot) to get high. Music was mostly folk music at first, then entering into the age of the early rock, as the Beatles became popular, then Elvis.

Boomers Start to Protest

These young students became rebellious then, partly prompted by professors that their parents were old fogies, and they should have freedom and live how they wanted, resenting anyone old, as their parents and any authority. They called the police pigs. This was the generation that was never going to get old. (Now with the "60s generation retiring, they have more aches and pains than their parents had).

These "flower children" lived together without marriage, partly because their parents would not support them and their chosen partner if they married and not wanted them to get married too young or when in school. Meanwhile, the socialist professors in the colleges encouraged this rebellion and had suggested they should act against authority, as well as the socialist leaning professors introduced socialism as ideal to them and their future. Their morals broke down, and play and fun were all they cared about. The students began to protest and have sit-ins. Those students are now the teachers and professors in the universities now and rampant working in government at the local and federal levels. For some reason, most vote Democrat and are very liberal. They want socialism here, thinking it would be great. And ideal. It has never worked and never will.

The Age of Flower Children and Hippies

Long hair for guys prevailed as the Beatles wore, so was considered popular to emulate. Girls wore long beads, long tie-dyed skirts, and headbands, with no bras. Sex was deemed free, and communes were born, where many lived together in communes, and moved back to the land, but not always living in harmony. Marriage was no longer deemed necessary for sex or even to have children. They were called flower children, those who lived in San Francisco in the Haight Ashbury District. Others were called hippies. This was a profound social and moral change for our country and is still having an effect on our way of life. This forever changed the landscape for San Francisco, starting it on a long liberal leaning course, until now it is the most liberal leaning city in the country.

J. F. Kennedy Elected President

In 1959, John F. Kennedy, a senator from an illustrious rich family from Massachusetts, was elected president. He represented a younger, charming president, along with his wife Jackie, who was considered the most beautiful and fashionable First Lady ever in our history. It was deemed the Age of Camelot, ushering in an era of Kennedys in public office for a long time. He was generally fiscally conservative in his lowering taxes and in supporting businesses. The old-time Democrat.

John Glenn Orbited Earth and We Plan to Land on the Moon

In 1962, John Glenn orbited the earth for the first man in space to do that, a landmark feat. With this achievement, President Kennedy declared we would have a race to the moon and attain our leadership in space as well as around the world. As we know, Kennedy's dream did come to fruition when we actually did send men to the moon on more than one occasion. Now Obama has cut the space missions and will only allow small robots to land on Mars and other moons, instead of people in voyages. He does not want America to feel great and strong. Or be the leader as we have been in the past.

The Cuban Missile Crisis

The Cuban Missile Crisis in 1962 was one of the most perilous crises in modern times. Russia had started building missiles in Cuba, daring the United States to do anything about it. JFK, his brother Robert, Attorney General, and staff spent many days developing a means to curb this aggression. With missiles that close within range of the US, it was a very dangerous time. The US brought in battleships causing an embargo around Cuba, with their large guns pointed toward the missiles, and dared them to continue placing those missiles in Cuba, within range of our eastern coast. Khrushchev, President of Russia, finally backed down at the last minute when he realized that the US was serious in deterring this threat. It was brinksmanship at that point. After the fiasco of the Bay of Pigs, Kennedy redeemed himself with this threat to Russia. This isolated Cuba and kept the Russians at bay for taking over our country.

Landmark Supreme Court Decisions

There were some landmark Supreme Court cases in the '60s, when the strict scrutiny standard was employed which allowed that all religious activities were permissible unless the state had a very compelling interest to restrict certain activities. The Establishment Clause, which states that no law based on religion would be employed by Congress, combined with the Free Exercise Clause prevailed for the first time in the 1963 Court Case, *Sherbert v. Verner*. In 1962, school prayers were banned by the Supreme Court, stating also that devotional Bible readings in public schools were unconstitutional.

President Kennedy Assassinated

In November 1963, we saw in horror the assassination on TV of President John F. Kennedy in Dallas, Texas. That was indelibly written on the minds of everyone, especially the young boomers then, of actually seeing something like this on TV. We were all glued to the TV for three days as they played over and over all of the drama around this horrendous act. To add to the drama and horror, his supposed shooter, Oswald, was then shot to death, when being escorted to another jail, as we watched it play out on TV. Those alive now still remember that day and weekend, the horror as this drama played out on TV; the first time most Americans had witnessed an actual assassination of a president, and not any president, but the shining one that the country loved. That changed the course of our ship.

We will never know how Kennedy's presidency would have actually been viewed as it ended so early.

Vice President Johnson stepped into the office of president and, in fact, was sworn in inside Air Force I, even before it took off from Dallas to go back to Washington, taking the president's body with it. We still remember seeing on TV Jackie Kennedy there on Air Force I, at the swearing in, with blood still on her pink suit, from when President Kennedy was shot riding in his limousine. This was the end of Camelot and a shock to all in the nation. All of this reflected another sudden change of course for our ship.

The sixties also ushered in the start of Women's lib. Liberal protesters advocated for women's rights and for an amendment to the Constitution for this. A women's advocacy group called NOW was protesting for this to be ratified in all the states as another amendment, however, not all of the states would ratify it. This group espoused women's independence from men, that women should have careers, while women homemakers were scorned. More mothers went to work, thinking this was what women should do, should have a career, thus changing the dynamics in their families, plus two-salaried families changed the economical dynamics of the country.

"The War on Poverty," designed by President Lyndon Johnson, initiated the creation of the Office of Economic Opportunity. This was the beginning of the largest expansion of entitlements. It was the beginning of huge welfare benefits as we know it by now. Congress, which we voted for, voted this entitlement in. It has grown out of proportion to our ability to pay for it, with much widespread abuse.

Martin Luther King Assassinated

On April 4, 1968, famous Civil Rights leader, Martin Luther King, Jr., was assassinated. MLK believed in peaceful protests in promoting equality in our country. This was another shock coming on the heels of President Kennedy being assassinated, culminating in desegregation ordered by the Supreme Court in 1969. This was a time of racial crisis and of desegregation to end the segregation practiced especially in the south in our country.

First Man on the Moon

One of the greatest achievements of the '60s was a first, when Neil Armstrong walked on the moon and raised the US flag in a feat never before imagined as consciousness in the possibilities of space escalated. No other country could nor has been able to accomplish going to the moon. NASA funding was strengthened as more space flights were planned.

We moved ahead of Russia with this feat in the race for space began, and we indeed eventually landed a spacecraft on the moon with Armstrong's famous broadcast from the moon. Another feat was not only landing a craft on the moon, but being able to take off and connect with the mother spacecraft in space and safely return to the earth. This hurled the United States as the world leader in space and in technology.

Congress Declares War for Vietnam and Voting Rights

The Vietnam War was brewing, causing anxiety all over the world. A US destroyer had been attacked in the Gulf of Tonkin in 1964. Congress resolves that President Johnson be given authority to use all power to repel attacks on US Forces. This resolution formed the basis for massive escalation of US military action with our Declaration of War. Most of the later '60s and early '70s were an age of rebellion, of protests, but also of different rights being established. Voting Rights were passed by Congress in 1965 to be sure voting rights was to equalize standards for voting in all fifty states. It was an era of change for the country—an era that changed the course of our Ship of State, in many different ways.

Race Riots Break Out

In 1965, race riots in Watts area of Los Angeles, resulted in widespread fires, thus escalating the civil rights in that area. Malcolm X, a black leader, was shot and killed, leading in 1966 and '67 to more race riots in many major cities. Thurgood Marshall became the first African American on the Supreme Court, another milestone and change of course for our country, as well as balance of the Supreme Court.

The '60s saw the Vietnam War escalate and the protests from the Boomers as well as protests from the black communities, with riots, and burnings.

It was a dangerous course for our Ship of State to continue down the voyage. Our ship was rocking back and forth, not sure what course to take. It was a stormy decade.

By 1969, the Vietnam Peace talks start, but the war was not to end until 1973. It seemed to drag out forever.

We saw Golda Meir become Prime Minister of Israel, the first woman prime minister. Some of the oldest prestigious colleges, such as Yale and Colgate admitted women amid protests of the male students.

This was an era of rights, civil, women's, and changing demographics in the country, thus changing our votes as a result, as we began to have voting blocs of groups then, such as the black vote, the women's vote, the Southern vote, and the white vote. Why not just the American vote?

In 1969, the Supreme Court ordered that all public schools must be desegregated. This caused riots, especially in the South, and as a result, it bred unrest in the country as it became even more divisive.

No Ship in the Bottle Waiting to Get Out

The changes coming about during the '60s, having been a profound change in course, have strongly influenced even now by who is in Congress and as president and what course our ship is taking.

Too many in Congress are a product of the rebellious '60s and '70s, the yuppies of that era. Many are liberal secular socialists and '60s activists, who are bent on changing the course of our ship.

They have a totally different viewpoint of how our Ship of State should continue and what course they think it should be on.

How different their votes are today in Congress, with more lack of bipartisanship cooperation, than ever before. Well, to the liberals, evidently, bipartisanship means the Republicans should give into them; therefore, if they do not, then the liberals need not negotiate with the Republicans. It did not used to be that way, or at least very little. Bi-partisanship helped us win WWI and II, helped us get to the moon, and other great achievements. But it only works if <u>both</u> sides are willing to give and not be "it's my way or the highway!" Or the Republicans must give in to the so-called wiser liberal elites.

CHAPTER 18

Nixon Presidency:
Vietnam War Protests,
Civil Rights of the '70s

Approved by the Senate in 1970, giving the president broad powers to wage war with the lifting of the Gulf of Tonkin Resolution, was another change of course for our ship. The war had amassed 543,000 troops in 1969, but Congress had not lifted the resolution yet. This was the largest number of troops in the war. We had just had two World Wars, so why were we in another? The draft had been invoked again, and the war was still going strong while the Civil Rights movement in the South was profoundly changing our country. Even though the Civil War in the 1860s during Lincoln's presidency (a Republican) had been fought for the freedom of the slaves, there was still much discrimination going on, especially in the south.

Vietnam War Protests

By the late '60s, the Boomers decided to protest the Vietnam War, well underway by then. So there were sit-ins, flag burning, and burning of buildings. I was working in an office in the early '70s in Berkeley, California, at the time the center of protests, when the Cal at Berkeley students burned down People's Park and other buildings. I had a hard time getting out of town after work, with the smoke dimming my vision along with many roads closed.

Massive escalation of the United States military effort, combined with nightly TV coverage of war and opposition of liberal news media was in our faces, so that escalated the anti-war movement. Anti-war demonstrations became widespread, mainly in California, but soon all over the country.

The college students and grads were protesting the war and protesting most anything going on. Many young men had been drafted by then and were off to the jungles. We were neither trained nor equipped to fight this type of guerilla warfare and were outnumbered by the natives, who were used to the jungles and that type of fighting. There were too many rules for our troops of where they could go and not cross over into North Vietnam across the border, yet the North Vietnamese could come across with impunity. The uniforms at first were not working right for there, as they stood out in that jungle terrain, so the camouflage uniform for the army was constructed. The military are still wearing the camouflage uniform on bases and in Iraq and Afghanistan. The only difference there was the coloring of the camouflage was lightened to blend in more with the desert terrain.

In 1970, 440 universities and colleges were closed or on strike in protest against the Vietnam War. This caused considerable disruption to the student's education as well as in the communities surrounding the schools.

Voting Age Changed to 18

In 1971, we saw a Constitutional Amendment (26) lowering the voting age to 18. Congress ratified this. The thinking in the country was if so many hundreds of thousands could go to war at 18, then why could they not vote. That profoundly changed the course of our ship, as it changed the voting demographics as many tended to vote more liberal, so more Democrats were voted into Congress and in local and state elections.

The Nixon Era: The Late '60s

In 1968, Richard Nixon had been elected as president. His helping brought an end to the Vietnam War was one of his signal achievements. But in 1972, when he was running again for president, some of his re-election campaign managers broke into the Democratic Headquarters at the Watergate Buildings, and when they were found out, the source was traced back to Nixon's headquarters.

It was covered up by Nixon and his staff. When this was exposed, there were threats by the Democrats in Congress to impeach Nixon. To avoid impeachment, Nixon resigned much to the country's surprise, being the first president to ever resign from office. From then on, the scandal was referred to as Watergate. This was the start of many things being called (prefix) Gate. Nixon was replaced by his vice president, Gerald Ford.

Ironically, Johnson had done the same thing to Goldwater's campaign headquarters, but nothing was ever said then. If you are a Democrat, you can get away with more.

Many years later, after historians reviewed his record, they deemed Nixon was a fairly good president after all. Nixon had worked to thaw the relations with the Chinese and made a start when the US Table Tennis team was in Nagoya, Japan, in 1971 for the 31st World Table Tennis Championship on April 6, when they received an invitation to visit China.

This was unusual given that several high-profile American citizens, such as Senator Eugene McCarthy, had expressed interest in visiting China after the 1968 election, but even he could not have a trip arranged for him despite his office. One of the Chinese players and one of the American players became friendly, which was unusual. The US team finally was allowed by China's Chairman, Mao Zedong, a table tennis player, himself to come into his country. On April 10, the team and accompanying journalists became the first American sports delegation to set foot in the

Chinese capital since 1949. The meeting was facility to the National Committee on United States-China relations. Two months later, Richard Nixon visited China, and then Mao Zhuan Zedong visited the US, as the head of a Chinese Table Tennis delegation in April of 1972. However, China's attempt to reach out to countries through ping-pong diplomacy was not always successful. Nixon, through our US athletes, and Zedong's interest in ping-pong, was able to thaw relations with China, so from then on it was called the Ping-Pong Diplomacy. This opened up trade in Asia again.

Another rocky voyage for our Ship of State. Events and actions can change the course of our ship.

Partly as a reaction to Nixon's potential impeachment and resignation, many more Democrats were voted into Congress, as a result thus controlling Congress for forty years until 1994, when the Republicans took over both houses. We voted for this course, but was it a wise course?

Vietnam War Finally Ends

The Vietnam War ends in 1973 to the relief of a war-weary nation. My own son, in the Marines by then, was ordered to go to Vietnam in 1971, but unexpectedly got his orders changed at the last minute. He ended up as an MP at Hunters Point in San Francisco, occasionally doing honor guard duties at funerals and special occasions for the military. His buddy in his unit who was sent to Vietnam never came back.

The Vietnam War was one of defining moments in our course, splitting the country, and the pain caused, for the first time, the public to blame the soldiers returning from the war, and unfortunately many were spat upon and treated disrespectfully. This was noted by the time we went to war again in Iraq and Afghanistan, so that now no matter whether our people agree with the war or not, we do not blame the soldiers, and now the military is generally treated with respect, especially those returning from the wars.

We owe our freedom to these fine military willing to fight for their country over the centuries since our existence. Over and over, they have been willing to give their lives to allow us to live free. How are we repaying these fine young persons? By not voting is saying they have given their lives or sustained major injuries in vain, as if we don't care. We are saying we don't care what course our Ship of State takes. Imagine willing to give your life for your country when many millions don't even bother to vote?

Voting is one of the few citizen duties we are asked to exercise.

CHAPTER 19

Supreme Court Landmark Decisions of the '60s and '70s

What murky waters our ship is wafting into now.

Roe v. Wade Some significant Supreme Court Decisions in the '70s changed our course forever. One of the most famous still being used in political debate and still a divide in the country over is *Roe v. Wade*, wherein the Supreme Court said that abortion was legal in <u>some</u> circumstances. This has been often taken to mean that any abortion, no matter what the circumstances. Part of the country looks at abortion as murder and the other looks at is as a "woman's right to choose." Yet these same people are against cruelty to any animals, even tiny insects, or the safety of the spotted owl in environmental fights, and yet also the death penalty, which is to say no murder there, but murder is okay for millions of growing embryos in the womb (see research on this decision).

Prayer in Schools which was deemed uncon-stitutional was another landmark decision by the Supreme Court that has affected and divided the country. Madelyn Murray O Hare, an atheist, who was also a Marxist, brought this to the court in 1963 and almost single-handedly forced the decision that prayers must be taken out of the schools. One person can make a difference. But not always for the better of our country.

This has gone on so long now, that even at grad-uations, prayers cannot be said. However, Congress invokes a led prayer every time they go into session.

Bible Reading Mandatory in Schools. The elimi-nation of this brought many protests from churches, when the Supreme Court determined this to be unconstitutional. But now, this is so extreme that no child can bring a Bible to school or even say a prayer before he eats at school. Recently, a pastor was arrested for reading his Bible on a park bench.

These decisions of the upper court can stay with us for a long time and change the course of our country. We do not vote for our justices of the Supreme Court and they serve for life.

Again, the Justices who voted for these laws were appointed by presidents whose ideology was along the lines for which these Justices voted for. Are they for the better or a planned execution to take God out of our country? This country was founded on faith by God-believing founders, and most people were people of faith that had positions of leadership until the early 1900s when that started changing. Is that part of the reason our Ship of State is floundering on the seas of time, trying to find its course? Yet we voted for the presidents knowing of their ideology and the type of Justices they would probably appoint.

CHAPTER 20

Reagan Elected: '80s, Age of Peace, Smooth Sailing Again

Our ship hits smoother waters and changes course, right rudder: Full Steam Ahead!

Ronald Reagan Becomes President

Our country voted and President Reagan (Republican), actor and former Governor of California, was elected in 1982, replacing Jimmie Carter, who had proved to be pretty inept as a president. His more liberal views of the direction and of the economy were not working well for him, and he was more of a micro-manager than a strong leader. Carter, former Governor of Georgia, had even determined the schedule of whom would play on the tennis courts at the White House. The economy floundered and unemployment in 1982 had risen to 10 percent, the highest it had been in forty years, which no doubt was one of the main reasons that Carter was not re-elected.

President Reagan, a charismatic leader, former Democrat, and a capitalist, found he had inherited a mess, so he set out to bring the economy back. Interest rates had gone up to 21 percent and the housing market was hurt badly by this. Reagan worked to bring the rates back down and to grow the economy, working well with Congress. He was able to work across the aisle and accomplish much during his presidency. Speaker of House Tip O'Neill was a good leader, though he and Reagan often differed in the way they wanted the votes to go, they could come to the table and work it out.

Reagan only had the Republican Senate for six years and one whom we had voted for and in his own party. He lowered taxes and business flourished bringing back the economy. Reagan is used as an example of a great president who accomplished much. Some historians rate President Reagan as our eighth best president.

The first act Reagan performed, as he was taking office, was to bring back the fifty-nine Iran hostages, from the US Embassy there, since President Jimmie Carter had been unable to accomplish their escape.

This showed the world right away that President Reagan was a real world leader and a strong one.

Reagan Addresses the Cold War with Russia

Reagan, working closely with Pope John Paul, a Polish immigrant, who understood the problems in the Soviet-controlled countries, was able to work with bringing down communism in the satellite countries that the Soviets had taken over. He addressed the Cold War and met with Russian leaders.

One of his most memorable speeches of Reagan's was at the Berlin Wall, which had separated Germany since World War II, when he said, "Tear down this wall, Mr. Gorbachev!" It was shortly after Reagan left office that the wall finally came tumbling down uniting East and West Germany once again. This was symbolic of tearing down the overreach of the Soviets to try to dominate the world and force Communism on all of those countries. Another change of course, for our country, as well as for the world resulted in allowing more freedom for the people in many parts of the world.

Cuban Refugee Movement

Some of the other more important changes in the '80s were: the Cuban refugee movement where so many tried to escape the dictatorship regime of Fidel Castro in Cuba and were immigrating to Florida in all kinds of make-shift boats. Some of the boats sunk or did not make it, with its occupants drowning. The US allowed them to come and live here, but eventually had to turn some away. This forever changed the complexion of Florida and surrounding states and changed the demographics of the vote, as most became US citizens.

First Space Shuttle

In 1981, the first reusable Space Shuttle, Columbia, was launched, flying for 54 ½ hrs. around the earth and landed on its wheels at Edwards AFB in California where it was piggybacked on a larger plane back to NASA launching site at Cape Canaveral in Florida.

This very successful space exploration and accomplishments added to our supremacy in the world and to our quest for more space exploration. The idea then was to plan for a space station, so that these reusable shuttles could take astronauts to the station, while building it and bring them back again. Congress voted for more money to go into the space program. In addition to space conquering, many techniques, technical innovations, and new materials employed in the space program and on the ships were later used in medicine, especially in machines for diagnostics like CAT scans and MRIs and in greater understanding the physiology of the body, especially under stress of outer space, and in the later computer technology, which was used in the space program. New or improved materials used for space was also later used in industry.

Our votes for Congress paid off to start and to continue the space program, as the whole world benefitted from it. It put the US on the map as the most inventive and competent country in the world.

The <u>Equal Rights Amendment</u> called ERA was defeated in 1982, when only thirty-five states of the then forty-eight ratified it. This was a blow to those who had been protesting for it for a long time. The votes in the states to not pass this Amendment changed the course of the country. This Amendment has never been brought up again since then.

Major Supreme Court decisions in the late '80s and '90s, with a divided court, were *Texas v. Johnson* in 1989. A man named Johnson was arrested for burning an American flag, which, in Texas, was illegal. In this important case, however, the Supreme Court established that his demonstration conveyed a particular message, and it was supported by his right to free speech, under the First Amendment. Flag burning in protest was carried out often after that.

In 1992, *Lee v Weisman* declared official-sanctioned, student-led school prayers were unconstitutional, with Sandra Day O'Conner providing the swing vote. O'Connor, appointed by Reagan, as a Justice was thought to be more conservative, but often voted with the liberal block, providing a swing vote.

CHAPTER 21

The 1990s, Bill Clinton, Scandals and His Moving Center with the Republican Revolution

Woe is the course of our ship, when we are not sure where to turn the rudder. Our ship rights itself with a new Congress.

William Jefferson Clinton was elected by our votes to the presidency in 1992. He was very charismatic. "I feel your pain," he would tell us, and make it really believable. He succeeded where no other Democrat president had since Franklin Roosevelt, as he was re-elected to a second term. Clinton also defied his critics in surviving an array of personal scandals, yet turning the greatest fiscal deficit in American history into a surplus (with the help of a Republican fiscally-conservative Congress, whom we voted for in 1994, and which became the first Republican Congress in power for forty years, with their Contract for America).

Clinton was able to move to the center (after being advised by his advisor, Dick Morris, who is now a conservative columnist, enough to work with his Republican Congress and with Newt Gingrich, capable Speaker of the House, who led the Republican Revolution).

HillaryCare Proposed

Early in Clinton's first term, his politically active wife, Hillary Clinton, wanted universal health care passed, so she lobbied for it strenuously. It did not pass, setting Clinton back in what he was trying to do to obtain health care reform. It has ever since been called HillaryCare.

Clinton was able to effectively use American forces to stop the ethnic cleansing wars in Bosnia and Kosovo and ended up presiding over the greatest level of economic prosperity since the early 1960s, with the leadership of the Republican Congress and their *Contract with America*.

This was the era of the Republican Revolution.

A significant Republican Party success in the 1994 midterm elections resulted in a net gain of fifty-four seats in the House and a pickup of eight seats in the Senate. The clear leader of the revolution was Republican Congressman, Newt Gingrich, who became Speaker of the House as a result of the victory. The day after the election, Democratic Senator Richard Shelby, of Alabama, changed parties, thus becoming a Republican.

The gains in the seats in the midterm election resulted in the Republicans gaining control of both the House and the Senate in January of 1995. Republicans had not held the majority in the House for forty years, since the 83rd Congress (elected in 1952). Our votes put them there, and it paid off so that by the end of the 1900s, we ended with a surplus and a good economy as a result.

Large Republican gains were made in statehouses as well, with 12 gubernatorial seats and 472 legislative seats across the country. Prior to this, Republicans had not held the majority of governorships since 1972. In addition, this was the first time in 50 years that the GOP controlled a majority of state legislatures.

The result of all of this was that Clinton benefitted greatly with this revolution, as the sweeping changes Congress made, they were able to get him to pass the changes which, were genuinely for the welfare of the country, like cutting, spending, and balancing the budget. Clinton gets credit for the spending cuts and reform, however, and he did work with Congress on these reforms. Clinton even worked with Congress to eliminate many welfare programs in that people would have to train and go to work after being on welfare for three years.

When campaigning, Clinton sought to focus on issues supported by the middle class, such as government spending to stimulate the economy, tough crime laws, and jobs for welfare recipients and tax reform that shifted the burden to the rich. He was also a typical Democrat in that he was for gun control, converting military expenditures to domestic purposes, for environmental laws, equal employment, and national health insurance and rights for gays.

Clinton Survives Scandal

Clinton surprisingly also survived the humiliating but unsuccessful impeachment trial by the US Senate with the infamous Lewinsky scandal. Ms. Lewinsky testified that she had had sex several times with Clinton in the Oval Office. She had kept the dress with his dried semen still on it, which was proven later it was his through DNA tests. Clinton first denied it with his. "I never had sex with that woman!" Later, he said that it was oral sex, and therefore, it was not sex. And it depended on what the word "is" is. He also was going to be impeached for perjury to the Grand Jury. But the impeachment trial was not successful.

Clinton fashioned himself as a "New Democrat" and has frequently been referred to as the "Comeback Kid." All of this made him the second president to survive impeachment. Few presidents have both raised more questions about the standing of the presidency and yet at the same time, presided over a long period of continuing prosperity.

However, he had the Republican Congress to thank for that. He was willing to move enough to the center when his advisor at the time, Dick Morris, advised him to do that and to work with them. Morris later changed to the Republican Party and is now a political advisor for the Conservative media and working in supporting Republican campaigns, as well as a sought-after advisor during the elections.

Clinton succeeded in foreign affairs by working closely with Northern Ireland between warring Catholics and Protestants and helping them to gain peace once again. He failed to end the genocide in Rwanda and the peace talks he worked with between Israel and the Palestine Liberation Organization became dissolved into a renewed and more dangerous round of strife for that region. The Democratic Party owed its strong renewal to Clinton as titular head of the party, as it appeared it was going in a good direction with Clinton leading it.

Clinton Appointments to the Supreme Court

Clinton appointed Ruth Bader Ginsburg to the Supreme Court, whom his wife Hillary had lobbied for. Ms. Ginsburg was a true liberal and most all votes have found her on the liberal side. She has suggested that International Law to be used as precedent in the Supreme Court decisions. That would be dangerous for maintaining our sovereignty.

International Peace Parks Here

One of the things that few people know about and was not voted for by us was by executive order the turning over of some of our National Parks to the UN by Clinton as International Peace Parks. I have heard that the Statue of Liberty was also designated as an International Peace Park. Look at the map of Montana and see the Glacier International Peace Park on the border of Montana and Canada. This was taking executive power way beyond what it is constitutionally supposed to do without our voting or Congress voting on it. Where does it say presidents can give away land to the UN? Or foreign countries manage our parks?

Generation X, the children of the Boomers, were young adults or teenagers during this decade, while the oldest members were nearly forty as the decade closed. They were not as extreme in dissident as their parents had been, but most had gone to college so soaked up the ideologies of their more liberal professors. Generation Y were children, preteens, and early teenagers during this decade.

The Dawn of the Information Age

The '90s is often called the Dawn of the Information Age. It was not until the late 1980s and '90s that computers became widely used by the general public. The mass mobilization of capital markets was the beginning of the widespread usage of new media such as the Internet. That along with the changes with the breaking down of the Soviet Union in its power led to a realignment and consolidation of economic and political power across the entire world.

The '90s was the dawn of current postmodern age, even though the first traces of post modernity take place in the '40s. We saw improved living standards in as much that Eastern Europe, Latin America, and South Africa became more prosperous. Instead of being called third world nations, countries like South Korea and Ireland became so economically successful they were called first world nations by the end of the '90s.

The Hubble space telescope floated in space in the '90s, signaling vast success in researching outer space, the planets, and stars.

The signing of the Oslo Peace Accords in 1993 was another peaceful resolution.

The *www.com* Revolution

The ingenious World Wide Web became popular and gained much popularity all over the world. It helped with first the e-mail popularity, where one could e-mail anyone all over the world for instant and very inexpensive communication, plus looking up any information on the internet. Businesses soon developed their own web page for advertising and social networks began. Blogs of all kinds came into being, as information channels. Personal dating through the internet became popular, while computer surveillance became used in warfare and in criminal investigations. Video gaming came in, along with the computer generation, appealing greatly to the young

At first, the government was the only entity to have large mainframe computers, along with the military, then banks started using them, and large businesses, but then it became possible for the general public to own one. At first, they were fairly large but became smaller until laptops came in and now we have even smaller ones, with the iPad and the iPod. Books are being read with the Kindle reader, called e-books. Microchips used in computers have found many other uses in technology and in personal use, such as in cell phones. Social networking like Facebook and Twitter was introduced and used all over the world.

The '90s was a time of economic growth, inventiveness, and greater communication throughout the world. It was a time of prosperity and with computers all over the world changing the ways that we communicated. This would surely affect the vote and demographics again. Instant news and political blogs flourished giving us as well, as the news media, instant information to report.

Bill Clinton ended his terms as president in January 2001 and some seem to think as popular as any Democrat president since World War II. He has worked in international aid, creating the William J. Clinton Foundation to promote international causes, such as prevention of AIDS and global warming. (Which may now be deemed corrupt and under investigation.) In 2009, he became the United Nations Special Envoy to Haiti and after the 2010 earthquake in Haiti, he teamed up with Geo. W. Bush to form the Clinton Bush Haiti Fund, for aid of that ravished country's inhabitants who were suddenly left without homes or food.

Clinton has had several major health concerns with a bypass and lately some stents put into his heart, but basically, he stays healthy and travels to other countries, goes on speaking tours, has built his presidential library in Arkansas and writes books.

His wife, Hillary, was appointed by Barack Obama to be Secretary of State, when our votes did not let her win the presidency, having lost her bid to Barack Obama in the primaries. It was a bitter pill for her to swallow as the plan was that she would help Bill to become president and then it would be her turn. His scandals and almost impeachment deterred her from even trying to run when he left office, so she quickly set up residence in New York and ran for the Senate and won. She thought that this would be a springboard for her own bid for presidency later.

She had declared that she will not remain as Secretary of State through another term even if Obama wins in 2012.

Some caution that we need to look at is the relationship between the Clintons and our last

President Obama, on the grand scale, all are working toward a world-controlled, Statist, UN-controlled society.

Dangerous Treaties Might Sink Our Ship

Hillary seems to be only somewhat well regarded now, and no one can really declare what she actually did as Secretary of State. She is viewed with mixed emotions. However, she has been working with President Obama and the UN with the Small-Arms Treaty to get small arms taken away all over the world and the turning of our sovereignty over to the U.N. through international treaties. Another treaty about to be voted by the UN is the Treaty of the Seas. If passed and ratified by our Congress, it would give the UN full control of all our seas, including any offshore drilling or use of the waters, even near our shores. That, too, would be extremely dangerous and take our sovereignty away. Hillary Clinton is much more of a socialist than Bill ever was. She is probably much more ambitious than her husband. Their daughter, Chelsea, recently was hosting a cable network TV program, may have political ambitions someday.

CHAPTER 22

The 2000s, George W. Bush and 9/11, and Two Wars

Our Ship of State hit deep waves of discord over voting for the 2000 election.

President Bush came into office on the heels of one of the most controversial elections in 2000. He was running against Al Gore, former vice president for Pres. Clinton. The election was running close, when in Florida, it was the deciding factor of the electoral votes. Al Gore decided to call for a recount, but selectively chose just certain few solidly Democrat-leaning counties to hold the election recount in. There was much confusion on how to count the votes as many were punched with holes in them, so they were counting hanging chads as votes.

Along the way, this was legally challenged and the fact that not all of Florida was being recounted, so it wound its way quickly to the Supreme Court to make a decision. The Court decided <u>unanimously</u>

that just counting a few chosen counties was not constitutional, but they voted then 5 to 4 on how long before the votes were to go to the Electoral College. Many, especially in the news, misconstrued this that the Supreme Court voted 5 to 4 with the majority being more conservative that voted in favor of George W. Bush. This caused a divide in the country with the liberals declaring that George W. Bush was not a legal president. However, as we know, George W. Bush succeeded in winning his re-election without any help from the Supreme Court

On 9/11/2001, our Ship of State encounters shock and awe as it is cruising near the coast of New York, when it sees planes flying into the Financial District Twin Towers of New York City.

This was a most shocking disaster. His was the first time since the Revolutionary War that foreign enemy had actually attacked the US mainland and on our soil yet. What audacity!

Planned by Al Qaeda, a terrorist organization, under the leadership of Osama bin Laden, we watched in horror as it all unfolded on TV, and many in person in New York watched in person in horror as first one plane drove right into one of the Twin Towers, then as it started to catch fire and to collapse, then again in shock when another passenger plane hit the other tower. Luckily, many people in the building were able to escape, but about 2,500 died. People were even jumping off to their deaths from the higher stories rather than be burned to death. Many of our finest first responders were either killed or wounded.

9/11/2001 Attack on the World
Trade Center and DC

On Tuesday, the United States suffered a devastating attack against New York City and the Pentagon in Washington, DC. At this time, it is reported that four large passenger jets are destroyed with the presumed loss of all souls on board. Each of the twin towers of the World Trade Center in New York were hit by hijacked commercial jet aircraft and destroyed.

The Pentagon in Washington, DC, was also struck by an aircraft and set ablaze, and one of the wings of the building partially collapsed. The national emergency Continuation of Government plan was activated, with key government officials evacuating to a secret Bunker in Mt. Weather, Virginia. An atmosphere of crisis engulfed the country. (www.apfn.org/the winds/2001/09/terror/attack.html)

This changed the course of our ship overnight!

What horror to watch. Orders were given quickly to ground all planes in the country, which may have saved more buildings from being hit, as it was rumored that more planes had planned to take off and hit other targets.

But wait, that was not enough; a little later, we saw pictures of another plane diving right into the Pentagon building, killing hundreds more. Then we got breaking news that another plane which had been hijacked, was turning around, and heading for Washington, DC, reportedly to hit the State Capital Building, when the passengers, after some had heard on their cell phones that the buildings in New York and the Pentagon had been hit by planes, then decided to ram the cockpit and try to take back and land the plane, if they could.

While they were not successful in landing the plane, as they could not subdue the terrorist pilot in time, they at least stopped the plane from heading toward Washington. Sadly, their plane crashed in a field in Pennsylvania, and none survived. Reports by cell phone to family members gave us a clear understanding of what happened on that plane. (That forever changed the way passengers respond to terrorists hijacking planes or anyone disrupting the pilots or the airline attendants. Several times since, passengers have intervened and subdued someone who was completely out of hand and causing serious problems on planes.) No US planes have been hijacked since. They know now that the passengers will not just sit there and let them take it over.

President Bush had been reading to a school group in Florida when one of his aides whispered to him what was happening. He was stunned, and it took a few minutes for him to decide what was best to do. He left the schoolroom and talked on the phone to the vice president and security in Washington and was advised to head out but not to come to Washington then as news was there was another plane on its way headed to DC. His Air Force One plane headed west and landed at one of our air force bases, waiting until it was deemed safe to return to DC.

Our ship took another course, headed out to sea, and anchored to ponder the shape of our Ship of State and determine what course then to take.

It soon became clear that when Al Qaeda claimed responsibility for these attacks that we must do something about this.

President Bush in a famous appearance among the rubble in New York of what was left of the towers, proclaimed to the workers with a bull horn and by TV to the world, "the whole world will hear from us." We could not stand by and allow our country to be attacked and do nothing.

President Bush decided with Congress to go into Afghanistan, the hiding place of Al Qaeda leader Osama bin Laden. We were able to rout some of the Al Qaeda, who were hiding behind the Taliban and causing much terror in Afghanistan, so they mostly headed over the border into Pakistan.

Then before the war was finished in Afghanistan, President Bush wanted to go into Iraq and get rid of Saddam Hussein wherein our intelligence estimated that Hussein was gathering weapons of mass destruction. He had already used gas on some of his own people, so he was considered an enemy and was a cruel dictator.

After hearing testimony, Congress agreed to allow the President to go to war if he felt there was justification. Saddam Hussein was chased out of Baghdad by our troops and the country fell into the hands of the US troops. No one could find Saddam's hiding place for a long time. Through US intelligence, he was eventually captured by our troops who found that he was hiding in a hole in the ground. He was turned over to Iraq officials and eventually tried, found guilty, and hung. The weapon of mass destruction or nuclear missiles were never found, but Saddam had two months, while we were, not very secretively, preparing for war, in which to hide them either deep in the ground or be taken to nearby Syria. Satellite pictures during that two months' time period showed very large trucks hauling something large in the direction of Syria.

The war continued on there and in Afghanistan in an attempt to bring democracy to terrorist run nations. But the Taliban and Al Qaeda and some of the insurgents kept on fighting and planting roadside bombs, killing many of our troops as they drove by on the roads. The whole war became bogged down by that point, causing many political problems for President Bush.

Katrina Floods New Orleans, Changing Our Course Once Again

Then in 2004, Katrina, a devastating hurricane storm, hit New Orleans, and the waves broke the canals around the city, flooding a great deal of it. Evidently, the mayor and the Governor of Louisiana were not prepared for a disaster. President Bush called the governor and asked if she needed federal help and she said not. He could not send the Feds in unless the governor asked for their help.

Many refugees from the storm were not housed in a stadium, which was not equipped for relief nor had any supplies available. Sadly, pictures in the paper and on the news, showed busses lined up in the water that could have been used to evacuate people, and the plight of the persons having to stay in that stadium. Many persons drowned as they could not be taken out fast enough by the rescue helicopters. Some chose to stay with their houses only to find the waters overtaking their home, and they either were drowned or climbed on roofs to try to hail for help. Helicopters were flown around the city looking for anyone needing help, as well as rescue boats on the water.

This disaster hurt President Bush, as some held him responsible, as they claimed the levies were not kept up by the federal government and were unsafe. He was put on the spot because they said he did not land in New Orleans right after the flood, as he was coming back from California. He chose not to at that point as he felt it would be a distraction from the rescue operation, because of all the security needed if he, as president, landed, therefore choosing to go a few days later. His FEMA appointee, Brown, made a lot of mistakes, causing embarrassment for Bush and had to be fired. But now as several major disasters have hit several of our states in the last three years, President Obama took his time in visiting the sites of serious disasters and nothing is much was ever said. It all depends upon who is president and whether they are Republican or Democrat or not.

The liberal media has a way of not noticing anything wrong if a president is a Democrat, but if he is a Republican, then report everything even if some of it is not very factual. And often without any research or investigation, but just offering opinions.

The Housing Meltdown

A few years earlier, Barney Frank and Chris Dodd in Congress, chairmen of regulations, in charge of housing market regulations, decided that everyone should own a home, so wrote regulations that banks must loan to people who were actually not qualified. Eventually, this caught up with the banks when people could not pay for their mortgages, causing a housing meltdown by 2008. A bailout stimulus bill was voted for in Congress by then to bail out the banks. Other financial factors here and in the world were happening at the same time. This all affected Wall Street, and the financial markets started losing money.

Our ship seemed to be heading into a recession stream. Can we steer our way out?

Bush Appointees to the Supreme Court

President Bush appointed Justice John Roberts to be the Chief Justice when Chief Justice

Rehnquist died in 2005. Rehnquist had led a remarkably stable Court—for the eleven years preceding his death, the composition of the Court remained unchanged—the longest such stretch in over 180 years.

Bush also appointed in 2005 former US Court of Appeals, Judge Samuel Alito to replace retiring Justice Sandra Day O'Conner. Both of these appointments reflected closer to the somewhat moderate conservative ideology of President Bush, but both men were also extremely well qualified constitutionalists. This complexion of the court accounted for other 5 to 4 decisions.

Landmark decisions in the 2000s by the Supreme Court were *Stenberg v. Carhart* in 2000 which voided laws prohibiting late-term abortions and *Lawrence v. Texas* 2003 which struck down laws prohibiting sodomy. Another controversial decision for the Rehnquist Court in 2003 was *Greutter v. Bolinger* which upheld affirmative action.

Democrats Take Back Congress in 2006

In 2006, as a reaction to the wars going on and seeming to drag out and to President Bush by the Democrats, the Congress changed, once again, due to our votes, so that now the result was a majority of Democrats in both Houses. Once again, the spending started spiraling, and more favors passed out to pet projects, earmarks, unions, and lobbyists.

CHAPTER 23

The Reign of Obama Himself, "The Anointed One," and National Health Care

Our ship is way off course; the icebergs are in sight in the distance. Can we avoid hitting one? Our periscope sights the dangers ahead. A new captain has come on board. Rumor is that he has never captained a ship before, and, in fact, has had no experience on the sea or in navigation, but he may have worked with pirates in the past, bent on boarding our ship and capturing it.

By 2008, it was an election year, but not a normal election year as for the first time, an African American (at least part half) was running for president. (Later information is that Obama was only ¼ African American with ¼ being Arabic, and in fact his name is Arabic and not African at all). If even that part is true, there seemed to be many questions about his heritage and identity as well as where he was actually born for sure.

He came up from nowhere, although he had been an unremarkable senator in the Illinois State Legislature, he was appointed to take the place of a senator leaving Congress, and had not been in the US Senate long when he started running for president. No bills were written by him in either Chicago or in our Senate. He voted "present" many times, it was reported. Could we not assume then that this man could or would not make decisions? He started running against Hillary Clinton in the primaries. This person, whom nobody knew, had spoken at the 2004 Democrat Convention and people were impressed with his speech. Through a serious of strange coincidences, such as where his campaign money came from, he gained on her, and in the end, he won enough votes, through caucuses, etc., to win the Democrat primary, thus upsetting the very strong Clinton machine

This new candidate promised "hope and change," which sounded so good, especially for the young. He became almost rock-star popular, as he campaigned across the country. The idea of our first "black" president especially appealed to the young and to the liberal mainstream media.

For the first time ever, our liberal national media did not even vet this candidate. There are still questions of proof of his eligibility, of his social security number, which comes from Connecticut, where he has never lived nor worked there, and of his selective service registration, where records of that have been destroyed. In fact, there have been several court cases asking for proof of all of his past records and to determine his eligibility, but they all get shoved aside. Somehow, many of his records have been erased or not allowed to be researched. He had committed contempt of court for not producing his records even when a court has asked for them or for him to appear. Who else can get away with subpoenaed requests for records and not produce them nor to appear in court when subpoenaed and not be imprisoned for contempt of court? When he had been pressed, Obama released on the internet his latest birth certificate from Hawaii, but recent forensic analysis from Canada has discovered that this certificate appears to have been manipulated and therefore may not be authentic.

Who or what is behind protecting this president, and he, earlier, as a candidate? Any other person running for president would not have been considered eligible in the first place and would have had to produce his records and be vetted by the media. He won't even release his college records. What is he covering up?

Some suspect it is because he was given a foreign fellowship or scholarship to go to Columbia University. If that were proven, it would no doubt prove he was not an American citizen. If he traveled to Pakistan on a world tour (as in his own words in his book, that he was a very poor college student), when a US passport would not have been allowed to travel with into Pakistan then, so he would have had to travel with either a British passport, as his father was Kenyan, which was owned by Britain or an Indonesian one. He was adopted by his stepfather who was Indonesian and lived there several years. Usually, in adoptions, you have to give up any other passport and take that of your father's or of his country. There are still many questions surrounding the citizenship requirements to be president of the United States. His supposed natural father was from Kenya and therefore a British subject, so that alone would make our president ineligible, according to most authorities on the constitution.

The next conundrum not mentioned in any news sources of note in our nation: Barack Obama, in 2005 as a freshman senator from Illinois, went on a Congressional fact-finding tour to Perm, Siberia, in Russia, with Senator Richard Lugar (R-Ind.) to verify the destruction of mobile missiles and their launch platforms under the Cooperative Threat Reduction Program (CTR)

The trip was uneventful, that is, until it was time to depart the Russian military base where these inspections took place. All of a sudden, Barack Obama and Senator Lugar were confronted and held by Russian authorities, while the Russians sought permission to search the aircraft they were traveling in.

Senator Lugar does not make mention of this incident in his after-action trip report. This was found strange. Numerous foreign news sources in Italy and other nations reveal that Barack was being held and questioned for espionage as being a spy for Britain. This is curious behavior from the Russians because the Cold War ended in 1991 and our nations have more to gain with mutual cooperation than hostility toward each other. This type of behavior was the custom during earlier times of *detente* between our nations, though not in 2005. What passport was he traveling with then, and why was he questioned for espionage as a spy for Britain? There are more and more questions being raised about the president's past.

The first two years of the last president's term went smoothly enough, with Congress holding a Democratic majority, except for the recession, which still haunts his presidency. At first, he talked Congress into another stimulus bill, promising the result of it would bring us out of the recession and make more jobs. He then bailed out the banks and the car companies, taking some of them over and firing their CEOs. Since when does our government or president own private companies and fire CEOs? Does anyone know where most of the stimulus money went? Most of it, according to a Fox News Special in 2010, is reported to have gone overseas or to favored entities. The economy certainly did not improve as promised. He said he was going to cut in half our national debt, but it has raised over 5 trillion during his first term.

Obamacare, What a Nightmare

Our president's new government mandated Health Care Bill, in 2009, which he had little or nothing to do with writing it, was passed over the protests of most of the country. In the secret of night <u>without any input from the Republicans</u>, the Democrats in Congress put together this government-mandated health care bill, some 2,700 pages, and passed it, with no vote at all from any Republican and no information out to the public as to what was in it. Many arms were twisted; bribes and threats were accomplished in order to get ALL the Democrats to vote. Their hesitation apparently stemmed from those representing red states, who worried about their re-election chances if they voted for this controversial bill. Indeed, in the House takeover by Republicans in 2010, some of those Democrats found that they had lost their seats. This Obamacare, as it is now called, has defined his presidency more than any other event.

Obama had left the White House and was not even around during most of the process. This president, who promised transparency in his administration, and that all bills would be posted on the internet five days before being passed, yet allowed secrecy to prevail during the process with the public knowing nothing about what was in it until it was passed and then printed up. Speaker of the House at the time, Nancy Pelosi, told the media at a press conference, *"We have to pass it so we know what's in it."* Never have I heard such a dumb statement from a Speaker of the House. The 2,700-some pages had passed so fast, it just clarified what many people had thought, "How could anyone even read it?" Well, folks, that is what many voted for, a Congress that would pass this kind of law, that apparently even they did not read, and that the people did not want, in the manner in which they did.

Vladimir Lenin (builder of the Soviet Communist state) said, *"The key to a successful Communist takeover of a free society is for the state to get control of the healthcare system." Lenin called Socialized Medicine, "the keystone to the arch of the Socialist state."*

Fidel Castro even praised the passing of the National Health Care Bill, as he thought that now the US was coming closer to a socialist North America.

When radio host Paul Smith asked liberal Congressman John Dingell (D-MI), why it will take the government until 2014 to fully set up the Affordable Health Care System, Dingell said this: *"It takes a long time to do the necessary administrative steps that have to be taken to put the legislation together to control the people"* (Source: News Talk WJR Radio with Paul W. Smith 3/23/2010).

I am outraged that Obama continued to move forward with setting up Obamacare by hiring tens of thousands of IRA agents to police the mandates in this new law, in the face of the Federal Ruling being heard in the Supreme Court, that Obamacare or parts of it is totally unconstitutional.

The Tenth Amendment clearly states that *"the power not delegated to the United States by the Constitution, nor prohibited by it to the states are reserved to the States respectively, or to the people."*

American Founding Father and primary author of the Constitution James Madison explained in the

Federalist Papers (No. 45) how our federalist system of government was intended to work:

"The powers delegated by the proposed Constitution to the Federal government are few and defined. Those which are to remain in the State governments are numerous and indefinite."

Nowhere does the Constitution give the power to the government to mandate to the states what they must do, especially where it affects the Commerce Law.

"Lord, deliver us from Obamacare. That is enough to wreck our ship for sure." We are now asked why health care costs keep going up when we were told this new health care would make health care affordable for all. Because it is mandated by the government and actually they did not want it to work, so they could move in with Single Payer Health Care (all owned by the government) and, in this way, control ALL the people. They can then blame the insurance companies for the high costs, and if we just get rid of them, it would not cost near as much if the government ran it all. Think about the waste in anything the government runs, and the costs going up. Like the post office. Think of the efficiency of FedEx or UPS.

The Tea Party Protests

As reaction to the ramming of the Affordable Health Care Program in Congress, the Tea Party was formed in protest. This was a large peaceful activist group of a cross section of people across the country concerned about our country and what Congress was doing. They saw moderate RINO (Republicans in Name Only) Republicans voting with the Democrats in some of the spending bills. They held huge rallies, protesting what was going on in Washington. The outcome of this was they formed a grassroots movement and were able to get more conservative Congressmen voted into the House, taking it back again in 2010. The Tea Partiers played a large part in Congressional votes in Congress in 2012, to maintain the House and take back the Senate in this next election. Indeed! They did in 2014, taking back the Senate, as well as the House. The Tea Party played a large role in backing more conservatives in States and local elections in many parts of the country, as well. The Tea Party are large in representation in some of the candidates for the 2016 Republican presidential race are ones that were backed by the Tea Party or lean somewhat in that more conservative direction.

Liberals, such as comedienne Janeane Garafalo, called them a bunch of tea-bagging rednecks. "This is about hating a black man in the White House. This is racism straight up," she claims. However, CBS/New York Time news polls show that in April 2010, 37 percent of the

Tea Partiers are college graduates as compared to 25 percent of the general public and 56 percent earn more than $50,000 a year. When asked the leaders of the Tea Party their goals, the top four choices were: reducing the role of the federal government, creating jobs, lowering taxes, and cutting government spending. They are, indeed, depraved and desperate characters.

Foreign Policy

Foreign policy for President Obama was mixed. He still refused to defend Israel against the threats of Iran, only making cursory statements that he is working on it, while waiting for UN sanctions to work. He was our first president that had not strongly defended Israel since they took back their land in the '60s. Israel is our only ally in that part of the world and has been a strong supporter of freedom. Even in the form of dire threats by Iran to wipe Israel off the face of the map, as well as the US, President Obama does not seem to care or act. Yet he claimed to be a Christian, while most Christians support Israel. He seemed to think that appeasement is the best answer to their threats of developing a nuclear bomb and blowing up Israel, as well as the US.

Our president was filmed as he bowed to Saudi princes and to the Chinese dictator and to other dictators. He apologized for America. No president has ever apologized for America before. He even seemed to be ashamed of this country. He seems to be ashamed of Christians or Christianity, as he had all Christian symbols covered up that were behind him on the stage when he spoke at religious universities. While it has been the best country in the whole world, the most successful, and world leader since 1919, why would anyone be ashamed of this unique beautiful country? What had we voted for? What kind of a captain for our ship was this? He hates his ship?

Obama can be credited for the decision for the capture and subsequent killing of Osama bin Laden, however, and a big BUT, we found out from some Navy SEALs that Obama's administration and Defense Department knew where bin Laden was holed up a year before in 2010.

The administration basically did nothing about his capture until closer to the next election, and even then, Obama almost had to be made to make the decision, according to those informants that knew people in his closer circle. Even when the Navy SEALs were all prepared and ready to go in, he wanted it to go down closer to the next election, was reported. President Obama seemed to calculate all moves based on his election and politics.

In the Situation Room during
bin Laden's capture.
[from the public domain White House photos]

Is the Obama "Situation Room" Photo a Fake?

From the blog on May 13, 2012, from FellowshipofMinds.wordpress.com, according to the writer, we learn that now there is even some doubt that President Obama was even in the Situation Room during the Navy SEALs capture of bin Laden, as shown over and over on TV, contrary to what was shown in that photo. In fact, according to Gateway Pundit report that a Swedish news agency is casting doubt as to in their view of that group photo pictured whether the group were even in the Situation

Room, because of the height of the TVs in the situation room are much higher than their eyes are focused upon.

A Swedish graphics firm has even claimed that the photo of Obama was Photoshopped in later, as he looks much smaller than those by him, and his eyes are focused in a higher direction than the others. The light on his face is different than those close to him. The couple in the back of the photo, having lighter skin than those by them, was placed in there later, this source says, due to the placement of her hands, verified in a blowup of the photo.

At the time, when this photo was released, many of us observed how dwarfed Obama appeared, next to the other individuals seated around the table, with his head looking much smaller. Now he is a tall man, so should have been of the same height as Biden, or even taller, even though seated. Another observation is that Obama claims to be warm-blooded and hardly ever wears a jacket around the White House or in meetings, yet in this photo, he is shown with a heavy sports jacket on. Note that most of the other men are in their shirt sleeves.

All of this assumes that the assassination of bin Laden actually took place, or did it? Responding to a Freedom of Information Act request by the Associated Press, it has no records—not one photo, not one video, not even an e-mail—of bin Laden's death. The only photo shown has been one of bin Laden's supposed bedroom.

And why were there no photos ever released of his capture and of the reported shooting of bin Laden dead, as well as the reported burial at sea? The administration claimed the photos were too violent to be released and might incite problems in the Arab countries. This all leaves us with many questions. When earlier Saddam Hussein was captured and went to trial, there were photos all over the place of all of the proceedings. Obama is said to have been on the golf course during the time of bin Laden's supposed capture instead of in the White House. Since we do not have any real photo proof of all of this, then how or did it really happen as reported? How do we know?

To add to this mystery, on August 6, 2011, three months after the purported assassination of bin Laden, all thirty Americans aboard a Chinook helicopter were killed, including twenty-two members of the same Navy SEAL team with six who had reportedly assassinated bin Laden. Was this investigated as an accident, or are there rumors of foul play so no one would talk?

CHAPTER 24

President Obama's Abandonment of US Allies around the World

According to Bruce Herschensohn, a fixture in American politics, political radio and TV commentator, world traveler, and has been teaching at the School of Public Policy at Pepperdine University, in his book called *Obama's Globe*, he says Obama's Globe reveals how the United States Foreign policy has drastically changed since the 2009 Presidential Inauguration. The policies, he claims, have changed in a way that would be difficult to imagine under US Presidents Roosevelt, Truman, Eisenhower, Kennedy, Johnson, Nixon, Ford, Reagan, Bush (41), Clinton, and Bush (43).

Obama has abandoned our nation's friends, and we could count on this president to treat USA's friends as friends and adversaries as adversaries. Obama, in his first year in office, cancelled the agreement between the Czech Republic for a long-sought radar system to be based there for destroying missiles launched by our enemies. This was put in place by President Bush via his Secretary of State, Condoleezza Rice.

Our military was being decimated, due to the economy, we are told, back to about 1914 level, which we cannot understand, as this threatens the security of our country when we are still facing enemies on several fronts. While President Obama did not seem to be overly fond of the military, yet he took full credit of a military operation and leaped on this in his campaign of his military achievements as commander-in-chief. We saw all kinds of pictures of the capture of Saddam Hussein in a hole in the ground, of his trial, and of his hanging. Now that could have incited the Arab world for sure. Yet no pictures of the capture of the notorious Osama bin Laden, none even available to the Associated Press (AP). Curious indeed! More transparency?

Racism Is with Us Again

Not since the late '60s, during the Civil Rights movement, has racism prevailed. There is actually little there, yet the whites are constantly being accused of racism in a manner to make it look like all those who do not agree with this administration is a racist. Class unrest is what is being fostered here, too. This is typical Saul Alinsky playbook tactics, as was studied by many of the protesters in the '60s, whom, coincidentally, are now in charge of our administration, and many in Congress. It was anticipated that much more so-called racism and instigation of race riots will prevail before the next election.

On Taking Responsibility

President Obama does not appear to accept responsibility for anything negative, as is quoted in a recent Western Journalism blog. "He lacks the character to accept consequences, but will gladly shine in the light of success, even when he has nothing to do with it." President Truman, an old army sergeant, was famous for saying, "The buck stops here!" But with Obama, the buck stops with someone else he can blame. For nearly four years, he has blamed President Bush for the "mess I inherited." After a time, a president has to take responsibility for what happens under his watch.

It is quite clear that other presidents have inherited messes, such as President Reagan, but they did not spend their whole first term blaming their predecessor. Could possibly our last president, being raised mostly by his aged grandparents, who may have felt sorry for him because he was pretty well deserted by his father and mother, could they then have given into him and let him have his way and treated him in such a way that fed his ego? He also may be very insecure underneath. We know for sure that he is very thin-skinned, from his reaction to not being liked or to criticism. Most presidents just let it bounce off and pay little attention to the usual criticism. I do not recall another president being so thin-skinned.

Soak the Rich: The War on the Top 1 Percenters

The past administration aims to split the country with income redistribution. "The rich are not paying their fair share," our president states in campaign speeches.

According to *ctjreports, from ctk.org:*

The bottom 20% gets 3-4% of income and pays 2.1% of taxes.

The second 20% gets 7% of income and pays 5.3% of taxes.

The middle 20% gets 11.4% of income and pays 10.3% of taxes.

The next 20% gets 19.7% of income and pays 19% of taxes.

The next 10% gets 14.2% of income and pays 15% of taxes.

The next 5% gets 10 .1% of income and pays 11% of taxes.

The next 4% gets 14.3% of income and pays 15.5% of taxes

The top 1% of income earners gets 21% of all income in America and <u>pay 21.6 % of taxes. So much for the rich not paying taxes.</u>

Overall, the taxes we pay are almost completely flat with proportion of income.

<u>Nobody is paying more than their fair share</u>!

We need to be careful whom we soak. While the left keep lambasting President Bush's tax cuts that help Joe Millionaire more than Joe Lunch Bucket; without the Joe Millionaires in our society, Joe Lunch Bucket might be in the unemployment line!

Data collected by the Tax Foundation, a non-partisan research organization, indicates that among Americans who are subject to the highest income tax rate, two out of three, are sole proprietors of businesses. Cuts in taxes have made it less expensive for them to raise capital for new plants, equipment, and to hire new workers. Income taxes are levied on income producing activities.

If higher taxes are levied, business owners will have no choice but to pass on the cost to someone else—either the workers in the form of lower wages or the consumers in the form of the highest prices. Therefore, some portions of the taxes on business income and investment income that are aimed at the rich are actually met by workers and consumers, who are not typically rich, according to ctj reports. Now who is getting soaked? Are we being sold a bill of goods for this mantra?

On cutting Taxes Success

Looking to success of recent history, Presidents Kennedy, Reagan, and Bush all cut taxes across the board, providing increased revenue and jobs with sustained growth in the private sector. Our votes brought people into Congress and presidents who understood economics and that tax cuts enhance the economy. Puerto Rico's governor has developed successful austerity programs, even reducing his own salary and taxes, and their economy is growing fast now. He was interviewed on Fox News and he said that families would have to cut down if they had overspent, so why not a country?

Fair tax. Some of the candidates for 2016 have said they would change the tax code to either a fair or flat tax. And get rid of the IRS, a heavily bloated wing of the Federal Government. The fair tax would be that everyone would pay a certain percent of taxes on all consumer goods or equipment purchased. This way, the rich would buy more and the poor buy less, but everyone would be paying some taxes. No IRS along with its mountain of forms and no filing even. The tax rate would be 23 percent, out of every $100 spent.

The flat tax with less loopholes is a system with a constant marginal rate, usually applied to individual or corporate income. A true flat tax would be a proportional tax, but implications are often progressive and sometimes regressive depending upon deductions and exemptions.

Some say some agency like the IRS would have to collect it, but what about the Treasury Department? Let people file on a postcard and eliminate hundreds of thousands of IRS jobs.

On Wealthy Presidents

Some of our earlier presidents were very rich people in their own right. Washington was the wealthiest of all, yet by all historians, considered our best president. President Franklin Roosevelt, and even more recently, President Kennedy, came from rich families. This has never until very recently become an issue in the campaigns for president. Obama said, "Romney is rich and born with a silver spoon," but Obama is not? Obama himself has amassed a few million from speaking and from his books, and we do not know from elsewhere. That is close to a 1 percenter in my book. He constantly denounces the rich, and yet he goes to Hollywood with his hands out, to those who are some of the wealthiest 1 percenters. George Clooney, one of the richest actors in Hollywood, gave a dinner at his house in one of the most expensive areas in Southern California, to raise money for Obama's 2012 campaign. Then Obama's campaign released an ad demeaning Romney for being rich and from Wall Street and again talking about 1 percenters not paying their fair share, while he goes to Wall Street and Hollywood asking for campaign money with his hands out. Give me a break!

The Wall Street Occupiers

The "rich are not paying their fair share" mantra for the next election was the theme, when suddenly appeared the Wall Street Occupiers. No coincidence that suddenly they appear when it comes close to an election coming up. These dissenters constantly chant that they are the 99 percent and are against the 1 percent that have it all and that the rich should share and pay their fair share to them. The difference between these protesters and the Tea Party is that many of their protests ended up causing much damage to property, some becoming violent with many arrested. In Oakland, they even blocked the freight shipping in the harbor, holding up hundreds of trucks there to load up. Would you guess that hurts the economy?

With the Tea Party, there has never been any problem with the police or damages while protesting, and they don't leave a mess either. They do not camp overnight on public or private property either. The Wall Street Occupiers do not seem to be very organized or have any one message. Their signs reflect many messages. Most of the photos in the newspapers look like many are homeless or out on the streets. They may become more violent as the elections approach, as they were needed by the administration to foam discontent. It will be interesting to see if they get organized enough to promote people to run for office in the next election as the Tea Party has done. The unions seem to be behind them and helping them to organize. It was such a coincidence their suddenly appearing, that it looks a lot like community organizing, as our president used to do. So who is behind this movement? Will they have a serious effect upon the vote? They might have, but by 2015 you never hear from them, so they petered out.

But once again in the campaigns for 2016 for president, there was protest at the Trump rallies. Looks like Occupy Wall Streeters are reportedly being paid to protest again.

War on Women

There is the war on women being contrived next, as another class warfare way to glean the women's vote. The president knew he must get the women's vote to win. His administration seems to leap on anything that might affect women. Now knowing the state of the economy women should be concerned about it more than anything else. Most women are usually more responsible for making ends meet in their household. They should be concerned about their children's future. And grim as it may be, due to the huge debt that has been run up here, which they and their kids will never be able to pay, women should be doubly concerned. Women are concerned about losing their home, the high price of food and gas. Women should vote for the safety of their family and their peace of mind for the future. What next?

Women's rights have been played extensively for several decades now. That division over abortion in our country is still being played out in the political campaigns today, along with the Catholic Church wading in when our president recently announced in his Obamacare that Catholic or religious hospitals and church colleges must furnish birth control contraceptives, the day-after pills, and needed abortions to their insured. This caused a real upheaval and response from the hierarchy of the Catholic church. This is still to be heard in the Supreme Court.

Then some of the liberal women in Congress put a Georgetown University campus activist on the stand in Congress to state that her birth control in the three years at this elite, most expensive law school in the country would cost her $1,600. This caused a stir. When birth control pills cost only about $10 per month, then why $1,600, and where are her young men who should be the ones using birth control, which is safer for STDs and AIDS while those cost much less. Then President Obama waded in and said this law student's parents should be proud of her. It immediately became a crisis out of proportion, so that the Obama campaign used it to burnish women's rights as part of the campaign in order to obtain more of the women's votes. "Always take advantage of a crisis," states our president's former campaign manager, David Axelrod.

Actually, Republican women have been responsible for the 13th, 14th, and 15th Amendments. The 13th Amendment outlawed slavery, the 14th guaranteed equal protection under the law, and the 15th guaranteed voting rights for blacks (now called African Americans). Women have always played a remarkable role in our history. Republicans, at the request of Susan B Anthony, a Republican, introduced Women's Suffrage Amendment to Congress in 1888.

Liberals say they are the ones for women's rights, but more has been accomplished for women with Republicans than liberals and even more from Republican women. (Believe it or not!)

On Confidence in Our Voting

Did we have confidence in that president? We evidently did to re-elect him in 2012. Did we have confidence in Congress or in part of it? Our votes in both presidential elections and in Congress can change the course of our journey in our Ship of State—sometimes drastically.

"No confidence will kill Obama's re-election chances," said John Ransom of Townhall.com, a conservative blog think-tank. Consumer index, Bloomberg Comfort index, which asks people to rate the national economy, their personal finances, and the buying climate, reports that it has declined for the third consecutive week. About 56 percent of people rate their personal finances negatively, up from 47 percent and the highest elevation since November of 2011. The index stood at -40.6 in 2012.

This has established a trend that should be worrying to the president. Bloomberg says that the "measures for registered Democrats and Independents have dropped the most over the past two weeks after both reached the highest levels in more than four years."

How many times did Obama declare that the "recovery" had finally arrived? After buying from the White House more of the same *"Hopey-slash-Changey"* rhetoric that "the recovery has finally started." Even supporters were recognizing that on economics, this White House hadn't a clue, or maybe did not even care? The administration was still singing *"Happy Times Are Here Again."*

The *Wall Street Journal* reports that one economist says that the confidence numbers are a good predictor of the election results for incumbent presidents. The *Journal* also cites loss of consumer confidence and high unemployment for the defeats of incumbent Presidents Jimmy Carter and George H.W. Bush (#41). But somehow in spite of the economy, he won again.

On Power

Power will intoxicate the best hearts, as wine the strongest heads. No man is wise enough nor good enough to be trusted with unlimited power.

—Colton

Jefferson, in a letter, once wrote in 1811, *"I have never been able to conceive how any rational being could propose happiness to himself from the exercise of power over others."*

President Obama has often been called narcissistic. *Readers Digest*, March 2012, talked about the man in the mirror. They were quoting from psychology today.com and said, "Although narcissism generally peaks in adolescence and declines with age, psychologist Frederick Stinson conducted interviews with 34,653 adults and found that across their lifespan, men are more narcissistic than women."

"We live in an age," according to Jonah Lehrer, "that worships attention, which can inhibit imagination. Insight arrives only after you stop looking for it." Men like Napoleon, Richard the Great, Stalin, Mussolini, and Hitler were all considered narcissistic.

We have had a president enamored with his political gifts. When the leaders of Europe got together to commemorate the twentieth anniversary of the fall of the Berlin Wall, he decided not to go. But he did find the time to record a video message, which he graciously allowed the Europeans to air during the ceremony.

Giving gifts to heads of state has been going on here since we have had presidencies. They are usually of value or historical gifts. But when our last president went to England, the gift he gave the Queen was an iPod, which I am sure at the time she had no idea how to use and included in this thoughtful gift was his speeches for her to listen to. And he gave Gordon Brown, Prime Minister of England, a bag full of $5 DVDs, which would not work on their equipment in England. Who is in charge of protocol in this White House to advise the president on what are proper gifts to heads of state or queens?

In addition, it was reported that when our last president went to England for a three-day trip to meet with world leaders, it was said that he took with him twenty-five airplanes/helicopters, two hundred Secret Service, his own White House chef and staff, two hundred other persons, and thirty-five vehicles. This was not reported in our media, but the British press reported it and were actually embarrassed by this show of power. They said, "Why even the Queen, when she goes on an extensive trip, does not take along anywhere near that large an entourage." They laughed at him and his grandiosity living—especially when the US is in the Great Recession.

How Our Country Was Founded and the Duties of the Government

Our founders envisioned a fair and balanced government, with a small government. The government's main job was to defend the country and for the safety of its people. They developed the Legislative (Congress), the Executive (presidency), and the Judicial (Supreme Court), with each having their part to perform. They saw this as no one branch having power over the others or to usurp their power above what it was meant to be. They saw grave danger in an imbalance of power. They knew our country would not survive well if these branches become out of balance, which would be a guarantee that our country would not function well or could even fail. They understood human behavior, which never changes.

Over the years, we have seen the judicial usurping great power and sometimes "making law" which is the job of Congress. And Obama exercised more and more executive power and decisions without consulting Congress. The only other president who tried to assume too high a level of executive power was Franklin Roosevelt in his proposing Congress to vote to allow him to appoint more than nine Justices to the Supreme Court. This unconstitutional idea did not even go over well by some of his own party leaders, and it was voted down. Even then, Roosevelt was able to appoint eight justices in his unprecedented nearly four terms, thus packing the court with his New Deal Democrats for a long time. Most presidents appoint from one to three Justices.

President Obama had mandated more executive orders than any other president in our history. He used the excuse that Congress will not cooperate so he will just go around them as "we cannot wait." The problem is that he had full control of Congress his first two years, with it being a large majority Democrat, and yet he went around them and was still is going around Congress with a Republican Congress, with continual executive mandates carried out mostly by his pack of czars, which are not appointed nor approved by Congress.

The Sunshine Laws: Transparency in Government

President Obama promised the most transparency in his administration, yet there is far less. According to the *Economist*, 5/26/12, he also said he would not prosecute whistleblowers, yet he has several.

These Sunshine Laws are called FOIA laws. The data shows that in states with strong FOIA laws, such as Florida, politicians are less likely to be corrupt, and those that are corrupt are more likely to be caught.

"Sunlight," Supreme Court Justice Louis Brandeis wrote nearly a century ago, "is said to be the best of disinfectants."

Scott Peck, in his book, *People of the Lie: The Hope for Healing Human Evil*, writes that people who are caught up with evil are, first and foremost, liars. Peck explains that such people lie not only to everyone around them, but to themselves as well, "deceiving others, as they also build layer upon layer of self-deception." Over and over, we have seen this president misspeak the truth. Saying this may well remind us of the terrible mistake we made in electing him. What have we voted for?

In fact, President Obama said more than once that the military is his, but it belongs to the country. He had said they are to salute <u>him</u> and pledge to <u>him</u>. (Wonder what he plans to do with "his" military when they all come home from Iraq and Afghanistan?) He wants many of the military bases closed now, but what did he plan to use them for? It is reported that the plans were to use them for concentration camps to put dissidents in, and that is anyone who disagrees with the administration or liberals in positions of authority or dares to speak out. Thank goodness, he did not have time to take these disastrous steps.

Another blog in 2012, from Western Journalism, shows that there was a strong possibility that Barack Hussein Obama Sr. (½ African American from Kenya) is not Obama's father after all. There is a man named Marshall Davis, an avowed communist from Hawaii. Davis is said to have had an affair with Obama's mother, during the year in which he was born, and even indecent photos of her were reported to have been found in Davis's home. Barack, in his book, tells us his mother was four months along with him when she married Barack Sr. his father, who was a poor student from Kenya in Hawaii. Now some think it is possible that this Davis is his actual father. Photos of each show President Obama looking more like Davis by far than his reported father, Barack Sr. Davis was his (Obama Jr.'s) mentor and friend in Hawaii. Obama even mentions Davis in his first book, as a friend and mentor, who helped him a lot. Could Davis have had early influence on Obama and his socialist thinking? Did Barack know that Davis might be his father? Was having a partly black father more expedient for his planned future? Perhaps Davis helped him to go to college in the States and who paid for his expensive world trip to Pakistan and other areas when he was, according to his book, supposedly a poor student at Columbia University?

Someone or persons must have groomed Obama for a long time to have had aspirations to be president. This did not just happen, this man coming out of nowhere. There are so many questions about "just who is Barack Obama?" Upon questioning, the general public had no idea who he was or little about him. I suspect his grandparents spoiled him to death, as felt sorry for him sort of abandoned by both parents. And they may have raised him to think highly of himself.

It was so highly unusual for this unknown state legislator from Illinois to make a keynote speech at the 2004 Democrat Convention. Who asked him and why? Were plans even then being laid for him to run in 2008? Then suddenly, this inexperienced unknown, whom the liberal media did not vet at all, is running for president and is able to break down the powerful Clinton machine to win, no small feat.

Major Supreme Court Decisions Since 2009

President Obama had the opportunity to appoint two Supreme Court Justices to replace two that retired. He chose two women, whom Congress finally agreed upon, but who reflected his worldview and were both very liberal ideologues. One was Sonia Sotomayor and the other, Elena Kegan, who had no judicial experience. These two replaced two fairly liberal Justices, so the court remained in a mainly 5 to 4 balance, as the Justices seem to generally vote much of the time in their own political ideologue or the ideologue of the president whom had appointed them. Why are they there? Supposedly according to the Constitution, the Judiciary are not there to make law but to interpret the Constitution, only. Not to be a political body. Now Obama had a chance to nominate another with the unexpected death of Justice Scalia in February of 2016. He may nominate one, the Republican Congress stalled any decisions until after the 2016 election so that a new president can appoint a new Justice. It is his right to select someone but also the right of the Congress to not vote for any and to forestall it as has been done many times in the past. If Obama had gotten his appointment and it would probably be a liberal, it would no doubt tip the Supreme Court to 5 liberals, thus affecting all decisions for a generation or two to come.

Justices are not there to vote their political ideology, but too often now they do. That is why so many decisions are 5 to 4.

Citizens United Case Changes Campaign Funds

The Citizens United Case, under *Citizens United v. Federal Election Commission 558 U.S.50 (2010)* is a landmark decision by the US Supreme Court which held that the First Amendment prohibited the government from restricting independent political expenditures by corporations and unions. The nonprofit corporation Citizens United wanted to air a film critical of Hillary Clinton and to advertise the film during television broadcasts in apparent violation of the 2001 Bipartisan Campaign Reform Act commonly known as the McCain-Feingold Act or BCRA .In a 5–4 decision, the court held that portions of BCRA violated the First Amendment.

The decision reached the Supreme Court on appeal from a July 2008 decision by the US District Court for the District of Columbia Section 203 of BCRA defined as "electioneering communication" as a broadcast, cable, or satellite communication that mentioned a candidate within thirty days of a general election or thirty days of a primary and prohibited such expenditures by corporations and unions. The lower court held that BRCA applied and prohibited Citizens United from advertising the film *Hillary the Movie* in broadcast or shown on or paying to have it shown on TV within thirty days of the 2008 primary election. The Supreme Court reversed it striking down those provisions that prohibited corporations (including nonprofit corporations and unions from spending on electioneering communications). The case did not involve the federal ban on direct contributions from corporations or unions to candidate campaigns or political parties which remain illegal in races for federal office.

Our former president, apparently, did not like this decision, as in his State of the Union message in January of 2010, he pointedly made remarks of derision and accusations to the attending Supreme Court, about this, causing Justice Alito to mouth, "Not so!" and most of the members of the court to look askance. I have never known of a president lambasting the Supreme Court in a State of the Union speech before Congress. Has he no respect?

Another historical case in 2012, that was before the Supreme Court, was about the National Health Care Law. It was brought by twenty state Attorney Generals in support of the states not considering the mandate in the Obamacare Health Bill to be constitutional. Some lower courts have upheld this as being unconstitutional, so it went all the way up to the Supreme Court. It is a violation of the Commerce Law is the state's case. In the questioning, the Justices appeared to question much in this law, and it has appeared they may not be too much in favor of the mandate and even might throw out the whole case as unconstitutional. The case was decided in 2013. They did not throw out the whole law but did say states could decide on the State Aid they offered under Obamacare.

Apparently, this upset President Obama, as this was his healthcare law voted in by his Congress that was to be his legacy. However, if the Supreme Court had thrown it out, this could cause him problems in his election. In a press conference and in speeches, he chided the Court and in effect threatened them "that if they threw this out, there would be dire consequences." He has threatened them twice now in speeches.

This is unheard of—a president threatening the Supreme Court. As we stated before in this chapter, socialism/communism and fascism all took hold of the health care in their country as the main power to control, so this was a very important law to be passed by his Democratic Congress on his way to enjoining socialism for this country. He had to have it passed in his first two years of his term as he had no way of knowing if Congress would remain totally democratically controlled after two years.

Our president uses people and then throws them under the bus, as he has done to his former mentor and pastor that married them and baptized his kids—the Reverend Wright. He also threw another supporter, Oprah, who threw herself into his campaign, only to find herself not welcome in the White House as a visitor, mandated by Valerie Jarrett, Obama's advisor, and Mrs. Obama treated her with determined coldness.

Are we getting the picture of how close our ship (country) is getting to the iceberg now?

CHAPTER 25

Was Obama the Worst President in History? The Legacy of Barack Obama

There's two hundred reasons that Barack Obama was the worst president in history, according to authors of this book Matt Magales and Mark Noonan.

They are a few as follows.

1. Decline of American optimism
2. Domestic policy flip-flops
3. No Wall Street or banker prosecution
4. Betraying the victims of Hurricane Sandy
5. The government's response to California Central Valley
6. Drought: Blames plight of farmers on global warming
7. The guilt response to the BP Oil Spill
8. Cutting Medicaid to states defunding Planned Parenthood

9. Skyrocketing college costs: increased by 8% despite campaigning on increasing Pell Grants

10. Racial quota for school discipline: Establishes a new bureaucracy to enforce disproportionate outcome in school discipline

11. Radical attorney generals, like Eric Holder

12. Giving up the US Control of the Internet which assigned domain names

13. Net neutrality—ignoring the desires of American people in promoting human freedom—taxing internet use and more government control of the internet

14. Releasing criminal aliens who entered the US illegally

15. The Border Crises Dream Act through Executive Order

16. Executive amnesty granting amnesty to illegal aliens

17. Common core through bribery—Federal monopoly on education

18. Inaction on housing foreclosures causing the 2007/2008 financial crises

19. Collapse of home values, bailing out failed Freddie Mae and Freddie Mac lenders transferring bad loans to the FHA, just moved the disaster around.

20. Obama's Supreme Court appointees, Sotomayor and Elena Kagan, both had radical pasts

21. War on coal. Energy bills went up under Obama

22. War on oil. He lavished taxpayer's money on "green energy." Gas was $2 a gallon when he took office using the oil spill in Gulf of Mexico gas prices spiked to $4 a gallon. In California to $5 as they add a lot of state tax to the gas.

23. Title 1X abuses. Altered interpretation of law using force of government –expanded definition of sexual harassment, treating student gender identity as student's sex, so all public schools allowed students to use the bathroom making them gender identity—all without assent of Congress

24. Climate change radicalism—He said in 2008 Democratic convention, "We'll be able to look back and say this is the moment when the rise of the oceans began to slow and our planet began to heal."

25. An opaque administration. As campaigning, Obama declared he'd have the most opaque administration in history by posting all bills online for five days, but he broke that rule only five days into his administration.

26. Excessive use of taxpayer funds. Vacations. Being on frequent vacations. So lavish that we need guess whether he views the presidency as the most important job in the world or a way to have a swank lifestyle.

By March 2015, they took thirty-eight vacations—not including his golf outings (three hundred times) but not only numerous vacations but also costly to taxpayers, tens of millions of tax dollars have funded the Obama's lavish vacations. Nothing but the best for them. They stayed at the finest hotels and resorts. Michelle's trip to Spain cost taxpayers $467,000 and an African safari with her girls cost $424,000, to name just a few lavish ones. While Eisenhower and Geo W. Bush vacationed at their rather simple farms and Reagan and Johnson to their ranches.

And on and on for a total of two hundred different items. Get the drift?

CHAPTER 26

Romney vs. Obama: The Election of 2012

We faced a crucial election in November 2012. This was a serious potential turning point and the race was between two people whose worldview was totally opposite. We need to understand the distinction between these two candidates. This was one of the most important elections of our time or even in our history. It could have been the turning point in our voyage for our ship and determines if it will hit the iceberg.

We are facing something far worse than a national disaster; in fact, all at once, have been streaming across our country—a veritable tsunami of deeds, in many cases, questionable constitutional rules and edicts. It is like the shock after a disaster strikes. Like "What happened?" God sends us the natural disasters perhaps to remind us how powerful He truly is. What about this storm taking over our country?

Obama came to us as a community organizer and an ideologue, a socialist, and from academia and law, but with no experience in business or the capitalist economy. His world, for a long time, was in academics, a polar opposite, and one more designed for philosophy than business. Like his past, he believes that a great nation must invest in human capital through education (everyone must go to college), through National Health Care for control of the people and infrastructure (shovel-ready jobs delivered by the government). His associates have been mostly socialist advocates, who have espoused or actually worked in revolutionizing our country during the '60s. Born revolutionists.

How did they plan to create jobs?

Republicans believe in lowering taxes as JFK, Reagan, and Bush had done stimulating the economy, and even earlier when Calvin Coolidge and Harding in the early '20s, lowered taxes and the economy was better. Conservatives want to get rid of nuisance regulations that keep businesses from starting up and prospering and to establish a business-friendly climate so much of the jobs can come back from overseas, where they had to go due to excessive government and state regulations. They believe in state's rights and that the economy will right itself if we just get the government out of everything. Excessive regulations are what stymie business growth, that and high taxes on the job creators.

The liberals believe in human capital, raise taxes (soak the rich), and put more people to work in the government or for the government. They want the government to control all. They are the party of NO! They are against growth, against the military/ wars, against creativeness, against equal opportunity, against job growth, except in the government area, and against individualism.

The Party of NO

Everything is NO! No incandescent light bulbs, no eating and obesity, no school lunch brought from home unless <u>they</u> okay it, no energy unless it is clean energy (no fossil fuels, coal, natural gas, or nuclear). No rights to protest or speak up unless it is what they believe or you agree with them, no business, no capitalism, no jobs, no gas cars, only electric ones, no use of energy, except solar and wind, no low-priced gas, no guns, and on and on. They want high-speed rails but don't care what happens to our infrastructure. Ever noticed the potholes growing in all of our highways? They want the rest of the voting masses to go on some form of entitlement, so then they in turn will vote for them in appreciation for the largesse.

The Obama Economy

Jobs lost: 740,000
How much they borrow each day to fund Obama's spending sprees: 3 Billion
Current federal deficit (second largest in history): 19 Trillion

(fourth consecutive trillion-dollar deficit)

Added to national debt since Obama became president: 5.9 Trillion

By 2022, expected national debt (Obama's 2013 budget): 25.9 Trillion

Our deficit by end of May 2012 was 1.9%, and we lost our credit rating.

The US has always had an AAA credit rating. We even had an AAA credit rating during the Great Depression in the '30s and throughout the costly World War II. But now, <u>for the first time in America's history, Standard and Poor's credit rating agency has taken away America's AAA credit rating, it says, because President Obama and Congress have failed to control spending and because the current mounting federal debt (now over 15 trillion) is unsustainable.</u> Many economists say the US federal debt situation is now worse than Greece and that the US economy is on the brink of collapsing under the weight of our $15 trillion national debt, according to Liberty Guard in Washington, DC.

A baby born in America today owes $45,000 on the national debt. If Washington continues to pile up the debt at the current rate, a baby born in 2021 will owe over $84,000 on the national debt. Is that fair? Most generations have wanted to leave the world better for their kids, now it will be a lot worse.

Obama claims he cut the debt by 2.5 trillion. But when he was inaugurated in January 2009, the federal government's debt was over 10 trillion. As of the close of business in February 14, 2013, the federal government's debt was over 16 trillion. Thus since Obama had been president, the federal debt at that point had increased nearly 6 trillion. <u>That is more than all the debt accumulated by all the presidents from George Washington to Bill Clinton.</u>

CHAPTER 27

The Years We've Prospered Were under the Republicans, <u>NOT</u> the Democrats

I n studying political history, actually, during our more prosperous years, was when Congress was controlled by Republicans, like in 1922; in the '50s under Eisenhower; in the '80s under Reagan when they controlled the Senate and when they controlled the Congress from '94 to 2006, when they controlled both houses for <u>the first time in forty years</u>.

Contrary to what the liberal ideology believes, Republicans, as a pattern, guiding Congress and the presidency with their ideology, then provide more fiscal responsibility, and that cutting taxes and investing in our businesses <u>does work.</u> That has been the periods in our history that have been more prosperous, in spite of what the liberals and liberal media would have you believe.

About the only exception was during President John F. Kennedy's short time as president, but Kennedy was fiscally conservative and cut taxes. The campaigns now demonize anyone that is even somewhat rich running for president, where several of our best presidents in the past were rich or came from wealthy families, such as Washington, considered the # 1 best president by historians—the wealthiest of all the presidents, and Thomas Jefferson, and Franklin Roosevelt.

At this point, Romney had been demonized for being "born with a silver spoon," even by our president, who has said this in campaign speeches to the college students. Romney's dad accumulated most of the family's wealth which Romney inherited some, but he has also worked for his money. Obama is now worth a few million himself, so some would call him rich. He looks to the rich, Wall Street cronies, movie actors, and other wealthy donors, such as George Soros, to help him in campaigns while he demonizes the rich.

In addition, Republicans became a party under President Lincoln, who was our first Republican President. Republicans formed this party because they were against slavery. After the Civil War, Republicans passed the 13th Amendment, to outlaw slavery, and 15th Amendment to guarantee rights for Negroes (African Americans now). Most of the slave owners in the south and the Ku Klux Klan were Democrats, not Republicans.

Romney was unapologetic about America's exceptionalism!

The Republicans have proven in the past that capital investment will improve the economy. To do that, they cut taxes, allowing the free market to correct itself. They and Romney believe that too many regulations cause businesses too many problems and therefore businesses send jobs overseas where they have far less regulation. California loaded with regulations has lost considerable business to other states and overseas.

Congress has yet to renew the research and development tax credits, after letting them expire in 2011, Alter says, "Both candidates want these credits to be renewed." Partly due to this, the rate of growth in R&D for business spending we are getting behind other nations now. Because of major companies investing overseas, more and more global interests are driving investments.

The race then is about the huge differences in ideology between the capitalist individualists, freedom-loving Republicans, and the liberal-secular Democrats socialist worldview. The way the Republicans want to deal with the economy was the accepted way of life in our country until Roosevelt's New Deal in 1932 where many "make work" government-controlled programs acted as the precursor to more and more government controlled jobs. Yet even then, there were periods under Republicans where the economy strengthened.

There are vast differences between the parties, the liberals on religion, at least Christianity, and the freedom thereof, as was determined in our Constitution and lived with by our Founding Fathers, who were very strong people of faith. They did not want a state-owned church but for people to worship as they pleased. Many of the liberals are secular, non-religious, atheists, and want religion taken out of the public square in any form, nor prayers or reading the Bible at schools, nor prayers at events, such as graduations. Crosses on private land are often not even allowed now, and court battles have taken place over their allowing them to remain. Now there are differences over social beliefs, such as abortion, gay marriage, pornography, and any censorship of movies, TV, sexual content, or violence. The left has convinced the courts that all of this is perfectly okay and should never be censored. Family movies with good wholesome stories generally bring in the most at the box office. Can you hear Hollywood?

"Everything must be politically correct" is the ideology of the left, so that everything must be PC now. The right does not adhere to that either. First of all, it is idealistic to think that everything must be "politically correct." How on earth did we survive since 1776 without "political correctness" until the last thirty years or so, when the idealist liberals/ unions and teacher's associations introduced it in the schools, and then Hollywood picked up on it.

Clean energy and going green investments went sour.

Democrats who think clean energy (like Solyndra) will solve all our energy problems and want to invest in health care, education, and more government control of it all, thinking this will automatically create growth. Republican capitalists believe in individual rights, in controlling our own destiny through innovation, hard work, and the American dream where anyone has the opportunity to make good and work their way to be successful, with as little government control and influence as possible, which is the way our founders envisioned when they developed the Constitution and helped make this the greatest country in the world ever since 1919. Republicans are respectful of the environment in which they live, but the EPA and environmentalist activists have gone overboard until this is their religion. They worship animals and the environment above people. They are their golden idols.

Unions and Welfare and Entitlement Programs

Then the unions came along to make things fairer for the worker, which at first was good, until union bosses accumulated too much power, control, and money, therefore, as a result corruption ensued. Then the strikes became ugly as the unions controlled more and, with huge amounts of money, lobbied Congress and give big contributions to the Democrats.

When welfare became the norm, more and more people went on the program encouraged by social workers and liberals and found they did not even have to work. Now, due to the loss of jobs, the economy and the illegal immigrants we have almost 40 percent on some form of welfare entitlements. Our candidates will have to deal with this out of control entitlement in any new presidency, as the rest of the country is not in a position to bail out almost half of the rest.

Social Security was enacted by Congress in the '30s, with the idea that the employee would have a proportional amount taken out of their pay in order that by age sixty-five they could start to draw on this for help with their old age, making old age more secure. Old persons often had to live with family or go to the "poor house" and lived a life with little dignity. This money was to go into a trust fund, but there were no teeth put into it not allowing Congress to tap into it. It was based on the fact that people would not live too many more years after sixty-five, if that long, but the Trust Fund has been dipped into by Congress over and over until now there is hardly any, if any at all, left. Due to modern health care and greater understanding of good nutrition, people are living far longer than was expected, so that they have many more years to draw on the program.

Social Security is expected to run out before 2035, if not sooner. A future president and Congress will have to deal with this huge problem, too. With the largest generation, the Boomers, reaching retirement age now, this program will run out even sooner, with far less people in succeeding generations to pay for the huge population of retired Boomers. One way suggested is to raise the retirement age for receiving Social Security benefits. It is sixty-six years old now and should be raised to sixty-eight. People are working longer and healthier, so age sixty-eight is reasonable to retire and start drawing Social Security.

Taking entitlements away in a severe austerity program can cause huge protests, yet this must be addressed and soon. We have seen what happened in France and Greece when austerity programs were underway by more conservative leaders. Yet these must be dealt with because it is either that or we go broke soon. Then there is nothing left to go around for anyone.

Recently at a college seminar, millennials were asked what word that starts with an "E" best describes their generation. There were all kinds of guesses. Exceptional, Eager, Elite, Evolved, Exciting, Entrepreneur, Esteem? No! What the facilitator wanted was the word ENTITLEMENT! Yes, this is the generation of expected entitlements. Free college. Free vacations. Free home with their parents. It is a given that they expect entitlements given to them at all occasions. They are the ones who each got a trophy for just playing the game in Little League instead of winning. They were spoiled by their parents who catered to their every whim and were called the helicopter parents, as they hovered over them all the time. They took them to all kinds of games, ballet, school, and whatever they wanted to do, without any effort on their part. They played with their friends on play dates the mothers arranged. They should have no hardships at all.

They expect to walk into high-paying jobs without coming up the ranks or gaining any experience and to live like their parents do after many long years of work and effort. Why? Because Mommy and Daddy said nothing is too good for my son or daughter. And if they stay at home until age thirty, they never turn a hand to help out or pay for anything. But who is going to pay for all of this? What will they learn? What happens when Mommy and Daddy are no longer around?

Our demographics changed with the boomers being the largest generation yet had far less kids, so that now we have much fewer young workers to support the Social Security and welfare programs and the hungry government than we are used to. China, with their one-child rule for a long time now, has a problem with not enough younger workers to support their older people. Girl babies were often killed, or aborted, so that now there is a huge population of young men, who can't find wives so they must go to other countries to find one. Population advocates want the same curbs on our population here.

Romney had suggested an individual contribution or investment be made for retirement, as an option of not paying into Social Security. Congress has talked about raising the retirement age. Other measures are being bandied about, but nothing concrete has been enacted.

Our country was on the verge of bankruptcy and yet Obama's health care mandates and other social programs he wanted, like forgiving student loans, and everyone should go to college free, would cause even more of an economic collapse if enacted. If we continued to spend and borrow, then more people will go into dependency. Romney with a Republican Congress would have overturned some of these laws and mandates, replacing them with more reasonable laws.

International regulatory and international laws and treaties may sink our ship.

Obama was working with his Secretary of State and the UN on dangerous treaties that if ratified by Congress would take away our hard-earned sovereignty. These treaties are the <u>Treaty of Small Arms</u> taking away small arms all over the world. <u>The Treaty of the Seas</u> would put all the waters and seas into the hands of the UN to control, even up to our land.

Agenda 21 is alarming and is definitely comprehensive and global, breathtakingly so, says from the trenchesworldreport.com. It proposes a global regime that will monitor, oversee, and strictly regulate our planet's oceans, lakes, streams, rivers, aquifers, seabeds, coastlands, wetlands, forests, jungles, grasslands, farmland, deserts, tundras, and mountains. It even has a whole section on regulating and protecting the atmosphere. It proposes plans for cities, towns, suburbs, villages, and rural areas. It envisions a global scheme for health care, education, nutrition, agriculture, labor, production, and consumption—

in short, everything there is on, in, over, or under the earth that doesn't fall within the purview of some part of Agenda 21. Obama is in full support of this and federal land grabs in the name of <u>environmental concerns</u>. He and his administration believe human beings are earth's enemy.

The UN Knocking and Knocking Hard

Right now, according to ConservativeAction Alerts.com, May 9, 2012, forces are working to eradicate the United States Constitution and give regulatory and political power to the United Nations and their vision for a global, one-world government. This is NOT a conspiracy that MAY happen, it is in place as you read this.

Agenda 21 is a vast United Nations initiative that may already have been implemented in your town.

In the interest of saving the earth and creating a sustainable future, Agenda 21 will dictate

- What kind of car you can and cannot drive;
- Where and when you can travel;
- Where you can live;
- What kind of property you can own, if you are allowed to own property;
- What size family, if any, you can have

The American policy center reports that Agenda 21 means that:

"Every societal decision be based on environmental impact, focusing on three components; global land use, global education, and global population control and reduction." The liberals declare.

Obama signs executive orders declaring:

International law for the US with Sections 1021 and 1022 for the military arrests and detention of American Nationals without any due process of law

- The Act which allows unlimited spying on the American people by the government.
- HR 347 Trespass Law for the implementation of Sections 1021 and 1022 of the National Defense
- Authorization Act upon any citizen who dares to speak out against the insurgency.

Executive Order National Defense Resources Preparedness Act, which allows servitude to the dictator (yes, that is the wording) to confiscate every resource of the United States, and for those persons who refuse, to be put into servitude to the insurgency.

This is exactly what the Bolsheviks did to the Russian people in 1917. Now we have this new executive order for the implementation of international laws not legislated by our Congress. The next step would be to eliminate everyone who refuses to acquiesce to collective slavery.

What is actually being attempted here is a standardization of international law. It is an absolute violation of the Constitution for the United States to legislate our law outside of our borders.

Treaties Cannot Be Undone

What is worse is that treaties that are ratified by our Senate cannot be undone, according to our Constitution which says we must honor treaties. They are then the law of the land. This could easily be accomplished even if Obama does not win this next election, as they would have three months to do it in before leaving office. With a Democrat-controlled Congress at least until January, what is to stop them?

The liberals have been planning for this day for a long time and are frothing at the mouth, as they are so close.

Is our former president a Christian as he talks about? If so, why does he say we are no longer a Christian nation. Since when?

In 1952, President Truman established one day a year as a National Day of Prayer. In 1988, President Reagan designated the first Thursday in May of each year as the National Day of Prayer.

In June 2007, (then) presidential candidate Barack Obama declared that the USA "was no longer a Christian nation!" This year, President Obama cancelled the twenty-first annual National Day of Prayer ceremony at the White House under the ruse of "not wanting to offend anyone."

But on September 25, 2009, from 4 a.m. to 7 p.m., a National Day of Prayer for the Muslim religion was held on Capitol Hill beside the White House. There were over 50,000 Muslims in DC there that day. He prays with the Muslims!

Does it matter then if Christians are offended by this event? We obviously don't count as anyone anymore. Should this strike fear in the heart of every Christian and even many non-Christians, especially knowing that the Muslim religion believes that if Christians, as well as others cannot be converted, they should be annihilated! That means *jihad*, or killing the infidels. Their extremist religion, founded by Muhammed, tells them this is their duty. This is being taught in many of the mosques around the world, including here in the United States. They are trying to place Sharia Law here. What does that mean? Islamic Law is what that means.

Why are the liberal women going for this? When in the Islam religion, women have no rights whatsoever, can't go to school or out anywhere without a male escort, and must wear a burqa (long black robe), head cover, and veils? That is the only religion the socialist liberals allow now as all others are not politically correct. Why?

[http://www.islamoncapitolhill.com]

This is the perfect storm that the liberal/secular socialists have craved for over a century!

Was Obama the Great Destroyer?

According to David Limbaugh, author of NY Times' best-selling book *Crimes against Liberty*, in his new book, *The Great Destroyer*, about Obama's war on the Republic, he says "When it comes to our prosperity, our freedom, tradition, and our constitutional government, President Barack Obama has been the great destroyer—knocking down the free-market economy and the principles of limited government that have made America the envy of the world. He reveals the true costs of Obama corny capitalism scandals—it's even worse than you think. Limbaugh tells how Obama spends our economy into oblivion while relentlessly demonizing those who try to stop the bleeding. How the Obama administration has repeatedly, almost systematically, violated the Constitution to achieve its goals. Or how the Obama administration has empowered shadowy unelected bureaucrats to determine how we live and the successes they already have in doing that. In short, he says that the Obama administration is a real and present danger to America's future.

In the latest book on Obama, it is entitled *The Worst President in History: The Legacy of Barack Obama*, the authors Matt Maargolis and Mark Noonan espouse that there are two hundred reasons why Obama will be known as the worst president in history. However, when interviewed, Obama said he viewed himself as the fourth best president. (See chapter 25.)

Obama and liberals blame the Bush tax cuts in 2001 and like to espouse that by keeping taxes low, they believe that helped bring the crisis of capital investment. Republicans believe in capital investments. Our president is still blaming President Bush in that he keeps claiming that he inherited this mess. He blamed President Bush for nearly four years, while the deficit has climbed and climbed, more than doubled under his administration.

At what point does a president start to take responsibility? Reagan inherited a mess from President Carter

CHAPTER 28

Trumping the Trump

Donald Trump, Republican candidate in 2016, was an enigma. He was a phenomenon. He had come along, loudly expressing and declaring what a lot of people were thinking or might like to say.

Surprisingly, the Donald had become the GOP presumptive (pending the convention) nominee. Another Bull Moose, like the outspoken, "Old Rough and Ready," Teddy Roosevelt, who became our president in the early 1900s, and was a cousin of Franklin Delano Roosevelt. Often called "Rough and Ready." He was loud, brash, confident, and very outspoken, but he was able to win the confidence of the people then, as he was so different, and said it like it was. His motto was "walk softly but carry a big stick."

Perhaps our enemies might not be so bold with Trump in there. Just as the Iranians backed down to Reagan when he was being inaugurated and released the sixty hostages held under meek and mild President Carter.

According to a fairly recent letter in the *LA Times*, "You don't need to put Americans on a couch to explain his popularity." To many, it is a backlash to the Obama administration. To others, he is an Archie Bunker redux. Trump's slogan, "Make America Great Again," resonates with many Americans. People feel we have lost our greatness in the country and in the world. Americans want straight talk, not mealy-mouthed politically correct sound bites. They want a dash of anger when necessary. They want a Congress able to get things done—yet who won't sacrifice their basic principles in order to merely compromise what the liberals and Obama believe and want.

Maybe we have had enough of these types of politicians. The big silent majority has been silent way too long. Maybe we have had enough of Washington.

Our last two candidates for the Republicans in the general election, McCain and Romney, were from the Republican establishment, and in 2008 and 2012 respectively, appeared to be timid, as they each bombed the general debates with Obama, regardless of their recent ferocity in debates with their fellow Republicans. We wonder what happened. Were they threatened? Were they intimidated? Or did they not want to be president after all?

What difference does it make if we have a Republican majority in Congress when they don't stand up for conservative values and are more con-cerned about PC (political correctness) or appeasing the president or liberals? Are they really representing conservatives and the constitution they have sworn to uphold?

The Donald does not need the money, lobbyists, or donors. He can then govern without being beholden to special interests. He has been working to improve the economy—citing real unemployment, not fake figures, as the Obama administration has done.

Trump might offend some heads of state, but maybe some need that. They have walked all over America, and Obama, way too long and don't seem to respect America anymore. America, which has led the world since World War I, has long been able to show our strength up until 2008, when Barack Obama took over the reins.

Would Trump have, working with Congress, signed or ratified any of these international treaties? I am sure he would not nor would a Republican Senate vote for these dangerous treaties that would replace our sovereignty. Yet we were being faced with an administration that was actively working on this.

Trump says that he is not interested in executive orders that would declare international law for the United States, but would depend upon our own Constitution. Trump wants to steer us back to what we were before. We needed more than to just win in 2012, but to continue to win for far longer until we have made a real difference in our ship's course, but he would need a Congress that wants this too.

A fence all the way along the border, as most countries have, might actually work and keep the people we don't want here from coming across the border from not only Mexico, but Central and South America, plus no doubt terrorists, murderers, and many drugs. We cannot afford open borders to all. No other country has that. He claims he will get Mexico to pay for it, but Mexico, including their late president, Vincente Fox said, "NO, they will not pay for a fence." Only in not so nice language. Why would they? They love all their people coming here, a lot less for them to take care of and most send home millions of American dollars each year to their families. In fact, it's Mexico's largest income.

The people in Washington who are against the wall, many have huge mansions, gated and in gated communities with high walls and locks on all doors. So if they protect their homes, why shouldn't we protect our country?

One of the reasons for the drought in California is the water usage, which is so much more with a huge population now. Our schools are jammed and taxes drained. Many of the people coming in get on welfare immediately and free medical, etc. (You don't get anything free if you come from another country and live in Mexico or Central or South America.) The immigrants of the past came here not expecting anything, embraced Americanism, and wanted to speak English. They wanted to become an American. They wanted to have the freedom here to get ahead. That is the difference in immigrants today and those that came in past centuries.

Thanks to Trump, the silent majority of Americans just might be getting it off their chest and feel they are being heard. We are concerned about our future and our children's futures.

Trump's recent dust-up with the Pope was handled pretty well. He is right; the world leader of Catholics should not make the decisions if he is a Christian or not. The pope said that Trump needs to build bridges, not walls, and that he is not a Christian if he does that. Well, it just so happens there are forty foot walls all around the Vatican, so who builds walls? If the Vatican were threatened by ISIS, one of the targets they would like to take out, don't you think they would call for help to a Trump president?

The Trump Organization has Trump as chairman, and president. Donald J. Trump is the very definition of the American success story, continually setting the standards of excellence while expanding his interests in real estate, sports, and entertainment. He is the archetypical businessman, a deal maker without peer.

He started his business career in an office he shared with his father in Sheepsherd Bay, Brooklyn, New York, working there five years—learning every aspect of construction. Then Mr. Trump entered the different world of Manhattan Real Estate.

In New York and around the world, the Trump signature is synonymous with the most prestigious addresses—the world-renowned Trump Tower, Trump Parc, Trump Palace, Trump Plaza, Trump World Tower, and Trump Park Avenue. The Jacob

Javits Convention Center and total exterior restoration outside of Grand Central Terminal as part of conversion of Commodore Hotel into the Grand Hyatt—the Ritz Carlton, the Plaza Hotel in Central Park South.

The Nike Town store is owned by Trump, adjacent to Tiffany's. Until 2001, he owned the land under the Empire State Building, which allowed land and lease to be merged for the first time in fifty years.

His Trump International Hotel and Tower on Manhattan West Side, *Conde Nast Traveler* magazine named it #1 hotel in the US. And its innovative concept has been copied worldwide.

(This author has the privilege late October 2020 to attend a political/Christian conference at the Trump Hotel in DC, which Trump rebuilt the Old Post Office Building into that hotel.)

He went into Chicago and built Trump International Hotel and Tower/Chicago, awarded world's best business hotel.

He is co-owner of the Bank of America Building in San Francisco, one of the most important office buildings on the West Coast.

Mr. Trump's holdings include Trump National Golf Club, in Westchester, New York, a signature golf course, residential development, on the 250-acre estate of Katherine Graham at Seven Springs (of *Washington Post* and Rockefeller University) to be developed into a world-class luxury housing development. He developed one of the largest parcels of land in California which fronts 2 and ½ miles along

Pacific Coast (Palos Verdes Estates) called Trump National Golf Club/Los Angeles, voted #1 golf course in California. Seventy-five luxury estates will follow. I have personally had lunch and happy hour there. The staff says Trump really treats them well when he visits.

He more recently developed Trump International Golf Links in Scotland and now one in Ireland. It opened July 2012. Since then, he has developed several more golf courses, plus his hotel collections all over the world, including one in Istanbul.

Trump restored the old Central Park New York Skating Rink. He restored the rink in four months at only 1.8 million of the city's $200,000,000 cost. He created the condo boom in New York versus the co-ops that were more prevalent.

Trump is an accomplished author. His fourth book, *The America We Deserve*, was also a best seller. He is a member of Board of Directors for Police Athletic Association, Chair of Donald J Trump Foundation, Co-Chair of New York Vietnam Vets Memorial Fund. In 1995, he served as Grand Marshall of the largest parade ever held in New York, which celebrated the fiftieth anniversary of end of WWII. He hosts the annual Red Cross Ball at his Mar-a-Lago Club in Palm Beach. In January 2012, he received American Cancer Society Lifetime Achievement Award.

In April 2015, Mr. Trump received the Commandant's Leadership award from the Marine Corps— Law Enforcement Foundation, given to him by General Joseph Dunford Jr., Chairman of Joint Chiefs of Staff.

In June 2000, Mr. Trump received his greatest honor of all—the Hotel and Real Estate Visionary of the Century.

To say nothing of his *Celebrity Apprentice* TV show which he departed from, when he started campaigning in 2016. He was also producing TV and cable TV programing via his LA-based company Trump Productions LLC.

In 2005, he launched his Signature Collection, including tailored clothing, dress shirts, ties, cuff links, eyewear, leather goods, and belts. Trump Home was later introduced to include furniture and mattresses. He has introduced two new fragrances.

Trump is one of the highest paid speakers in the world today and considered the smartest names in the world in real estate and the world of development.

So Why Not Trump Again? I, like a lot of the country, like his spunk. He's doing what he said he would do, and he does not back down, as so many presidents have done to even our enemies. He does not need to do this. He had it made, but he really does care for his country and thinks he would bring her back to greatness. And just maybe, he already has a large start on it. He was making great inroads in the economy about best in many years until the shutdown with the coronavirus stopped the economy all over the world. He loves a challenge and to win. I believed he would beat Hillary. And he did.

So if anyone can bring back the economy, Trump can do it again.

Do you believe this is a man who can get unbelievable, difficult things done?

To negotiate these very difficult processes required with city, government, and countries all around the world to achieve his developments, well, it would be a piece of cake to negotiate with foreign leaders, either friend or foe.

You don't have to be a politician to accomplish all that is necessary to be a president. Having business, executive, negotiation, and economic visionary skills is probably far better and more economic.

Also, he's paid his own way in his campaign so he owes no one. He has played into the disgust of the regular folks with the establishment, Washington, and the party elites. The blue-collar folks who are getting hit on hard.

"Trump knows exactly what he's doing," writes Doyle McManus in *LA Times*, February 24, 2016. McManus goes on to say that the Republican establishment has finally woken to the danger it's in. Donald Trump was the party's nominee for president. How is that possible?

Trump was able to win most primaries with no more than 35 percent of the vote because the GOP field was so fragmented. But there is another reason Trump was doing so well: he's turned out to be a disciplined candidate with a clear strategy. He's not the unguided missile he once appeared to be. His attacks on other candidates may have looked petulant, but now it's clear that they were calculated. First his sights were on Jeb Bush, but when he faded, Trump moved his sights to Cruz, who was trying to steal Trump voters. "Ted is hanging around the top too long." Each candidate caved to Trump's popularity.

Trump said he would get rid of incompetent politicians, halt illegal immigration by building a wall on the US-Mexico border (which he declares that Mexico will pay for), and stop losing to other countries. He says he will build up the military, which Obama had decimated. Trump seems to speak out and then back down a bit. So he has softened his message in some areas. After surprising conservative voters by not defending Planned Parenthood, he promised that he would block federal funding for the group if it continued to offer abortions and selling baby's body parts.

The pattern is for Trump to grab media attention by saying something outrageous—and then takes a step back as if to say "I did not mean it literally." That free media strategy has enabled Trump to dominate the debate. Plus, he bypasses the liberal no-news media by tweeting. It's his way to get the word out, bypassing the liberal media who abhor him so report on their opinion not the news.

His campaign is self-financed, so he says, but he has accepted about 26 million he has collected from individual donors. He does not collect from Super PACs as the other candidates do. Therefore not beholden to anyone, but to the general electorate.

While the hallmark of Trump's campaigns has been giant rallies, he's used the names collected from those events to mount a massive old-fashioned telephone drive to get out the vote on election days.

His campaign is not all that chaotic. It is well-designed of old and new that makes good use of the candidate's reality-TV strengths.

Trump is still uncivil and mendacious. He's still the most unconventional president we've seen in a long time, but part of his crazy genius is that he's not as unconventional as he pretends.

These were the questions of that time. On the minus side, having sung his praises, is he a real Republican or a Democrat in sheep's clothing, as he has supported quite a few Democrats? Has he really changed his position on many social issues or is he saying he has to get votes? Would he turn more liberal once in office? We already know the answer to that. Was he running for the fame and his name, or is he sincerely concerned about the direction of this country and can he change much at all? Can anyone? Can a CEO who is used to a lot of control, find himself frustrated in the political processes, and where he has not as much control as he thinks. We just don't know. I think he just might turn out to be one of our best presidents in a long time. Unconventional, but maybe that is what we need now. I do know he would make a far better president than Hillary Clinton, whom I have studied and researched her history for years. He did not have to do this at all. He would be far richer and life be far easier if he had not run.

CHAPTER 29

Trump Comes Along and the Rest Is History: Election of 2016

B eating out all the Republican candidates, picking them off one after one, Donald J. Trump, businessman, but no politician, lands the 2016 nomination for president. Against all odds. Could he beat the Democrats chosen number one, Hillary Clinton? Well, the polls up until election day had Trump behind Hillary. But who believes in polls, as most are slanted. Much to Hillary's "glass ceiling" surprise and the media, who were in tears, Trump won.

A few months before the election, a prophecy by a fireman was reported that he said God told him that Trump would win. He said the prophecy came to him years before anyone knew that Trump would even run. He didn't tell about his unique prophecy until in August 2015. I remember hearing on

YouTube about it then and I had cold shivers as I really believed what I heard.

Trump won the electoral vote, even though Hillary won the popular vote, and to this day, she says she won over Trump. After the election, she went on a tour and wrote a book as to why she lost the election, blaming everyone and everything but herself. She was a lousy campaigner, with her nasally Midwestern voice, and her campaign had no meat, only trash Trump and his voters, whom she called a basketful of deplorables. She was lucky to get only a few hundred to her rallies, which she held about one a week, as she had to rest between. She did not have the stamina for president. Whereas Trump held several rallies in a day with many thousands in attendance and with long lines outside.

Trump's message was to *Make America Great Again*, to bring back the greatness it had always been known for, especially after the two World Wars, in which we literally saved the world and rebuilt several countries. The premise for America was freedom and to be the best country ever founded in the world.

Trump has striven to bring back that reputation, with his thinking of America First for a change as former presidents seemed to have almost put her last. He has worked on the economy, the immigration problems, the rebuilding of the military which Obama had almost decimated, to rebuild relations and negotiate with foreign countries, with strength, and to bring troops home from Afghanistan, to help our vets, to rebuild our economy. He renegotiated

NAFTA and made the other countries pay their fair share; he negotiated the trade agreement between Canada, the US, and Mexico, which Congress finally passed.

There have been no wars in over 3 and ½ years now. He walks softly but carries a big stick. And the other countries recognize that now. North Korea slowed down their nuclear progress and quit lobbing missiles toward Japan. Don't mess with Trump or America. China has a lot of respect with Trump in their trade dealings.

From what I can see, we are far better off with a businessman than a politician. Running this country is like being the biggest CEO in the world, so a business background works best for that. America's president is the number one leader in the world.

Obama never even ran a lemonade stand, so knew nothing about business or enterprise. He had never even worked, spending his time going to school. On free scholarships. Or wherever he got his money. He would never release his school records which would have proven from what country he used on his application as to how he got his scholarships.

Trump has appointed two conservative judges to the Supreme Court, as they were known for being constitutionalists, Neal Gorsuch and Brett Kavanaugh. He has appointed many as the circuit judges. More so than many other presidents.

Trump suggested the start of a new branch of the military called the Space Corps. Some generals have not liked this. The reason is that we will have to defend our right to some space, and someday, there will be space wars. We need to plant our flag on Mars as we did on the moon, and Trump wants a manned space mission to Mars.

CHAPTER 30

The Scariest Reason Trump Won

According to radio talk show host and well-known commentator Dennis Praeger, "There are many reasons why Donald Trump won in 2016, but the four most cited are the frustrations of white working-class Americans, a widespread revulsion against political correctness, disenchantment with the Republican establishment and the unprecedented and unrivaled amount of time the media afforded Trump. They are all valid. But the single biggest reason is this: the majority of Republicans are not conservative. Conservatives who opposed Trump kept arguing that Trump is not a conservative and has never been one. But the argument meant little or nothing to two types of Republicans: the majority of Trump voters who don't care whether he is a conservative and the smaller number of Trump voters who are conservative, but care about illegal immigration more than all other issues, including his many and obvious failings."

We ask then what happened to the majority of Republicans? Why aren't they conservative?

The answer lies in America's biggest and scariest problem: most Americans no longer know what America stands for. For them, America has become just another country, a place located between Canada and Mexico. But America was founded to be an idea, not another country. As former Prime Minister Margaret Thatcher put it, Europe was created by history. America was created by philosophy.

Why haven't the past three generations of American known what America stands for?

The biggest reason is probably the influence of left-wing ideas. Since its inception, the socialist Democratic left has opposed the American idea and for good reasons. Everything the American idea represents undermines leftist ideas. And the left, unlike most Americans, has always understood that either the left is right or America is right.

America stands for small government and a free economy (and therefore, capitalism) liberty (which therefore capitalism) (which therefore allows for its inevitable consequence); inequality, the melting pot ideal and a God-centered population rooted in Judeo-Christian values (so that a moral society is created by citizens exercising self-control, rather than relying on the state to impose control). Only America was founded on the idea of small government. But the left is based on big government.

America was founded on the principle that human rights come from the Creator. For the left, rights come from the state.

The American Revolution, unlike the French Revolution, placed liberty above equality. For the left, equality is more important than all else. That's why so many American and European leftists have celebrated left-wing regimes, from Stalin to Mao to Guevara to Castro to Chavez, no matter how much the regimes squelched individual liberty. They all preached equality.

It took generations, but the left has succeeded (primarily through the schools, but also through the media) in substituting its values for America's. While the left has been the primary cause, there have been others. The most significant is success.

American values inspired so much success that Americans came to take that success for granted. They forgot what made America uniquely free and affluent. And now it's not even accurate to say they forgot because the current generation never knew. While schools (starting with the universities) were being transformed into institutions for left-wing indoctrination, American parents ceased teaching their children American values (starting with not reading them the most popular book in American history, the Bible).

Schools even practically stopped teaching American history. When American history is taught today, it is taught as a history of oppression, imperialism, and racism. Likewise, there is essentially no education on civics, once a staple of the public-school system. Young Americans are not taught the Constitution or how American government works. I doubt many college students even know what separation of powers means, let alone why it is so significant.

So then, thanks to leftism and Americas taken for granted success, most Americans no longer understand what it means to be American. Those who are called conservatives because they wish to conserve the unique American idea are the only ones who actually appreciated our rare country. But conservatives now constitute not only a minority of Americans, but a minority of Republicans. That is the primary reason Donald Trump—a nationalist, but not a conservative—was the presumptive Republican nominee.

However, after over three years in office and from strong influence by conservatives, President Trump is governing more like a conservative and fighting the establishment Republicans. I feel personally that his whole outlook on life has changed considerably after being president—an awesome responsibility and that he actually feels closer to God and prays. He encourages the Prayer Breakfast. Under Obama, the National Prayer Breakfast was eliminated. I feel certain that he can see that religion and faith have a place in American philosophy and that he understands this now.

CHAPTER 31

The Battles of Hillary versus Sanders

The difference between Clinton and Sanders widened in Iowa, in 2016, as they battled with fierceness, exchanging sharp words.

Health care is a divide between the two. Clinton proposes tweaking the present Obamacare to improve upon it.

Sanders, the elderly Vermont senator, who appealed greater to whites and young voters, proposes a fully government-funded plan, that would be paid for by taxes on all but the poorest Americans.

"We finally have a path to universal health care," said Clinton.

Sanders says a Medicare plan for all program does provide in this country health care for every man, woman, and child as a right. "This would get rid of the power of campaign donors," he states. He says super PACS, pharmaceutical industry, and private insurance companies are pouring hundreds of millions of dollars into campaign contributions and lobbying.

Clinton defended herself as tough on Wall Street. Sanders casts himself as a leader against the current political system. He says, "I don't take money from big banks. I don't get personal speaking fees from Goldman-Sachs," meaning Clinton does.

"If Teddy Roosevelt were alive today, the Old Republican Trust Buster, he would say those guys are too powerful. Break them up," says Sanders.

Sanders appeals to the young who are college age. They believe socialism is just what we need here. After being hammered (brainwashed) for years in the schools and even more in the universities under socialist professors, they believe that socialism is good for everyone, so we have several generations who now believe in socialism for this country, actually knowing little about what that would mean for them. Little do these young know that socialism is the same as communism, Nazism, and any other country run by a dictator where no one owns any property or money, and all are told what to do by the government, and all work for the government, and by the way, you are killed if you protest or dissent. Ask anyone from one of these countries why they ran away and came here. They will tell you exactly why. For the freedom they can have in America. They will tell you that socialism/communism is really horrible.

I know several from Cuba, who say communism/socialism there is really horrible, so they escaped and came to America or their parents did.

I met a gal who escaped from Russia during their large communist reign and she tells horror stories of what socialism means there. Putin is planning to start another Cold War and make Russia a large communist owned country as they take over more, smaller adjacent countries once again. Communism/socialism is run by a dictator and Putin is salivating to become a dictator there. Then he has his sights on the United States to take over. He is already trying to take land around Alaska and the Bering Sea for their own territory.

So what would we have with a Sanders or a Clinton president? Socialism from both, but Sanders is even more liberal than Hillary. It sounds good to take away money from the rich and give it to the poor and redistribute the wealth. But who is responsible for most of the jobs? Who is responsible for the economy to be as good as it has been? Not the poor. And if you gave it all to the poor, it would soon be gone, and then a few others would invest and use the money sensibly and rise to the top. Then you would have rich and poor again.

Under both, terrorism would reign. Our enemies are not going to pay any attention to either of them. The terrorists only deal in fear and both of these candidates, unfortunately, did not generate fear. We would be easily taken over. Imagine Hillary dealing with Putin or China's dear leader or North Korea. She would probably get mad and throw a vase at them, starting WWIII.

CHAPTER 32

Hillary's Many Scandals: Skirting the Law Again

If you go just by experience, Hillary Clinton was well positioned to become a president. She was a lawyer, then wife of a president. It was understood that Hillary would be next as soon as Bill's terms were over to run for president, but the turmoil over Bill's scandals in the White House deterred her plans at that time, so she ran as a senator (although they say she "carpetbagged" in suddenly moving to New York to run in a district). She won the Senate seat. Then in 2008, she ran for president, but Barack Obama, a newcomer, won.

To appease her, as she was second place, and often a president will appoint the second place as his vice president to run with him, he apparently did not want Bill in the White House. They are not known for liking each other much. So he appointed Hillary as Secretary of State, which she served as for four years. What she did as secretary remains to be seen. No one has been able to really tell what she accomplished, other than travel a lot. It did seem to appear that her meetings with heads of states, and apparently steering things in their direction, benefitted the Clinton Foundation. She is now worth 45 million. So much for them being poor when they left the White House. If they were, it was from trying to defend Bill in all of those lawsuits from the females who claimed he was a predator toward them and made sexual advances, even one or two declared rape.

Hillary shrugs the scandals off as mere distractions or it is just a "vast right-wing conspiracy" manufactured by the Republicans to do them in. This was a term she used during her husband's administration in the '90s to describe the ideologically driven partisans who developed a massive following investigating alleged Clinton misdeeds. Though Bill lied before the grand jury, he was not indicted. And the impeachment proceedings went through, but he was not formally impeached. Many people said his misdeeds were of his sexual adventures were personal and not worthy of a reason for impeachment. But it was not that, it was the lying before the court. He perjured himself and got away with it.

How can Hillary get away with all of the scandals and even alleged murders, misuse of government emails to the point of jeopardizing our national security—as she always seems to wiggle out of each of them?

Scandal seems to follow the Clintons. Yet they get away with it all. Why? For one thing, the media will not vet them and have always loved the Clintons. The media is trying to influence each election with whom <u>they</u> choose, regardless of the voters.

As Hillary sought to reboot the Clinton brand, she forgets and waxes nostalgic about earlier times when in the state she's is in at the moment, by reminiscing what she did when there before. But does it then remind people of how long ago the Clintons have been doing this. Some call Hillary a candidate of yesterday since it's been more than two decades since the Clintons first campaigned nationally—a long length of time. As she tried to frame her family's political history, it may come back to bite her. It is laced with scandals. The young view her as the chaperone at the ball, rather than relating to her as one of them. "She is so yesterday," some of the young have said.

Eight Years Later, Bill Clinton Is Causing Headaches for His Wife Again

"Former president Bill Clinton greets others at the Puritan Backroom on January 4, 2016, in Manchester, New Hampshire. Bill spent the day campaigning for his wife, then Democratic candidate, Hillary Clinton," according to Abby Phillip of the *Chicago Tribune*.

Halfway through his forty-minute stump speech, Bill Clinton arrived on the topic of Bernie Sanders's proposal for single payer health coverage—and became annoyed.

"Every time we try to have a debate on this, they say, 'You don't understand. We're creating a revolution. You're getting in the way. You are part of the establishment,'" Clinton drawled, with more than a hint of frustration in his voice. "God forbid we should have an honest discussion on it."

Then Clinton changed course again.

"That's not the point I want to make," he said hastily, before refocusing on his principal assignment: delivering a positive message for his wife's candidacy rather than attacking her opponent.

In his post–White House years, Clinton has become a coveted Democratic surrogate. But when it comes to his wife's campaigns, something else can happen; he seems to lose it. It was true in this crucial nominating state in 2008 where Hillary Clinton lost badly to Barack Obama. And it's been true this month when the former president has reemerged as a potent but unpredictable advocate, who sometimes helps his wife's cause—and sometimes doesn't.

In Florence, over a weekend, the crowd of more than 650 would get a glimpse of the Bill Clinton who had broken free of the reins earlier in February, in the closing days of the New Hampshire primary race. Then Clinton accused Sanders of running a dishonest campaign and the media of coddling him.

This was not seen as helping Hillary. Her campaign aides emphasized that the former president's role was to positively reinforce her message, not be an attack dog. But that has proved difficult for Bill Clinton.

"Bill Clinton is an incomparable genius when it comes to politics, except when it comes to his wife," said former Obama strategist, David Axelrod. "It clouds his judgment." Axelrod thinks it is because he loves his wife and because he believes she is the best candidate in the race. "He is proud of what she's done, and he can't believe that people don't see it," Axelrod said. "He can be super effective for her. Where he is not effective is where he has these histrionic episodes."

A day after that outburst in New Hampshire, the former president let it be known he wished he was free to say more. "The hotter this election gets, the more I wish I was just a former president and just for a few moments not the spouse of the next one," he proclaimed.

Sometimes, it's the tone and apparent vitriol in Clinton's voice that seem to hit the wrong note. Sometimes it's his actual argument, which doesn't always mesh with what his wife is saying on the same day, somewhere else on the campaign trail.

This writer's take on this, after observing Clinton's stance and expressions when Hillary was sort of claiming victory, like in Iowa, my guess is that Bill really does not want her to be president. He is so happy with his freedom now, wandering around the world and hobnobbing with the princes, the rich, and the parties, that to be chained to the White House as the First Man, is not what he really wants and to be scrutinized with everything he does. I have read, where they made a pact a long time ago that she would help him become president, via the governorship of Arkansas, and then it would be her turn and he would help her. Therefore, while he feels beholden to that promise, yet he does not like it at all. Bill looks tired, aged, and his voice is weak. He is only sixty-nine, but looks a lot older. Could he be inadvertently sabotaging her campaign as he did in 2008?

When Hillary Clinton launched a new broadside against Sanders recently, she focused on his criticism of President Obama, her pitch, targeted at Obama supporters, attempted to cast herself as more loyal to the president. Enter Bill Clinton, at an appearance that Thursday in Memphis.

"The economy is rigged," Clinton told the crowd, appropriating one of Sanders's favorite terms because you don't have a president who's a change-maker…with a Congress who will work with him."

It sounded like he was blaming the sitting president for it and agreeing with one of Sander's central arguments about income inequality. Once again, the former president was on the wrong side of the headlines. Clinton allies mounted a familiar defense, trying to tamp down the significance of what the former president had said.

"What Clinton was clearly trying to say is that the GOP has thwarted President Obama at every turn," said longtime Clinton ally, Paul Begala. "Any fair reading of President Clinton's comments proves that."

Even on the friendliest turf, Bill Clinton can run into trouble. His wife's campaign considers him an enormous asset in South Carolina and in other Southern states with upcoming contests, where he is hugely popular among the African Americans and moderate whites, who make up a vast majority of the Democratic electorate.

Yet even here, he can do damage. Days before the South Carolina primary eight years ago, Bill Clinton called Obama's candidacy a fairy tale. His words plunged Hillary Clinton's campaign into a racially charged tailspin, and she went on to lose the state's primary by nearly thirty points. The blowback from that experience is one reason the Clinton campaign this year is trying to keep him focused on a positive message.

"I don't think it's his job to vet her opponent. It's the job of the media," said Iowa-based democratic political operative Jerry Crawford, a longtime ally of both Clintons. "I think he is at his best when he is talking about Hillary."

Bill Clinton's power on the trail is hard to dispute, but it's also hard to measure whether he is succeeding at persuading voters to support his wife. He draws large energetic crowds and nearly as much media attention as the candidate herself.

Clinton's popularity is driven in part by older voters who recall him as he once was: an energetic, electrifying young politician. But he has also aged dramatically. His words come more slowly and in a raspy voice. His slim stature and drawn features show the toll of age and a stringent diet.

The battle for South Carolina was fierce among young voters, who showed in Iowa and New Hampshire that they are open to supporting Sanders.

For young voters like Joshua Keith, a twenty-eight-year-old African American and a small business owner in Florence, Hillary Clinton still needs to win his vote. Asked whether Bill Clinton's endorsement of his wife will make a difference to him, Keith, a former Obama campaign volunteer, replied, "Not really. The last time he was in office, I was twelve, maybe," Keith said with a shrug. "I don't think it impacts the younger voters. I don't think that the Clinton name has the stronghold that it once did."

Hillary's Associates

Once an intern in the White House and an activist for Muslim student affairs, Huma Abedin has risen up to be Hillary Clinton's closest aide and vice chairman of her presidential campaign. She goes with Hillary everywhere she goes. Hillary bragged how Huma had taught them all about the meaning of Ramadan and how peaceful the Muslims really were. She and Hillary are joined at the hip. Another advocate of Islam and Ramadan celebration in the White House was Grover Norquist, a Republican. Huma is, or was, married to the famous Anthony Weiner, who served in New York's 9th Congressional district, who was made to leave Congress after a sexting sexual scandal. He later ran for Mayor of New York, as he at the same time admitted to sexting again. He lost, nevertheless. He was also being investigated as running a sex trafficking and child molestation ring.

Now does this make sense to elect a president whose constant companion and advisor is an avowed Muslim?

Hillary has been known to associate with questionable people in the past and be involved in shady deals. Others who go against the Clintons or are supposed to testify against them might find themselves dead in an airplane crash, car crash, committing suicide, or disappearing. It has been documented that over sixty persons mysteriously have had something like this happen to them that were acquaintances or enemies of the Clintons or about to testify against them as a witness. Yet this is completely ignored by the media. How many do you know that have mysteriously died?

Upon questioning, even by the liberal media, Hillary now says she "<u>tries</u> not to lie." Talk about lying. She will not come out and say she has lied. She is a proverbial liar, as she has been called, often, so that after a while, she probably no longer recognizes the truth. About 60 percent of the people say they do not trust her and believe she has lied continuously.

For a good book on Hillary, read Dick Morris's book on *Armageddon*. Just released. *How Trump Can Beat Hillary*. Morris was Clinton's political advisor and knows the Clintons better than anyone. He claims Hillary is the most unfit and the most corrupt person to ever run for the office of president. She has been so insulated for so long, that she has no idea what the real world is like. She has a retinue of staff and helpers, who do everything for her. They buy her clothes and tell her what to wear, they bring everything to her. When she goes out, it is in large Secret Service cars, taking her anywhere she wants to go at any hour. She lives like a queen. And at our expense. She does not pay for all of this help.

The Clinton Foundation pays for all airfare for the Clintons. Including Chelsea, her husband, Bill's brother Roger, and Hillary's brother. They all take money from the Clinton Foundation, which there have been calls to investigate it, for misuse of non-profit. Very little is spent on the projects and programs they incorporated it for. Most is spent on the Clintons. This must be investigated.

Some of the reasons Morris cites why Hillary should NEVER BE PRESIDENT:

- She is so corrupt: Always immersed in scandal.
- She doesn't know anything about our biggest problem—the economy stupid.
- She is governed by Gurus.
- She is rigid and stubborn. She allows nepotism.
- She will get us into a war to show how tough she is.
- Hillary and the Muslim Brotherhood are perfect together. Her No. 1 aid is connected to the Muslin Brotherhood.

- She flips, she flops, and she flips. Changes positions with the moon.
- She demonstrated her inability to be commander-in-chief in Benghazi.
- She is a compulsive, pathological, and serial liar who cannot be trusted to tell the truth to the American People.

Hillary's Latest Getting Off: Skirting the Law AGAIN

Why is it that the Clintons both skate the law, skirting it over and over and always getting away with it? The law is not for them. They are above the law. This has always been the case with them and now the latest email scandal, just as she gets ready to go to the Democrat Convention to be crowned the heir appointed (something she has planned to be since the fourth grade). She is exonerated by FBI Director Comey and will not be indicted for her knowingly mishandling her emails. She should have been indicted for her lawlessness in handling her emails as Secretary of State.

Bill got involved, when he just happened to be on the tarmac at Phoenix Airport where the Justice Department Attorney General Loretta Lynch was in her plane, and he boarded and spent half an hour so they said talking about golf and grandkids. Talk about fishy. That was totally improper and probably illegal since Bill was under investigation and as was his wife with that investigation Lynch was in charge of, the email scandal, and the Clinton Foundation.

So what happened there? What was promised or threatened? It sounds rigged. That was no accidental meeting.

Then the next day after the announcement clearing Hillary, she flies to North Carolina with President Obama on Air Force One to campaign with him. At our expense. At over $200,000 per hour for one way, plus Secret Service and cooks and air attendants. Then to rub it in more, he lets her use the podium where his presidential seal is hanging, to make her campaign speech from, as if she was already president.

Obama proceeded to tell us that Hillary is the most qualified person, man or woman, to ever run for the presidency. Now when he was running against her and later even when she was Secretary of State, he really did not like her. But he wants his legacy of tearing down America to continue. Yet for the 2020 election, strangely, Obama has not endorsed his former vice president, but seems to be leaning toward Bloomberg, former Governor of New York.

Hillary was grossly negligent, to say the least, but she has been in the public domain and in government and in law, so she knows what is legal or not. The FBI finally questioned her for only three hours and not under oath, a real short time for something that serious, on a Saturday holiday for the Fourth of July weekend, and then announced that while she was negligent and careless, that they were not going to indict her or let it go to a grand jury. This came as a surprise to a lot of people as it looked like they were going to prosecute. Even the FBI Director Comey (appointed by George Bush as FBI Director) indicated a lot of wrongs happened, but that any prosecutor would not prosecute her. He admitted that what she did with her emails, by using a private server and later deleting 30,000 of them, stating they were personal, was poor judgment. In addition, about her State Department emails, she stated they were not classified, then later she was saying they were not marked classified.

She was using several devices in foreign countries where it could be easily hacked into, which could have led to our enemies knowing the information and hacking into them. She said she did it for convenience to only use one device, yet pictures of her as Secretary of State show her using more than one device. Can you imagine her with government secrets and the nuclear code?

So much to most everyone's surprise, even the liberal media, she got off scot free—again.

CHAPTER 33

A New Book Tells All on Hillary By Gary Byrne, Secret Service

Byrne was Secret Service and posted outside the Oval Office when Bill Clinton was president; in his book, he portrays Hillary as too "erratic, uncontrollable and occasionally violent: to become leader of the free world." The allegations from Byrne, a twenty-nine-year veteran of the military and federal law enforcement, threatened to derail her campaign days before she is to clinch the Democratic presidential nomination. Byrne describes Hillary Clinton as acting friendly one moment and raging the next. She screams, throws things, hits Bill with vases or phones and whatever she can find. He said Bill and the White House staff lived in fear of Hillary. He said Hillary has a Jekyll and Hyde personality that left White House staffers scared stiff of her explosive—and even physical—outbursts.

Byrne claims Clinton is too erratic, uncontrollable, and occasionally violent to become commander-in-chief. He describes Hillary as switching quickly from friendly to angry in a moment and repeatedly screaming obscenities at her husband and anyone around, including the Secret Service.

"Hillary is now poised to become the Democratic nominee for President of the United States, but she simply lacks the integrity and temperament to serve in the office," Byrne wrote. "From the bottom of my soul I know this to be true. And with Hillary's latest rise, I realize that her own leadership style—volcanic, impulsive, enabled by sycophants, and disdainful of the rules set for everyone else—hasn't changed a bit." (And she accuses Donald Trump of being "temperamentally unfit" for office. The pot calling the kettle black?) He said he felt obligated to write this book now to try to warn the people about what they might get.

Hillary Clinton's campaign downplayed Byrne's book and compared him to Edward Klein, author of last year's *Unlikeable: The Problem with Hillary.*

"They say Gary Byrne joins the rank of Ed Klein and other authors in this latest in a long line of books attempting to cash in on the election cycle with their nonsense," spokesman Nick Merrill said. "It should be put in the fantasy section of the bookstore." A spokeswoman for presumptive GOP presidential nominee Donald Trump suggested Byrne's book would be grist for his campaign as he prepares to face Clinton in the general election.

"The issue of temperament is more of a problem for Hillary Clinton," said spokeswoman Katrina

Pierson. "I don't recall Mr. Trump ever screaming at the Secret Service, calling them pigs, throwing vases across the room and clawing the face of his spouse, which Hillary Clinton has been reported to do," she told CNN.

According to the *Daily Mail*, Monday, June 20, 2016, reporting on a book by Bill Clinton's former lover, Dolly Kyle, that Hillary once called disabled children at an Easter egg hunt "f—— retards" and referred to Jews as "stupid k——s" while Bill called Jesse Jackson a damned n——r. Rumors of Bill's trysts with black women were rampart in Little Rock. Yet they profess to have been supporters of racial equality. When Hillary moved to Arkansas, she looked down her nose at what she viewed as ignorant hillbillies. Kyle said they called Hillary "Chilly Hillary" and the "Warden." Hillary loved to tell Bill about her sexual adventures with her female college roommates. She did not like men or sex with them, including with Bill, so Kyle said. Also, Bill Clinton profiled Hispanics and allowed them to be stopped by the Highway Patrol and profile them as drug dealers. Yet they pretended to be for them to get their vote.

CHAPTER 34

How Justice Scalia's Untimely Death Affected the Campaign and Election of 2016

What difference does it make if a Supreme Court Justice dies? Especially now before a major election?

Well, it probably would change the whole game. Not only in the campaign but in the decision of who is elected.

All will be campaigning on the importance of their party winning in order to get a new justice appointed in their like political mode.

Congress did delay their confirmation process. So hopefully a conservative president coming in would appoint a more conservative constitutionalist for the bench—a long shot—as they could also be accused of delaying the process. This confirmation could easily change the balance of the Supreme Court. For quite a while, there were four conservative and four liberals and Kennedy who sometimes was the swing vote—so many decisions came about 5 to 4. Even though the judges are not supposed to vote their political persuasions, but they do.

So if Obama had appointed one, it would be a liberal, so most decisions would end up 6 to 4, pushing the balance of the court way to the left.

I don't think many realize the incredible impact that the death of Justice Scalia was going to make from then on, not only affecting the campaign, but the election of 2016. This was completely unexpected at this time. First of all, there is suspicion on how his death was handled at the ranch in Texas where Justice Scalia was visiting. His death was pronounced officially by an official in the nearest town, and she did not even see his body yet went by what the police told her on the phone, that he was dead and it appeared no foul play. She decided not to order an autopsy. Now normally, when anyone important dies suddenly, there is automatically an autopsy. Who knows if there was foul play or not.

Scalia was the first justice in sixty-three years to die while serving. Most retire. The average age has risen considerably since the first appointment. There have been 112 people appointed to the Supreme Court, since the Court was established in 1789. For its first 180 years, it was mostly made up of white male Protestants. Prior to the twentieth century, a few Roman Catholics were appointed. Concerns about diversity were mainly geographic diversity. The twentieth century saw the first appointment of a Jewish Justice, African American Justice, a first

Woman Justice and Italian American Justice. There is no minimum age.

From 1789 to 1970, in the past, most Justices served an average of 14.9 years, now those who stepped down served an average time of 25.6 years. The retirement age jumped from an average of 68 to 79. The youngest Justice appointed was Joseph Story at age 32 and the oldest was Charles Evans Hughes, at age 67. Oliver Wendell Holmes, the oldest to serve, stepped down at age 91. The typical presidential appointment for one term has been one appointment opportunity instead of two. Increase of life expectancy and with the reduction in responsibilities by modern justices as compared to the earlier justices results in much longer potential terms of service. This has led to proposals such as imposing a mandatory retirement age for Supreme Court Justices and predetermined term limits. Any changes would require a Constitutional Amendment, a long-drawn-out process.

There has become a tradition called Thurmond's Law, that if a justice retires or dies in the year before the next election, that it can be filibustered by the Senate, who normally confirms or votes down the president's selected appointee, to delay, so that the new president can make the appointment. Now the Senate has filibustered this appointment. He says he is determined to get the process done as soon as possible, and he well may make a recess appointment. If he did, they would only be in for the end of the next court term. According to Jonah Goldberg, recently in the *LA Times*, "Democrats have been blowing up the appointment process since they turned against Robert Bork in 1987. Sen. Charles E. Schumer (D-NY) gave a blistering speech in 2007 vowing to do everything he could to prevent George W. Bush from appointing any more conservatives to the bench. He said that John G. Roberts Jr. and Samuel Alito Jr. were quite enough for one President. Switch that from Roberts, Alito and Bush to Elena Kagan, Sonia Sotomayor and Obama and you have McConnell's position now. Any claim that Republicans are the first to break the peace is as absurd as the suggestion that Obama is blameless for the polarization and meanness in our politics."

In the meantime, the court vote will be 4 to 4 on most issues. If a tie vote, the case goes back to the lower courts, whose ruling stays. So this is not good for all cases either. There are several key cases before the Supreme Court right now that may be delayed.

How did this affect the campaign? The candidates talk about all of this and the conservative ones say they want it delayed, then those who think it should be done right away will accuse them of blocking the progress, so that may affect some moderate or Reagan Democrat votes. People like Cruz and Rubio say they will filibuster it in the Senate and try their best to block Obama being able to appoint another liberal Justice, preferred by Conservatives. The ramifications of another liberal justice is great, as then many issues that the Republicans don't want will pass, so that more and more America will become a socialist state.

As far as the election, and should the appointment not have been made, then the Republican candidate will be accused of blocking the appointment for political reasons. So much is riding on this. We don't need a packed court of liberals. What is sad is that the court has become a political arm of the liberal progressive movement. With too many Justice's votes orchestrated by their political leanings, instead of pure interpretation of the Constitution law. This can be seen by so many 5 to 4 votes, and the same people making up the five and the four. Over and over.

CHAPTER 35

Are There Two Americas?
Socialism versus Capitalism
Why Socialism Will Not Work

> *Socialism is a political and economic theory which advocates that the government will control your entire life.*
>
> —From *Ban Socialism in America*

> *Capitalism is an economic and political system in which a country's trade and industry are controlled by private owners for profit, rather than by the state.*
>
> —From former football coach,
> Lou Holtz, sportscaster and speaker

The Democrats are right. There are two Americas. The America that works and the America that doesn't. The America that contributes and the America that doesn't. It's not the have and the have-nots. It's the dos and don'ts. Some people do their duty as Americans, obey the law, support themselves, contribute to society, and others don't. That's the divide in America.

It's not about income inequality, it's about a political party that preaches hatred, greed, and victimization in order to win elective office. It's about a political party that loves power more than it loves its country.

That's not invective, that's truth, and it's about time someone said it. The politics of envy was on proud display when President Obama pledged the rest of his term to fighting income inequality. He noted that some people make more than other people, that some people have higher incomes than others, and he says that's not just. (Since he is now a multi-millionaire, wonder if he thinks he should give up his millions.) That is the rationale of thievery. The other guy has it, you want it, Obama will take it for you. Vote Democrat. (And you will get yours taken away.)

That is the philosophy that produced Detroit. It is the electoral philosophy that is destroying America. It conceals a fundamental deviation from American values and common sense because it ends up not benefitting the people who support it but a betrayal.

The Democrats have not empowered their followers, they have enslaved them in a culture of dependence and entitlement, of victimhood and anger instead of ability and hope. Obama's premise "that you reduce income inequality by debasing the successful" seeks to deny the successful the consequences of their choices and spare the unsuccessful the consequences of their choices. Because by and large, income variations in society are a result of different choices leading to different consequences.

Those who choose wisely and responsibly have a far greater likelihood of success, while those who choose foolishly and irresponsibly have a far greater likelihood of failure. Success and failure usually manifest themselves in personal and family income. You choose to drop out of high school or to skip college and you are apt to have a different outcome than someone who gets a diploma and pushes on with purposeful education. You have your children out of wedlock and life is apt to take one course; you have them within a marriage and life is apt to take another course. Most often in life, our destination is determined by the course we take. You raise a kid in a two-parent family, and you will have a better course.

My doctor, for example, makes far more than I do. There is significant income inequality between us. Our lives have had an inequality of outcome, but our lives also have had an inequality of effort. While my doctor went to college and then devoted his young adulthood to medical school and residency. I got a job in a restaurant. He made a choice, I made a choice, and our choices led us to different outcomes. His outcome pays a lot better than mine. Does that mean he cheated and Barack Obama needed to take away his wealth? No, it means we are both free men in a free society where free choices lead to different outcomes.

It is not inequality Barack Obama and the Socialists intended to take away, it is freedom. The freedom to succeed and the freedom to fail. There is no true option for success if there is no true option for failure. The pursuit of happiness means a whole lot less when you face the punitive hand of government if your pursuit brings you more happiness than the other guy. Even if the other guy sat on his arse and did nothing. Even if the other guy made a lifetime's worth of asinine and short-sighted decisions.

Barack Obama and the Democrats preached equality of outcome as a right, while completely ignoring inequality of effort. The simple Law of the Harvest, "As ye sow, so shall ye reap," is sometimes applied as "The harder you work, the more you get."

Obama would turn that upside down. Those who achieve are to be punished as enemies of society and those who fail are to be rewarded as wards of society. Entitlement will replace effort as the key to upward mobility in American society if Barack Obama got his way. He sought a lowest common denominator society in which the government besieges the successful and productive to foster equality through mediocrity.

He and his party spoke of two Americas, and their grip on power is based on using the votes of one to sap the productivity of the other. America is not divided by the difference in our outcomes, it is divided by the differences in our efforts.

It is a false philosophy to say one man's success comes about unavoidably as the result of another man's victimization. What Obama offered was not a solution, but a separatism. He fomented division and strife, pitted one set of Americans against another for his own political benefit. That's what socialists offer: "Marxist class warfare wrapped up with a bow." Two Americas, coming closer each day to proving the truth to Lincoln's maxim that a house divided against itself cannot stand.

"Life is ten percent what happens to you and ninety percent how you respond to it."

CHAPTER 36

What Is the Difference between Conservative Republicans and Liberal Leftists, Socialist Democrats?

Well, to understand the workings of American politics, according to the late political guru and commentator, Charles Krauthammer, "you have to understand this fundamental law: Conservatives think liberals are stupid. Liberals think conservatives are evil."

When media pundits and Democratic politicians routinely compare Donald Trump to Adolf Hitler and his supporters to Nazis, Fascists, and white supremacists, and more nicely Hillary's basket of deplorables, this stirs up anger and hate.

Unfortunately, such accusations escalate into mob violence, and enraged leftwing activists target Republican lawmakers, as they did US Rep. Steve

Scalise, who was wounded during a mass assassination attempt at a Congressional baseball practice.

Krauthammer goes on to say, "After all, if Trump actually were another Hitler, as leftist media and pundits have posited, virtually no form of 'resistance'—no lies, deception, obstruction, subversion, violence or armed revolution—would be morally off limits in the heroic quest to save the world from another holocaust. Indeed, all-out resistance would become a liberal imperative."

But Hitler murdered eleven million people. How many has Trump murdered?

We are dealing with screaming mobs while trying to eat dinner in various Washington, DC, restaurants, and in the case of former Press Secretary, Sarah Huckabee Sanders, actually being thrown out of the premises.

Representative Maxine Waters, even told her rally mobs that they must harass Republicans, conservatives, and Trump associates, family or friends or voters, wherever they are.

Why is the left so obsessed with defaming and demonizing, not only Trump but all those who dared to vote for him? Is the left so obsessed with power and their hysteria all about winning the 2018 and now 2020 elections? This is true, but maybe there's more to it all.

Charles Krauthammer, conservative pundit and political consultant on Fox News, muses that "we should remember the Ninth Commandment 'Thou Shalt Not Bear False Witness Against Thy Neighbor,' comes right up there with 'Thou Shalt Not Kill' or 'Thou Shalt not Commit Adultery.' These are all forms of stealing. Murder is stealing another's life, adultery is stealing another's wife and bearing false witness, slander and false accusations is stealing another's good name, credibility, opportunities, happiness and all too often his freedom."

Yet the left completely ignores this commandment. It is all about racism, sexism, homophobia, xenophobia, Islamophobia, and you name it! But then the Marxist creed is to sow chaos everywhere—divide and conquer.

CHAPTER 37

When Did the Democratic Party Become Socialist?

From Freedom Outpost on Google: What is the Democratic Party? Or what was the Democratic Party? Either way, it is NOT what it used to be, and many indications show that this party is neither for the people, nor for the US as we know it. In fact, they appear to want it to decline and fall so they can remake it into a Socialist (communist) state. It's not the party of John F. Kennedy. If living and running for president today, Kennedy would probably be running as a Republican as he would no longer recognize his party, as it has changed that much with the infiltration of the socialists, and that's right, actual communists. Kennedy would probably turn over in his grave if he knew how his party has travelled so far to the left.

The Democrat Party can trace its roots to Thomas Jefferson as he formed the original Republican Party, it was first known as the Democratic Republican Party.

The modern Democrat Party began during the War of 1812. It was originally anti-national bank by the 1820s. From mid-1830s to the War between States, Democrats were America's major party.

On Slaves and Racism. The Democrats supported slavery, were the slave owners of the plantations, and protested the Jim Crow laws and were against any blacks obtaining freedom. Yet today, they claim it was the Republicans who were slave owners and against the blacks having freedom.

There have always been slaves since time began in most other countries and even some white people were sold as slaves. Some want reparations for the slaves here in the Civil War era.

The 1860s

But my ancestors came from Europe, and at one time, the Vikings came down into Europe from Scandinavian countries, Norway, Denmark, and Sweden. They were known as the Norse or Norsemen. They were invaders and ran over a great deal of Europe, leaving a lot of blonds in their wake, especially in Northern Europe. They took white people as slaves. My ophthalmologist claims I must have a lot of Viking blood in me by the rare light color of the fundus behind my eyes. So therefore, I want reparations from the Scandinavian countries for the Vikings invading where my ancestors lived and took over their lands and bred with their women and made some slaves. Not much different than what happened to the North American Indians, yet people think there should be reparations for them. And slaves of North America during the civil war times were not unusual at all. There's no reason for reparations for blacks who were never slaves nor are now suffering any hardships because of what happened more than 160 years ago. Nor for North American Indians, as every country has been taken over by another country at one time or another since time began. That includes their people and their land. By treaty, by war, or by mutual agreement, or like by a trade. We probably all come from early invaders or were the invaded or made slaves.

So when did the Democrats slide down the road toward socialist/communist ideology?

Actually, after the First World War, during the '30s especially, quite a few Marxist professors from Russia came to the United States to do research and to teach in the universities, bringing their socialist agenda with them. Those same professors were in the classrooms when the rebellious '60s kids were in college, and the professors fomented their rebellion in that they championed Marxism and socialism and were against organized religion and against authority, even encouraging them to rebel against any authority. Thus, they spit at cops and called them pigs, spit on the returning vets from Vietnam, as they protested the war, and burned down parks, buildings, and cars in places like Berkeley, the worst cauldron for the fomentation.

It really began around 1944, when the six-time Socialist Party Candidate for President Norman Thomas stated, "The American people will never knowingly accept socialism, but under the name of Liberalism they will adopt every fragment of the socialist progress. America will be a socialist nation without even knowing how it happened."

The Socialists in the US did not achieve their full move toward making the Democratic Party more of a socialist party until they got a foothold in the '60s.

The '60s proved to be what was ordered. Fertile ground with the rebellious young. It was here where the new Left got its beginning.

But the magic figure for the Socialists was Saul Alinsky, a very good friend of presidential hopeful Hillary Clinton. In fact, she did her graduate paper on him.

Alinsky stated that to change a society, one had to first infiltrate the major institutions, the schools, the media, the churches, the entertainment industries, the labor unions, and the three branches of government. Then it would have the power to implement policies.

It was in the 1972 elections that the Democratic Party, through the use of the old New Left, made the final move by effectively eliminating its opposition, the centrist liberals, who had viscously opposed Communist totalitarianism.

Once the centrists in the Democratic Party were eliminated, the New Left took over and incorporated the "liberalism" word. It was here that Socialism began its move into the depth of the Democratic Party with Hillary Clinton actually writing letters to Saul Alinsky telling him how great his work was and that his ideas were working well. She carefully kept hidden from the masses during her campaign, running as a centrist, hiding her association with socialists and their movement.

It was during George W Bush's first term that Democrats wanted Campaign Finance Reform, but the Democrats were not interested in true reform, only in making sure they kept their biggest donors and, at the same time, keeping the Republican party from doing the same.

They did this by including a small provision called the 527 organization, which allowed ultra-radicals like themselves to give unlimited sums of money to only the Democrats. The 527 included George Soros, who was one of the leaders of the Shadow Party to include his own Move on.Org. It was after John Kerry lost the 2004 election that these groups stated, "NOW, IT'S OUR PARTY. WE BOUGHT IT, WE OWN IT!"

The Democratic Party of today is very far left and the top parts of the Democratic Party have been infiltrated by a vast number of Socialists/Communists, which is why the DNC could not differentiate between the Democratic Party and The Socialist Party.

Today's ruling Democratic Party faction, whose members included the so-called Shadow Party and its constituents themselves, call themselves, Progressive Democrats. These Democrats themselves have a left-wing faction in the House of Representatives which is formally organized into the Progressive Caucus.

The Democrat mayors and governors and leaders yield to the anarchists.

The leftist Democrats are saying the country is shameful. And the Left is saying this county has systemic racism. And watch out for the enormous power the left has—like with PC against us. Is there a way out of all of this? The left more and more claims its innocence. We, on the right, defer to the left, so the left challenges us to prove our innocence. The left wants to dominate. It's a culture war. We have to quit deferring to them and realize what they are really doing to us and to our great country.

This should trouble people who love their freedom and liberties because the Socialists do not like either one and will lie and steal to remove both from the United States.

The Communist Party USA urged their members to drop their communist label so they could work more effectively within the Democratic Party, actually so that Communists might someday be able to capture the Democratic Party entirely. They are very close to total control of the Democrat Party now.

Two anti–United States groups have now stolen the Democratic Party, and it now represents both the Socialist Party and the Communist Party.

Big lawyers, big labor union leaders, big green environmentalists, big insiders with billions of dollars in personal wealth and foundation grants—together essentially dictate what Democrats can and cannot support on many key issues. Special interest groups that donate to the Democratic Party are a part of the plans for the takeover, too.

These groups, along with rich donors, provide most of the campaign funding and workers, political and policy expertise, legal and regulatory muscle, and communication of the party.

This all has moved the party far to the left of mainstream America. They have used the power of the purse to co-opt the agenda of the Democratic Party.

The mainstream media aligned with both the Socialists and the Communists within the Democratic Party, and it refuses to allow this truth to be shown. They are carrying the water for the Democrat Party as an arm of the party. Unfortunately, many do not know this as they only listen to the mainstream news and hear only one side or mainly personal opinions, which may often be biased when they are not trashing President Trump.

The Democratic Party today is no better than the Democratic Party of the 1850s that wished to keep slavery, and later on, the Jim Crow laws, both of which hold not just blacks back but all other poor people. In every large city in America, which most have been under Democratic rule for a long time, there is much homelessness, much corruption, and holding of people back, places run down, and most have left the city that could keep it going. Think Detroit and

Chicago. Los Angeles and San Francisco, with their homelessness problems, are soon following.

The term shadow party is the 527 political committees promoting the Democratic Party agendas. Organized by George Soros, Hillary Clinton, and Harold Ickes, aided by the ACORN group (Obama's friends) key organizers are veterans of the Sixties Left.

It is time to take our nation back from these groups and let them know we don't want our nation changed into their way at all.

CHAPTER 38

What Has Crept Up on Us?

May I remind you that socialism sort of gradually crept upon us as we quietly accepted, at least halfway in order to not earn their wrath or even being jailed. May I remind you that the leftists deal in fear and threats.

Our kids are being taught in the schools to accept the entire social order as laid out by socialist leftist teachers and professors. They are being brainwashed. In many schools now, they are being taught the Koran—as the only acceptable religion, yet the Bible is banned from all schools and teachers in most cases may not even refer to it. If I had kids of school age now, I would home school or send them to private Christian schools as hopefully they would not be brainwashed by the leftist progressives/Marxist agenda. Yet with the pandemic of coronavirus, teachers and school districts are calling for a delay starting the schools until they can get more funds due to an Act of God. Now that sounds very Christian or religious, yet none is allowed in the schools?

This book is designed to inform, as that seems to be the biggest problem in this country is the lack of being informed by the masses. They watch or listen to the mainstream media and learn nothing of the truth or what is really happening. Just trash Trump is about all they hear. Or the personal opinion of the TV host. People are far less literate or well-read than they used to be.

Many have seemed to be asleep at the wheel and don't realize the dangers we are facing as a country and, for that matter, the whole world.

As President Reagan once said. *"Freedom is never more than one generation away."*

And finally, what you can do as a person and as groups to work toward changing our country back to more like it was in the peaceful '50s. Patriotism was popular then. Churches thrived. No one heard of terrorist attacks or church shootings.

Conservatives/Christians must awake and start thinking what kind of world will we leave our kids and grandkids?

CHAPTER 39

There Is a Revolution Going On in the US

"There is a revolution going on in the US propped up by three legs. Economic chaos, chaos through racial division, and chaos through class division all joined by one core element; Barack Obama and his stable of unelected czars. Obama is using the lessons learned in 1968 as the template for 2012, and many of those close to him, who were alive and activists in the late '60s, are now calling the shots for 2012."

"The administration and many others either directly or indirectly are engaged in covert activities with the Occupy movement, various labor protests, and other subversive activities inside the US," stated his source, Hageman said. "Using untracked campaign funds, they are paying people to infiltrate the various movements to cause physical destruction of property and disrupt commerce. That infiltration began last year, but has increased ten-fold already this year. My source added," Hageman said, "that they are using some lower level DHS agents to make the payments under the context of tracking subversives, but they are the unwitting subversives. It is like the *Fast & Furious*, but in the social realm," he added.

"Obama is using some high-profile people as pawns to foment this revolution." Hageman says he has heard through credible sources that Louis Farrakhan, '60s fomenter, is on the CIA payroll. Others have been armed as well, but Hageman says he is not prepared to identify them yet. Farrakhan is to coordinate the Blacks and the Muslims to prepare for riots this summer, using ANY means."

"They envision rioting starting in the urban areas first, such as New York, LA, and other major cities, followed by disruption of business and commerce. This will allow the DHS to mobilize their various teams into the streets of America, without the objection of the people, to protect us," stated Hageman's source.

"They wanted to restrict travel, if not through high energy prices, then by checkpoints and curfews mandated by rioting and unrest. They know it is just a matter of time that Europe will implode economically, and when it does, start counting the days before we see massive hyperinflation and the ultimate collapse of the dollar."

What will it look like in the streets of the US when they realize there is no money? Chaos.

"It is common knowledge that Socialism is not American and neither is the Socialists agenda. Of course, criticism of their bona fides plays into the cries of racism, despite the massive fraud perpetrated on the American people. Party lines are meaningless when the common object is in the revolutionary overtaking of America," Hageman's source said.

"One statement that really rattled me," Hagen wrote, "is that more than anything was the great number of those already in power actually wanted to see Obama stay in power. They say, this is what we've been working toward and we're closer now than we've ever been. If we lose now we might not have another chance."

"That administration was working closely with Bernanke, Chairman of the Federal Reserve, and Geitner, Secretary of Treasury, and others <u>not</u> to save our economy but to <u>outright destroy it</u>. Was the information that Timothy Geitner's father worked with Obama's mother in Indonesia coincidental? What we are seeing now is the fourth quarter of a game that started long ago, which also currently involves the Clintons. Obama would have been where was if it were not for the Clintons and to a lesser extent, Bush, but that for other reasons. Don't be fooled, the Clintons never left or lost power," he added.

"The power behind international financial dealings has been going on for decades, with such organizations as the Bilderberg Group, the Trilateral Commission, and people like George Soros, Henry Kissinger, and current leaders of big industry, and of big banks in the world. They want to put in place a global system of governance, including a common currency to replace the dollar. They are working toward this goal, and when this happens, it will cause chaos like never seen before in the history of this country."

The aspect of suspended elections could well happen, as we hit rocky shores.

"The surreal aspect of suspended elections won't look so surreal when you see any or the entire trigger points take place in the not too distant future," Hageman's informant said.

"Watch for a false flag. It will be carefully choreographed, but executed in a manner that will evoke the ugliest of reactions and create racial chaos in this country that will make the Watts riots in 1968 and the Rodney King riots pale in comparison. That's the third leg in this. Does the mass murder of policemen at Dallas in July 2016 mean more riots and more racial divisions? They are power hungry and they want to remain in charge," states Hagen's source.

<u>The end game plan for America is its destruction as a constitutional Republic with the assistance of the agencies under the DHS."</u>

"By the time this went out on the internet, my informant was worried for his own safety," Hageman said.

Could this be the end of the Republican Party?

Could we be imprisoned because we are people of faith? Could this be the end of the Republican Party or the two-party system? Could it be the end of freedom of speech, the end of talk radio and FOX News and internet blogs being censored, even our e-mail and Facebook, so that our information is stifled and we are arrested for speaking out, with total control of the internet, so that our every word or thought is monitored? Our food now is already monitored and our electricity.

Could all of our country be taken away? Could our seashores be claimed by the UN? By treaty, will the UN take away all of our private property, the seas, and the atmosphere? Would we even survive much longer? Think long and hard, America, what will you do when all of this very well could happen? How could it?

Could it be because we remained silent for the last, close to one hundred years, and allowed this gradual erosion of our, the best in the world, country?

Our Ship of State was in real dire straits and is it in troubled waters.

Could we have won a war if we were attacked with our military so drastically cut by Obama? Or because our economy was so bad we could not pay for the military might we would need or any defense in place to protect ourselves? Could our ship survive if we find we are a socialist/communist state, taken over by Sharia Law?

Thank goodness for our new Captain Trump turning our ship around as it is in smoother waters now. He has added to the military and to our ships around the globe and let the world know we are back now as a leader in the world. He says we will never be a Socialist country. As long as he is in charge, we will not be a socialist country, but what about 2024?

Our ship may not sink now, and it is sailing into smoother waters.

We have to keep on voting now in 2020 and onward and at all levels. Not only for president but for a more conservative reasonable Congress. We must educate our young in a far different manner, if we are able to change our course. They must learn history, as it repeats itself. We may not realize just how much in danger the future of our country is in. The way our debt is growing now, our children will have to pay off this enormous debt for most of their lives and their children's lives, even if this country survives for them. Do they realize this? What are we leaving our children?

Are we headed for the worst "Perfect Storm" that we have ever sailed into? Wake up, America! Before it is too late and change the course of our Ship of State before it hits that iceberg, crashes, and sinks.

Can America Survive?

What we have to ask ourselves when we vote: is can America survive to 2025? We have regained our shattered status in the world, but it will required a level of leadership this country has not seen for a long time. It will take all of us working together, speaking out, one person at a time, to millions literally <u>rolling up our sleeves and pushing on the rudder, hitting reverse and literally swinging our Ship</u> of State <u>bodily around to a renewed course, full steam ahead</u> to help our Captain Trump steer this ship on an even better course, to keep it the greatest nation in the world once again, with renewed energy and purpose to meet the challenges of the twenty-first century. To fight the "swamp" which is literally trying to sink us.

As we did in 2016, turning the ship around with our vote. We have a captain now who is steering our ship in the right direction for a change. We have a chance now to continue to pursue freedom, independence, and the values our founders envisioned for this great one of a kind country.

So full steam ahead now and steer our ship straight to freedom and the greatest port of all. *America*!

CHAPTER 40

Battle for the Soul of the Democrats and Trump Derangement Syndrome

After months of uncertainty and a sort of free for all, we may see just how determined the Democratic candidate will be. Still completely undecided until all states have had their primaries, so we won't know for sure, as of this writing, but it looks like Biden may be the candidate so far. The quandary is do the Democrats want to put forward a progressive who promises radical change or a moderate who would more slowly move to invoke the Socialist tendencies already culminating in the Democrat Party. Even if he has dementia, as some have reported. Both old white millionaire men. (Neither can beat Trump.) Either way, it boils down to a more leftist progressive platform.

This will be the most consequential presidential election of our lifetime. It's a battle between how this country might lean for a long time—

Socialism or Capitalism. To Republicans, the results of capitalism mean more growth, a better economy, and more independence in businesses, and to the Democrats, capitalism is evil and socialism is the only way to go so that the top tier income earners pay more, and they won't admit, yes, we the middle class pays for all the rest of the free goodies. You would see sky-high taxes.

The young say, "Well, it's government money that is free to us, for free education, and other free goodies," but they don't realize someday they will have to be the ones paying for it all. Who is the government? A rich uncle or an invisible multibillionaire or is it, we, the taxpayers?

The antidote for the Trump Derangement Syndrome, according to Adriana Cohen, in *Trending Politics*, says that when asked why she supports the president, as they think he's a racist, misogynist, homophobe, criminal, and for good measure, a bully. She says she laughs, "Because none of these things are true. Then she hits them with the facts."

"Like the allegation Trump is anti-women." Cohen continues, "Why has he created millions of jobs for women? The unemployment rate is 3.5, lowest in 66 years. The poverty rate has fallen to record lows. He's appointed quite a few women in his administration." (Your author indicates that when in the contracting business he hired a woman supervisor of a huge building complex, unheard of then). Financial independence truly empowers women, giving them more freedom. (Feminists like the allegation that Trump is anti-women so they will get the women's vote.)

Cohen goes on to say that "He invoked more parental leave for civilian employees. Nearly 7 million have been lifted from food stamps, allowing many women to transit from poverty to self-reliance and careers. The black employment rate is at a historic low. He's delivered on criminal justice reform, affecting blacks, initiated reforms that support the nations historically black colleges and universities. "

So how would a racist be?
- uplifting minorities and empowering them with enhanced housing and educational opportunities
- block grants
- given them small business loans
- jobs with higher wages and tax breaks
- while rebuilding their communities

Then how does this make him a racist? Only fake news says he is a racist.

Cohen continues, "Allegations of homophobia—Trump last year launched a global crusade alongside LGBTQ groups and human rights organizations to decriminalize homosexuality around the world."

Cohen says, "When I hear 'Trump's a criminal,' I remind people that in America everyone is innocent until proven guilty by a jury of their peers. Since the president has occupied the Oval Office, he's been subjected to a daily deluge of investigations, including a 22-month counsel probe that found insufficient evidence of criminal mischief. If any evidence, he would have been charged a long time ago."

Grasping for straws at this point, some Democrats will say, "Okay, I guess you're right, but he's still a bully."

"To which I respond," Cohen says, "that if you were to have the entire Washington establishment against you and the fake news media accusing you of treason and other accusations that are heinous, false, defamatory, and hurtful, wouldn't you fight back too?'

That's usually where the debate ends and they change the subject. Plain and simple facts should guide anyone voting, not blind hatred, fed by #Fake News Media, should be one's guiding light leading into the next election.

CHAPTER 41

How the Anti-Trump Resistance Erodes US Institutions

According to Kimberly Strassel, often seen on Fox News, in the subject in her new book, *Resistance (At All Costs) How Trump Haters Are Breaking America.*

"The anti-Trump resistance has devastated core American institutions and broken long-standing political norms in seeking to defeat and now oust from office President Donald Trump," says Strassel and columnist for *The Wall Street Journal.*

"What's wrong? We've been told for over three years that Donald Trump is wrecking the institutions (in an interview with *Epoch Times*) (a conservative newspaper)."

Where's the real wreckage? Where's the public faith broken in the FBI, and Justice Departments have fallen. That's because of Jim Comey and Andrew McCabe.

It's no lie that the Senate confirmation process for the Supreme Court is in shambles and will never be the same again after what happened to Brett Kavanaugh. He was put through the mill on false charges. Never have I seen a nominee for the Supreme Court put through that bad a situation in his nomination process.

The haters of Trump can't abide nuance. To the resistance, any praise of Trump is tantamount to American betrayal. No matter how qualified he is. Never has a president been so vilified before.

Schiff's Chamber of Secrets, closed-door impeachment proceedings. Farce attacks due process.

Hot dawg! The Republicans in Congress finally got some (you know what). They marched on Pelosi and Schiff's secret hearings as if they were storming the barricade in *Les Mis*.

While the Libs and mainstream media poopooed it all, the Democrats decided to make an inquiry vote. The bullies that they are, they were shocked to be called on their trickery.

So now Republicans can be in some of the hearings—but Schiff was appointed by Speaker Pelosi to decide on witnesses called. And the Democrats and Feckless Schiff were coaching the witnesses—unheard of in any Congressional hearings.

It's a distraction by Pelosi too. Her party sympathizing with our known enemy that our troops killed in Bagdad. They are feeling the heat but it's phony. The Democrats in on this said, "You'll have to get our permission first if want to call witnesses, etc."

Schiff's Chamber of Secrets, closed-door impeachment, farce attacks, due process.

Justice in America hangs in the balance. Republicans needed to push back on merits. It should be dismissed and be put to bed. As it was.

Ironically, the president did his duty.

Could we have won a war if we were attacked with our military so drastically cut by Obama? Or because our economy was so bad, we could not pay for the military might we would need or any defense in place to protect ourselves? Could our ship survive if we find we are a socialist/communist state, taken over by Sharia Law?

CHAPTER 42

Is Liberalism Dead?

I n Hannity Headlines on the internet on Monday, May 7, 2012, Emmett Tyrell Jr., Founder and Editor of the American Spectator, had just completed a book called *The Death of Liberalism*, in which he analyzes the past, present, and future of liberalism.

Liberals have carried on as a kind of landed aristocracy, gifted but doomed. They dominated the culture and politics of the country unchallenged from the beginning of the Cold War to the first Nixon administration. Has the political environment of the US acted as a warm and fuzzy incubator in which liberalism can grow or has the country taken a sharp turn? Tyrell advocates the latter as he points to the 2008 elections. Democrats have shown their true colors by putting us in additional trillions of debt when we are already in an entitlement crisis. The leader of this decline, President Obama is "a stealth socialist" and a leader such as Obama creates an unsustainable state because "in the Constitution there is life.

303

There is Energy. In *Statism,* there is only stagnation and death." The "good news" is conservatives always outnumber the liberals and now in some surveys they outnumber the moderates—that is, if we vote.

In a book called *The Righteous Mind. Why Good People Are Divided by Politics and Religion* by Jonathan Haidt—says in the revolution of morals, the difficulty people have in comprehending opposing political view. Haidt, a psychologist at the University of Virginia, in that progressive enclave, was troubled that his profession routinely demonized conservatism. So he set out to try to understand conservatives instead of demonizing them. His premise: We are all self-righteous hypocrites, mainly because we evolved that way. He envisions the human mind as an elephant bearing a rider. The latter may believe he is steering, but the giant beast below is actually in charge. The rider is our rational self; it exists only to serve the elephant, which represents the great mass of mental processes that occur outside consciousness.

Haidt cites an example. Back in 1989 controversy erupted over a photograph by Andres Serrano depicting a crucifix in urine. To conservatives, this was blasphemous. To liberals, the issue was censorship.

But what if the likeness was immersed in urine had been the Reverend Marin Luther King Jr.? Or Nelson Mandela? Then which side would you be on? Haidt did not have much to say about why we have become so much more righteous in recent years.

Why liberals do not understand conservatives. It has been said that conservatives understand the ideology of the liberals to a certain extent, but it does not appear that liberals have the foggiest idea where conservatives are coming from nor make any effort to understand them. That might explain the divisiveness mainly driven by the Liberal Democrats. The Democrat party has evolved and changed drastically from the old Democrat party under and up until John Kennedy. They have been taken over by the ultra-liberal leftist movement, who really has far more diverse ideologies than the older Democrats had. That is one of the main reasons that it becomes much more difficult to work in a bipartisan manner now. Yet Republicans kept getting blamed for not being non-partisan. They have presented bill after bill, but the Democrat Senate Leader, Harry Reid, would not accept them.

The Rich against the Poor: Class Warfare

Obama, in campaigning against Romney in 2012, was trying to paint Romney as the vulture capitalist, with Bain Capital, with a commercial of how Romney took over Bain and lost many jobs. The time for that commercial in question was two years after Romney had left Bain, to help more struggling companies with venture capitalism. And to top that insinuation of venture capitalists, Obama was found speaking to one of the biggest venture capitalists on Wall Street and raising huge amounts of money from them for his campaign. He demonizes the rich and Wall Street venture capitalists and yet holds out his hand for their vast amounts of money for his campaigns.

Is the thrill gone for Obama? What a difference eight years makes! Gone are the lofty goals and the inspired rhetoric. Instead, we have the stark reality of a failed presidency. His adoring fans are fewer now.

He had failed to unite Americans; he had ushered in more racial division than any president in recent history; he has inserted himself in controversies, beneath the dignity of his office, more than any other president. Most stay above the fray. His stewardship of the economy has been abysmal, and he has spent more money than all other presidents put together. We asked in 2012, can we really afford four more years of this? What about 2016?

We can change course drastically.

In a book called *Change*, Newt Gingrich tells us about several distinct changes our country has gone through in the past, so he believes change in course is possible again. Conservatives and Romney were accused by Obama and the liberals of wanting to go backward. Some of our most significant courses or changes in this country might have appeared to go backward, such as when Reagan took us back from a more modern liberal leaning economic mentality to more conservative values and balanced the budget. Though he inherited a bad economy, he turned our ship around, wherein it had been heading in the wrong direction. He had a Republican Senate to work with and was able to work with the Democrat House, but Democrats were far different then.

The change in 1994 when the Republicans took Congress back over for the first time in many long years, the economy came back and we ended up with a surplus. Things went well in the Bush years until 2006, when after that, two wars drained our capital, and then in 2006 when Congress was taken over by the Democrats <u>again</u>, then their bank regulations, by Barney Frank and Chris Dodd, which said banks had to loan to almost anybody, as all should have their own home. This was the NUMBER ONE REASON that caused the housing meltdown, spending increased and the budget was not balanced, so we ended up 2008 in debt and in trouble. The Senate, controlled by the Democrats since 2006 up until 2012, had not balanced a budget for three years.

We hear often, even from Republicans that the Republicans do not do anything and are the same as the Democrats. From the Congressional Report, we have the following information:

The Republicans in the House 2011–2012. They passed the following bills:

1. Repeal Obamacare.
2. Spending cuts to reduce the deficit, to ensure a balanced budget amendment.
3. Cut 6.2 trillion in government spending over the next ten years.
4. Cut 45 billion in non-defense spending.
5. Terminated 29.9 billion of TARP funding for failed housing.

6. Rejected the bill HR 1954 because it contained no spending cuts per the president's request.

7. The House in March 2012 passed a Budget Resolution.

8. The Senate, controlled by the Democrats since 2006, has not passed a budget for three years.

9. The Democrats controlled both Houses in 2008.

In 2014 and '15, the Republicans the "do lots house" passed 511 bills and "do little senate" 256. Obama has signed only 108 House bills and 37 Senate born laws. Nancy Pelosi, speaker of the House from 2007 to 2011, did not allow Republican bills to come to the floor, nor did Harry Reid, Speaker of the Senate, neither allowed the Republican bills to come to the floor.

When you hear anyone saying that Congress is the same, the Republicans do nothing, and are as bad as the Democrats, look at what they try to do while the Democrat-controlled Senate will not even hear them. While a few might be bad apples, generally, when the Republicans are in control, the economy bounces back. During Bush's first years until 2006, the economy, even with two wars going on, we were still okay. Then in 2006, the Democrats we voted in got full control, spent and spent, and by 2008, the economy was far worse, the housing market collapsed, adding to this the stock market was affected adversely.

McGary also writes in his book *Instantity*, "When I see this president Obama speaking with a similar air of sophistication, yet defiant, eloquence, as Mister Tibbs in Sidney Portier's *The Heat of the Night*, I envision this president saying, 'They call Me Mr. Fibs!' While watching Obama host a seemingly endless schedule of press conferences, meetings, and preemptive specials, my Mr. Fibs analogy helps me get through the barrage of baseless promises, hyperbole, and obvious incompetence with laughter and humor."

"Our president made many promises during his presidential campaigns and during the first six months in office. By my count very few (if any) of these promises have been kept," McGary states. "What does this mean? It means that we have been entranced by the many assertions delivered with eloquence and style without interrogating the substance—delivery or manifestations or outcomes. The promises on the stimulus, tax cuts for 95% of Americans, Transparency, Darfur, Automobile and Financial Institutions, Budget, Enhanced Interrogations, and National Security, were for the most part not kept and others blamed for the responsibility for these but not our administration," wrote McGary.

Americans may be more worried about our survival since the Civil War.

World Net Daily (WND), one of the largest blogs in the world, in their blog on May 28, 2012, states, "Millions of Americans feel they're living in a war zone, the bombardment coming their way daily. The bombardment of brazen presidential power brags, bows to enemy leaders insults to allies intentionally destructive economic and energy policies. Presidential hot mike gaffes proving collusion with America's enemies was an unintentional gaffe. No wonder Americans are more worried today about the very survival of their nation than at any time since the Civil War."

We need an experienced captain of our ship? Our country is a huge business. To be run as one.

CHAPTER 43

On Voting Rights and Voter Fraud

According to the ACRU, American Civil Rights Union, the radical left doesn't trust voters like you and me. They still haven't accepted the results of the 2016 election and they are terrified voters will make the "wrong" choice again in 2020.

They are using ever sleazy underhanded tactic they can to sway the results of the 2020 election, which is why the American Civil Rights Union (not the ACLU) is assembling our Election Integrity Task Force to ensure YOUR vote is counted.

What do leftists do when they can't win fair and square? They change the rules of the game. Just as they changed the rules in Congress during the impeachment trial.

The Democrat Party is pushing a legislative agenda all across the country that will completely dismantle our electoral system and allow for voter fraud on a massive scale. Like their campaign to repeal Voter ID laws. But most of their work has been quietly taking place behind the scenes.

Here's three devious tactics that the far left is employing to ensure they win in 2020.

1. Ballot Harvesting: Ballot harvesting is illegal in most parts of the country. But the radical left is pushing to change that. Democrats have already legalized ballot harvesting in California. And it resulted in massive victories for leftist candidates in the 2018 midterms.

    Here's how ballot harvesting works;

    Step 1. State send out absentee ballots and mail in ballots to voters. Each state has a different process, but in California, every voter now receives a ballot in the mail whether they asked for it or not.

    Step 2 Door to Door Campaign: Campaign operatives, union activists, and community organizers go door to door and collect or "harvest these mail in and absentee ballots on behalf of voters."

    You see, most states require that absentee ballots are turned in personally by the voter or a close family relative with your signed permission. Or mailed in. But under this scheme, anybody can walk into an election office and hand over truckloads of absentee ballots, no questions asked. They don't even need to provide any documentation or proof the votes they are turning in are legitimate.

What is to stop a campaign official from collecting or buying blank ballots from voters and filling them out themselves?

And what's to stop union activists from pressuring union members to hand in their ballots to prove they voted for the "right" candidates?

Ballot harvesting allowed California Democrats to flip at least seven Congressional districts in the 2018 midterms. They were able to flip seats that were held by Republicans for decades all because of these underhanded tactics.

2018 was just a trial run. Now that the radical left has seen how effective ballot harvesting was in California, they are pushing to legalize the practice nationwide.

But ballot harvesting is just the beginning.

2. Devious Tactic #2. Allowing felons to vote even if still in prison. Most states restrict certain felons and violent criminals form voting. Democrats know that convicted felons are more likely to vote for the far-left progressive candidates—which is why they've recently leveled a massive effort to give millions the right to vote [PC again]. Starting this year, 1.4 million felons in Florida will be able to vote—thanks to a

measure pushed through by the radical left in that fair state.

And in Virginia, Democrats are trying to push through an amendment for felons to vote—thanks to a measure pushed through by the by the radical left. And in Virginia, Dems are trying to push through an amendment for felons to vote.

If the Democrats should take over the Senate and White House, they will restore voting rights to all felons, countrywide.

3. Redistricting Reform

When the Democrats are not gaming the Russians for losing an election in 2016, they are usually pointing their finger at their new favorite gerrymandering.

For most of our nation's history, Congressional districts have been drawn up by the state legislatures. The Democrats were fine with this—until 2010, when they lost hundreds of state legislative seats, across the nation. The Dems lost control over the redistricting process, which takes place every ten years.

They are afraid the same thing will happen in 2020, so they have decided to launch a nationwide effort to change the way redistricting happens.

Obama's former Attorney General, Eric Holder, has recently launched a measure 35 million campaign to strip the state legislatures of their authority to set the boundaries of Congressional districts. Sounds like he may have gotten multi-millionaire George Soros to fund this move.

Instead, Holder wants a panel of unelected bureaucrats to have total control over the redistricting process.

The idea of having an independent commission set the boundaries of our Congressional districts might sound appealing to some. But the truth is, this is all just a cheap ploy to further weaken the states and make it easier for radical leftist candidates to win Congressional seats.

Congressional districts should be set by duly-elected representatives who are accountable to the voters—not a bunch of faceless bureaucrats (who can be bought off easily).

Eric Holder and his allies are trying to change the rules of the game. We must not let them succeed

THE RADICAL LEFT IS SPENDING MILLIONS IN THEIR CAMPAIGN TO DESTROY FREE AND FAIR ELECTIONS IN AMERICA.

By now, I hope you realize the threat being posed to our Republic and to you.

California has had this outside committee to draw up districts for several years now. Ex- Governor Brown's idea. How has it worked? More and more

Democrats are winning these Congressional seats due to the redistricting by this outside committee. Upon further investigation, since the committee is appointed by the Legislature, and a huge majority of it are Democrats, most on this committee were liberal Democrats. Democrats change the rules often to meet their cause.

CHAPTER 44

Is Politics Becoming
Blood Sports?

I t seems like the only thing that's guaranteed in this year's election is the litany of punditry after every primary. This undiscussed industry has helped make politics more blood sport than democratic exercise.

What are we looking for?

Were we looking for a problem solver, one who is versed in the economy and the ways of business or are we looking for a charismatic speaker who will tell us anything and do just the opposite, who apparently does not love America and wants to change us into something we don't even recognize, this inexperienced captain of our Ship of State, who is working to turn us over to the UN, who has a worldview? He may be looking for more than just being president of the US. He dreams of higher aims, to control, and who has almost a dictator type of personality, who sees himself as way more than he is. Ask ourselves, could our country if this regime had been allowed to continue would we end up with no two-party elections anymore?

Media and the Alinsky Code

Millions of American felt they were living in a war zone, and a lot of nonsense being spit out from the media and the administration, so it appears they are justifying it, enabling the subversion of Am, a language most America with a secret language of the left, a language most citizens do not understand, nor even recognize. Words can make the difference. This secret language comes from the socialist transformation as exposed in the Alinsky Code. Without this secret language, WND tells us, in the matrix of deceit and delusion enveloping modern America would soon disappear. Just as in the sci-fi film blockbuster *The Matrix*, and citizens would behold Barack Obama and his administration for exactly what they really are, committed revolutionaries of the radical left.

The Planned Re-Election of Obama, Revolutionary Style

That election of 2012 promised to be the bloodiest ever, the most fraudulent, and now there is a new report out by the Canadian Free Press. They say in their internet news blog in an article by Doug Hageman, that he talked to an informant from the

Department of Homeland Security that Obama and his czars and his closest progressive supporters are planning a manufactured insurgency against America, using the media to garner both sympathy and support for his unfinished goals. Hageman first disclosed the information that he had received the previous week from his source.

"The information went viral across the internet," he said.

People are starting to catch on as word is getting out, so they are starting to wake up, which is causing a lot of pissed-off brass!

Hageman has shown his handwritten notes of two pages to support the statements made during the interview. According to Hageman's source, there is talk among the highest levels of the uppermost echelon of the Department of Homeland Security, which he describes as effectively under the control of our president. During this call, he said that the DHS is actively preparing for massive social unrest inside the US this summer. Then he corrected himself, stating that "a civil war" is more the appropriate term.

"Certain elements of the government are not only expecting and preparing for it, they are actually facilitating it. The DHS not only takes its marching orders from Obama, but mostly from his unappointed czars, and from especially, Valerie Jarrett. Don't think for a minute that the administration is doing anything to stabilize events in the US. <u>They are revolutionaries and they thrive on chaos</u>," he added.

"My informant said he has not seen things this bad since he began working within DHS. He also told me updated information about a meeting taking place on May 5 at Chantilly, Virginia, with the highest level meeting of DHS personnel, which my informant learned about from another informant who was there at this meeting," Hageman said.

CHAPTER 45

Infanticide by Any Other Name

What on earth will the Progressives/Leftists dream up next? To violate our laws our Constitution and our very well-being, what on earth are they thinking of? This latest is shocking beyond all comparison. The actual killing or causing to be killed infants, either about to be born even up to the day before birth, as was recently signed into law by the State of New York. It is up to the doctor and the mother to decide the fate of that actual child. That is infanticide. Pure and simple. There is no other name to call it. Killing actual human beings.

Give them an inch and they will take a mile.

The Progressives have spent eons of time, with protests, and spending of federal money. They fight for the lives of wee snails, species of fish, and preserving the life of the spotted owl, but don't they care about HUMAN life at all?

They declare that late-term abortion is only if the mother's life is at stake, but that has been the excuse all along and that won't always hold water, either. Will the "party of death" soon declare that all late-term abortions are fine and somewhere down the road will they decide it's okay up until two years old for children to be put to death if the parents don't want them? (Believe me, two-year-olds can be real trying.)

In ancient Rome, parents who simply did not want their young children anymore were allowed to leave them alongside a road to die from exposure to the elements. Christians came to their rescue, only to be beaten and arrested. In more modern times, the Chinese, with their rule of only one child per couple, had put to death any infants born that were subsequent to the first allotted child. In some cases, girl babies were drowned as boys were considered more important.

As Governor Cuomo of New York, celebrated the passing of this bill, there were screams of happiness from many in the audience. They cheered and cheered. This would influence the *Roe v. Wade*, in case the Supreme Court revisited that landmark law. The way the law reads now, abortion is only allowed after twenty-four weeks, if the mother's health is at stake, but than can be interpreted broadly as it does not say mental health or physical health. Well-known gynecologists and obstetricians say there is no single fetus or maternal condition that would require late-term abortion. Delivery yes, but not abortion.

What's next? To legally kill children, then kill people whom you don't agree with? Or euthanasia of all older people even if they aren't real sick? To what end will this madness stop? Are the progressives going out of their minds?

We need to stand up and speak out in our churches, in our neighborhoods, in the media and online. We can stop this madness, but we must unite and call for it to be stopped. LOUD AND CLEAR! OUR VERY LIVES MAY DEPEND ON IT!

There is an all-out actual crusade alongside LGBTQ groups and human rights organizations to decriminalize homosexuality around the world.

That's usually where the debate ends and they change the subject. Plain and simple facts should guide anyone voting, not blind hatred, fed by #FakeNewsMedia, should be one's guiding light leading into the next election.

CHAPTER 46

On Colleges Today and Religious Freedom

C olleges today are increasingly collections of hostile identity groups, each clamoring against the crime of the other. Students are not invited to step out of themselves and to look at things as they have been understood by the best over time. If they did that, they would then learn and grow, not by invention, but by discovery, according to Larry Parnum, president of Hillsdale College (a conservative think tank).

We forget the fact that Americans who founded our country were mostly Christians, and they were devoted to both civil and religious liberty with the same intensity that they held their faith.

Those founders thought that liberal education should cultivate the practice of moral alongside the intellectual virtues.

Colleges should be about thinking and the refinement of the intellectual.

Humans not only think, but they do. This forms their character. They believed in freedom for the blessing of civil and religious freedom. These two kinds of freedom were combined and wholly supported for the first time in America.

Having come from England, where, as we know religion was not free, and run by the state—the founders set out to keep our country religious free. However, this has been misconstrued to mean no public form of religion ever, like no nativity scenes in the town square, or the Ten Commandments, which all or our basic laws come from, is no longer allowed to be displayed in public buildings or property.

Then along came the famous Johnson Act that declared churches, and especially pastors, could lose their tax-free status for speaking out on issues and on backing any candidate from the pulpit.

Fortunately, President Trump outlawed the Johnson Act so that now (according to conservative radio analyst, Craig Huey), pastors and churches can speak out from the pulpit on issues and on candidates and not lose their tax-free status—much to the liberal's disdain. The thought police don't like that at all.

In days long past, churches and pastors had a lot of influence in human behavior and in what was going on, sometimes denouncing and sometimes praising anything that might challenge the virtues and values of most of the country then.

Nowadays, some businesses have been arrested and lost their businesses, such as a baker because they refused to make an inscribed wedding cake for a gay couple. It's not as if that was the only cake decorator in town. But the homosexual couple sued them and won in the lower courts. The Supreme Court has upheld their status. Fighting this case took so much money, they were forced to close their business. And this is just one case.

The same determination to wipe out religion in the town square was when they went after Chick-fil-A, who closed on Sundays so the employees who wished to could attend church and worship God. Its owner, being a religious man, declared Sundays off. All you see now every day, except Sunday of course, are long lines of cars going into Chick-fil-A. At no time past in our history has the government ever shut down businesses for being open or not open on certain days.

The liberals are messing with our very foundation of beliefs. They must be stopped. Let's vote them out and STAND OUR GROUND!

A lot changed with the socialist/Marxist training from socialist professors and teachers in the schools. Along with the Industrial Age.

Christians have been persecuted since time began, almost. But we have prevailed—because it's the truth and God is on our side! Liberals cannot stand the truth or any authority; after all, God is the ultimate authority. (They have their own gods, such as climate change, which they worship).

The Obama administration tried to curb religion and sought to redraw the map of America's religion and society. He wanted religion relegated to "private space" with an individual's self-definition. However, he would gladly allow Muslims to worship anywhere and denounce all Christians. It seems pretty apparent he was really a Muslim after all.

The Obama administration and its dramatic concentration of power wanted our constitutional republic to resemble the statist governments for most of Europe—by emphasizing areas of health care and climate change, markets, and immigration. All supplanted to control by the government.

CHAPTER 47

The Impeachment Case Against President Trump

After three years plus of trying to find something to get President Trump on so they could get rid of him, including the bogus Collusion with the Russians, supposedly spying on the Clinton campaign, when in reality, it was the Clinton campaign and the Deep State (mostly people in the Justice Department that are bureaucratic holdovers from the Obama administration who worked out a collusion to undermine Trump's campaign). The Democrats became increasingly worried after they realized that with the loser Democrats running for president that Trump more than likely would win again, so they got desperate. After the Inspector General could find nothing to hang Trump on, with no reasonable proof that he ever colluded with the Russians to have anything to do with the Clinton campaign, that charge fizzled out.

This did not satisfy the Democrats under the leadership of Speaker Nancy Pelosi in the House, so they decided to try another approach. Impeaching the president. But on what grounds? Well, they scratched their heads and came up with high crimes and misdemeanors, without any real poof of anything and indeed voted in the House to impeach him, as they have a large majority of Democrats in the house. There were some investigations done in secret in the basement of Congress and talking to witnesses. There was a supposed whistleblower, but they never produced him and it turned out it was hearsay for him what he said. Well, you can't convict on hearsay.

The Articles of Impeachment as Outlined by the House Democrats

Article 1. Abuse of Power: In supposedly arranging a quid pro quo with the president of Ukraine in asking them to investigate the Biden connection to Burisma where his son sat on the Board with no knowledge of their business. The Democrats on the committee claimed he withheld funds for Ukraine pending the investigation. Which there we never any proof of. The Dems said this was done to aid Trump in his campaign

Article 2. Obstruction of Congress for blocking testimony and refusing to provide documents in response to the subpoenas in the impeachment inquiry

After countless investigations and hearing witnesses, held in secret in the House basement, with investigations taking place without any Republican Congressmen present or allowed to be there and not even the accused, and neither the president nor his lawyers were allowed to be there (guilty until proven innocent). Head of this investigative committee was one Congressman Adam Schiff. Colluding with him was Congressman Jerry Nadler.

When this committee did present this to the House, they called witness after witness to reaffirm their beliefs of the articles. Mostly professors and one ambassador, who had no direct knowledge of any of it. There was a supposed whistleblower whom they never brought in, so one could wonder if there really ever was one. They claimed that he had heard "that Trump did a *pro quid pro* with the president of Ukraine in a phone call." All hearsay.

No one witnessing had heard the actual conversation and long before that Trump had sent to Congress an actual transcript of the conversation. The transcript bears out the president's saying he did not do a pro quid pro. The president of Ukraine verified that no pressure was put on him and that he had received the funds not too long after the call. So what was the big deal? But even with this information, the Democrats in the House, led by Speaker Nancy Pelosi, Schiff, and Nadler, went ahead with the Articles of Impeachment. A vote was called for. No Republicans in the House voted for it. It was along party lines with a vote of 230 Democrats to 197 Republicans.

On Jan 25, 2020, Much Ado about Nothing

As the time got near to deliver the articles of Impeachment to the Senate, House Speaker Nancy Pelosi delayed delivering for several days and said would not deliver the articles to the Senate unless they planned to hold a full trial and other considerations. It wasn't enough the House had held a trial, then they wanted the Senate to duplicate a lot of it there. Well, House Leader Mitch McConnell spent no time in letting Ms. Pelosi know that the Senate would do what it pleased and no thank you for any suggestions or interference from her or any other members of the House. Thanks but no thanks!

After holding up the articles for twenty-two days, with Pelosi trying to dictate to Majority Leader Mitch McConnell how they should hold a trial, the house manager and aides and Speaker Pelosi made the procession across the Capitol at 9:30 a.m. to deliver the 28,578-page record of their case to the Senate.

Just who is picking up the tab for a lot of pure foolishness and nonsense? To put these impeachment records in some perspective, let's take a peek in the documentation, all just for the House Democrats in their zealous pursuit of the Impeachment of President Trump. This was a part of a grand deception to fool an entire nation.

If the record of their total efforts is 28,578 pages in length, that means that at least 11.43 cases of paper weighting a total of 285.75 lbs. It's not including the bindings and covers were consumed to document their secret SCIF depositions and prospective witnesses in the Capitol basement, the actual impeachment inquiry hearings themselves, the various House Committees deliberations, as well as the seven case manager's arguments before the Senate over a four-day period.

All of that to document the nonexistent evidence that the president should be charged with Abuse of Power for making a telephone call to a foreign leader, requesting that his contrary conduct and investigation of possible corruption and telling some members of his staff not to appear before the impeachment inquiry hearing in the House of Representatives, which he has every right to do under Executive Privilege, which he did not formally exercise.

Please bear in mind that no enumerated Constitutional crime was charged in the articles, so in order to come up with an Abuse of Power, the house managers concocted the novel legal theory that if you do something perfectly legal like making a phone call to a foreign leader, but that you did so for a personal reason (like putting heat on a possible political competitor in an up-coming election campaign), then a "corrupt purpose" was the reason for the call, hence an abuse of power for which you must be impeached. Rep. Adam Schiff (D-CA) who has headed this entire fiasco from start to finish for Speaker Nancy Pelosi (D-CA) is the novelist of this extremely dangerous concept along with Rep. Jerald Nadler (D-NY). At its essence, this ridiculous charge speaks not to a criminal act done but to a president's assumed state of mind during a perfectly legal action. Is Adam Schiff the Gypsy Fortune Teller?

This is nothing more than conspiring up an imaginary crime because they have NO case. What a colossal waste of time, effort, and treasure merely to take political revenge on a man who was elected by the people, whom they cannot tolerate because of his style, his beliefs and achievements, which they perceive as a threat to their own well-being and success, their agenda and to push for their socialism schemes, but which they then project as a threat to the safety and security of the nation as a whole!

The Democratic Party has declared the forty-fifth president as a threat to the nation, so dangerous, that he must be immediately removed from his duly elected office involuntary, and not allowed to stand for re-election or to let the people pass judgment on his performance.

We are dealing with irrational, vicious, and evil people who will say and do whatever is necessary to accomplish their political goals.

Was William Shakespeare prescient? "Much ado about nothing" is an apt description of the evil travesty we are currently witnessing. The Democratic Party needs to be taken to the woodshed this November as a just reward for their more than 3.5 years of sedition and treachery directed at one American citizen, who is sacrificially serving our nation. He does not even draw the president's normal pay.

Republicans across the board prepared for the impeachment case transfer to the Senate. While every one of them played an essential role in prepping the Senate for a fair trial, Sen. Ran Paul (R-KY) may have gone above and beyond the call of duty. He embarked on a mission to gather at least one-third of the Senate to support the notion of dismissing impeachment charges.

Paul got 45 Republicans on board with the cause. The Senator told the *Washington Post*, "There are 45 for dismissal, with about 5 to 8 wanting to hear a little more. I still would like to dismiss it, but there aren't the votes to do it just yet."

Now no matter what it seems that Donald Trump wasn't to be removed from office in spite of what the Dems want. However, Senator Paul still wanted to garner more support before moving to outright dismiss the charges (from RightWing.Org).

The first article, abuse of power, was rejected by a vote of 48 to 52 along party lines. The second article, obstruction of Congress, was rejected by a vote of 47 to 53. Senator Mitt Romney, Republican of Utah, was the ONLY member to break with his party, voting to remove President Trump from office. In fact, he was the only Republican to ever vote against a Republican president in an impeachment trial in our history. (This was no doubt out of jealousy and to grandstand as Romney had his chance when he ran against President Obama in 2012.) What a turncoat! He made no points doing that, and in fact, I heard that many of his Republican constituents in Utah were not very happy with him, as it appeared he was trying to make a name for himself, so perhaps so he can run again for President in 2024?

CHAPTER 48

Judges or Politicians? What Changed Senator Lindsay Graham?

There's a clash in this country between those who believe in the rule of law and a limited role for courts, and those liberals for whom a judge is just an extension of politics.
—Sen. Lindsay Graham.

Expanding on his reasons for now supporting the president, Graham says a pivotal moment came during the Senate confirmation hearings that he presided over for Supreme Court Justice Brett Kavanaugh.

After Dr. Christine Blasey Ford, PhD, a high school classmate of Kavanaugh's, accused the nominee of sexually assaulting her at a party during the summer of their high school years, with no proof at all and could not even remember where or when it happened, Graham exploded in an epic moment of anger and frustration.

"What you want to do is destroy this guy's life," he said, accusing committee Democrats of doing anything for power. "I was raised better than this."

Graham says ever since the Kavanaugh hearings, he has been besieged by people who come up to him in appreciation that finally "someone said what was on their mind during the hearings."

In following speeches to conservatives, Graham frames the Kavanaugh debate as the moment when he concluded that liberals and the national media hated not only Trump, but "they hate us." He then pauses and repeats the call. "They hate us." By that, he means God-fearing, patriotic mainstream Americans.

So it's not only Trump they hate, but all of us who dared to vote for him. Looking down their snobby noses at all the smelly unwashed Wal-Mart shoppers and any Christians. They know better what is good for this country, and it is them running the helm and not us ignorant lowly citizens and voters. The craving for more and more power will never be satiated. Power and control and therefore money. It's good against evil now.

Asked earlier this year if he trusted Trump, Graham responded, "I trust the president to want to be successful…and I want him to be successful under terms that I think are good for the country. And successful he will be in spite of all the flack, as he believes in our country."

Nowadays, some businesses have been arrested and lost their businesses, such as a baker because they refused to make an inscribed wedding cake for a gay couple. It's not as if that was the only cake decorator in town. But the homosexual couple sued them and won in the lower courts. The Supreme Court has upheld their status. Fighting this case took so much money they were forced to close their business. And this is just one case.

The same determination to wipe out religion in the town square was when they went after Chick-fil-A, who closed on Sundays so the employees who wished to could attend church and worship God. Its owner being a religious man declared Sundays off. All you see now every day, except Sunday of course, are long lines of cars going into Chick-fil-A. At no time past in our history has the government ever shut down businesses for being open or not open on certain days.

The liberals are messing with our very foundation of beliefs. They must be stopped. Let's vote them out and STAND OUR GROUND!

Christians have been persecuted since time began, almost. But we have prevailed—because it's the truth and God is on our side! Liberals cannot stand the truth or any authority; after all, God is the ultimate authority. (They have their own gods, such as climate change, which they worship.)

The Obama administration tried to curb religion and sought to redraw the map of America's religion and society. He wanted religion relegated to "private space" with an individual's self-definition. However, he would gladly allow Muslims to worship anywhere and denounce all Christians. It seems pretty apparent he was really a Muslim after all.

The Obama administration and its dramatic concentration of power wanted our constitutional republic to resemble the statist governments for most of Europe—by emphasizing areas of health care and climate change, markets and immigration. All supplanted to control by the government.

The founders of Hillsdale College—175 years ago—thought liberal education was the road to good living and good citizenship. But these very tenants have been severely challenged by an ever-growing liberal mob set out to destroy America and that for which it stands. While we hope, it will not become a socialist nation, there is that likelihood down the road, and then that is when the country will spiral downward fast. Average citizens will lose all they have. It's being taken over by nonbelievers who want to destroy our very souls. Colleges like Hillsdale will be no longer be.

We conservatives and moderates, who still believe in the greatness of America have been fighting for generations now, but the young have been so brainwashed in the schools, from pre-school on, to believing in liberalism, socialism and climate change and indoctrinated into values that we know will only endanger them from being virtuous citizens, believing in our everlasting God. So Bibles are banned and no prayers in the schools, yet they are teaching the Koran in many schools now, and that Islam is a good religion, while all others are banned.

CHAPTER 49

The Plight of the Black Community

While the black community have probably had it better than ever before under President Trump, at least until the unforeseen coronavirus erupted and most of the jobs were shut down, the blacks enjoyed the lowest unemployment rate in history. The Liberal Democrats led them to believe they are still being oppressed, and if you will only vote for the Democrats, they will give you of the largest of the government. You, then, not realizing that you will be part of the people paying for all of this. There is actually far less racism probably than ever before, but you would not know it when a few isolated cases come out on the TV of a white cop shooting a black man and no scenes of what happened prior to that happening. While that is not okay, in most circumstances, there are often extenuating circumstances, so judgment should not prevail until the facts are all investigated. And these few cases do not mean that systemic racism prevails in this country.

For a long time now, the black community have seen many on welfare, and kids living in single-family homes, without a father figure to emulate, especially for the black boys. For a long-time, welfare provided more money if the mother had more kids, so that was an incentive for these single mothers already on welfare to have more kids. Then many of their kids when get into high school often skip school or don't apply themselves, drop out, and get into drugs and gangs. I have learned this from teachers from the Watts or Los Angeles areas. The kids have not learned any respect that a father can teach.

Then these young guys look for gangs to replace this loss and emulate what they learn there. It is reported by black leaders, like Larry Elder, Candace Owens, black actors and singers, and others, that the black community is getting tired of the Democrats propping them up before every election while promising them the moon, then basically ignoring them for four years until the next election. So are you any better off?

Most of the largest cities have been ruled by Democrats for at least the last forty to fifty years, this too often causes moral decay and a lack of leadership, and money wasted in supposedly "curing" the problems, with possible corruption, and they say they are trying to make it better for the black communities, but crime prevails and often a lot of homicide shooting from blacks on blacks in their own communities.

(Tell me if Black Lives Matter when these black on black murders count?)

The majority of the homeless are blacks or so they say in Los Angeles County anyway. Then often the Democrat leader's answer is to build more expensive housing for the homeless. But that takes time and a lot of money. And sure, they have a place to live, but do you have the money or the ambition or income even, to keep up your gifted houses or condos? You need a lot more than just a house. For a temporary solution during the coronavirus, they were moving the homeless into pretty much vacant hotels and colleges, where they were vacant due to the lack of travel and for schools shutting down due to the coronavirus, but what happens when the hotels fill up again with tourists and the schools reopen?

Some homeless seem to prefer living on the streets or under overpasses or bridges, as they can do what they want with no rules. Too many times, they don't want to go to a shelter or facility or rehab, provided for them, as an interim solution, as too many rules.

Contrary to the media propaganda and sometimes the Democrat Party agenda, the Republicans were NOT the slave holders in the south, NOT the racists, and the Republicans freed the blacks through the Civil War, losing 620,000 of lives in total, and 360,022 from the North. Those lives are the payback for the reparation demands now going on to give back to the blacks for the slavery they endured. Even though none now living had to endure anything like slavery or even their near ancestors had.

The Republicans got the vote for the Blacks and voted for Civil Rights against the objections of the Democrats in Congress at the time. President Johnson, while in Congress, voted against Civil Rights. But once the Democrats realized they could get the black vote, by promising them all the largesse from the government, they decided to give them the vote after all. The Democrats cannot win a presidential election without most of the black votes.

What does this all mean? Sorry, folks, but the Democrats are seeming to act like slave holders of this time. They are literally holding the blacks as slaves, to their agenda and through their free programs, such as welfare, food stamps, etc. They are holding you back. You can take care of yourselves and have done that before.

Our founders who established the Constitution wanted freedom for ALL and were against slavery. While slavery has existed since time began, often the whites were the subject of slavery in some countries, like at one time even in Africa, as well as the blacks.

Many Black Americans are Christians, and for sure, you should be voting for the more conservative side that continues to help you, encourages freedom of religion, and encourages you to help yourselves, and one that gives you more freedom, less regulations, allows you to open businesses, get better jobs, and etc.

The country is more integrated than ever before, and most are used to this. I have not witnessed any blatant racism for many years. One of the best bosses I have ever had was a black woman.

It's like chasing a rabbit down a hole to keep on voting for the Democrats. They often talk a good talk, but don't always walk a good walk. Their policies are worn out and tried over and over and simply will not work. As they move closer now to real hard socialism, and it's coming, folks, they are getting more and more like bullies and try to control your every breath. With their PC and all kinds of other rules and what they push for, none of this works. Socialism will not work for the black community nor for the white community. Ask the people in Venezuela or in China or in Russia and Cuba, how it works for them.

CHAPTER 50

Promises Kept

Finally, there's someone putting America first as our forefathers and founders envisioned. They warned about getting into wars overseas and of danger of not putting our country first.

But that not all, we finally have a president taking a stand for our faith, our freedom, and our God-given rights.

Hopefully, the Adam Schiff show is over when his heralded impeachment trial failed. But now there's a rumor Shifty Schiff is starting an investigation into the way the president handled the coronavirus pandemic. And don't be surprised if over that there is another impeachment attempt. They simply will not give up. They were caught off guard and could not believe that Trump actually won, but he must be destroyed so they can go back to their gradual trek to take over our country and remake it into a socialist/communist state. Thereby granting more power and money to those at the top—the socialistic leaders like Pelosi, AOC, Bernie, Biden, Warren, Obama, and Schiff, and many others. Of course, the liberal mainstream media has helped fuel all of this dissent. Even during the coronavirus outbreak, they do nothing but send guess the President and try to diminish him by saying he is not doing all he can do and etc.

According to the Tea Party express leader Sal Russo, this may be the most pivotal election of all time. Liberals will do anything to win. Now you can expect voter fraud up the gazoo. The liberals are masters at fraud and deception, and since now so many states have mail-in ballots or government-run vote centers, most government and state employees are liberals, so of course they are going to do everything possible to change the 2020 election.

The left has proven that they will cheat and steal from their own liberal candidates, even. Just look at the mess they created in the Iowa Democrat caucus only a few weeks ago. Don't think for a moment that they won't do the same again and worse to Donald Trump and voters like you and me this November. It will undoubtedly be the most dishonest election ever. They are determined to win at all costs and get that monster Trump out of there.

That's the sort of nightmare that could put a Bernie Sanders, Socialist, or an Elizabeth Warren, Radical, in the Oval Office.

CHAPTER 51

America Has Undergone Enormous Change

This enormous change has occurred during the last eight decades of my life. Today America is a bitterly divided, poorly educated, and morally fragile society with so-called mainstream politicians pushing cynical identity politics, socialism (or downright communism), and open borders.

The president of the United States is impeached in a mock trial, with liberal Democrats in the House secretly holding hearings from witnesses and not even letting the Republican in Congress or the president or his attorneys know. But the Republican majority Senate acquitted him. All because the other side is afraid he will remove all the changes they have been able to instill, and besides, they really don't like him. He's not an insider or an ultra-liberal. He's more like Teddy Roosevelt, old Rough and Ready. Although the Democrats were more than willing to hold their hand out to him prior to his running to give them large donations for their races.

The once reasonably unbiased American media with such as Walter Cronkite has evolved into a hysterical left-wing mob not capable or desirous of presenting unbiased and truthful news information to the American citizenry.

How could the stable and reasonable cohesive America of the 1950s have reached this point in just one lifetime? Who are the main culprits?

Here's a list of the ten most destructive Americans of the last eighty years. There may be others just as deserving but these are the most prominent:

10). Mark Felt—Deputy Director of the FBI aka Deep Throat during the Watergate scandal. This was the first public instance of a senior FBI official directly interfering in America's political affairs. Forerunner of James Comey, Peter Strzok, Lisa Page, and Andrew McCabe.

9) Bill Ayers—Represents the deep and ongoing leftists ideological damage to our education system. An unrepentant American-born terrorist who evaded punishment, he devoted his career to radicalizing American education toward communism and pushing leftist causes. He ghost-wrote Obama's book, *Dreams of My Father*.

8) Teddy Kennedy—Most folks remember Teddy as the guy who left Mary Joe Kopechne to die in his car at Chappaquiddick. In reality, it is thought he really did the act of drowning while they strolled on the beach when he found out she was pregnant,

then moved her to the car and the story after that is a cover-up. He did not notify the police for several hours later on the next day, and he made several calls during the night. The real damage came after he avoided punishment for her death and became a major Democrat force in the US Senate, pushing through transformative liberal policies in health care and education. The real damage was the 1965 Hart-Cellar immigration bill he pushed hard for that changed the quota system to increase the flow of third world people without skills into the US. This essentially ended large-scale immigration of years past from Europe. Like Kerry, he sought Russia's aid in running against Ronald Reagan.

7) Walter Cronkite—Cronkite was a much beloved network anchor to some, who began the politicization and tainting of America's news media with his infamous broadcast from Vietnam that described the Tet Offensive as a major victory of the communists and significantly turned the gullible American public against the Vietnam War. In fact, the Tet Offensive was a military disaster for the NVA and Viet Cong, later admitted by North Vietnamese military leaders. Decades later, Cronkite admitted he got the story wrong, but he was too busy sailing and hanging out with the Kennedys and it was too late. The damage was done.

6). Bill and Hillary Clinton—It's difficult to separate Team Clinton. Bill's presidency was largely benign as he was a relative playboy and fiscal conservative who rode the remaining benefits of the Reagan era. But his sexual exploits badly stained the Oval Office and negatively affected America's perception of his presidency. In exchange for financial support, he facilitated the transfer of sensitive military technology to the Chinese, gave Korea nuclear capability. Hillary, a Saul Alinsky acolyte, is one of the most vicious politicians of my lifetime, a real "godmother," covering up Bill's sexual assaults by harassing and insulting the exploited women and peddling their influence around the globe in exchange for funds for the corrupt Clinton Foundation. She signed off on the secret sale of 20 percent of the US uranium reserve to the Russians after Bill received a $500,000 speaking fee in Moscow and the foundation (which supported the Clinton's regal lifestyle) received hundreds of millions of dollars from those who benefitted from the deal. Between them, they killed any honor that might have existed in the dark halls of DC, and it aided the rise of political corruption of presidential degree.

5) Valerie Jarrett—The Rasputin of the Obama administration and devout terrorist. A Red Diaper baby, her father, maternal grandfather, and father-in-law (Vernon Jarret who was a close friend and ally of Obama's mentor, Frank Marshall Davis) were hardcore Communists under investigation by the US government. She was in in Obama's ear for his entire political career, even living in the White House with them and pushing a strong anti-American, Islamist, anti-Israel, socialist/communist, cling-to-power agenda.

4) Jimmy Carter—Carter ignited modern-day radical Islam by abandoning the Shah and paving the way for Ayatollah Khomeini to take power in Tehran. Iran subsequently became the main state sponsor and promoter of international Islamic terrorism. When Islamists took over our embassy in Tehran, holding hostages, Carter was too weak and unknowing hot to effectively respond, thus strengthening the rule of the radical Islamic mullahs for many years to come. Ronald Reagan got the hostages released from Iran immediately after he took office.

3) Lyndon Johnson—Johnson turned the Vietnam conflict into a major war for America. It could have ended early if he had listened to his generals instead of to automaker Robert McNamara. The ultimate result was

a) 58,000 American military deaths and collaterally tens of thousands of American lives damaged; and

b) A war that badly divided America and created left-wing groups that evaded the draft and eventually gained control of our education system. These young groups hated authority, the police, and religion.

Even worse, his so-called War on Poverty led to the destruction of American black families with a significant escalation of their welfare use and policies designed to keep poor families dependent upon the government (and voting Democrat) for their well-being and rest of their lives. He deliberately created a racial holocaust that is still burning today. A strong case could be made of putting him at the top of this list.

2) Barack Hussein Obama—Obama set up America for a final defeat and stealth conversion from a free market society to socialism/communism. He has never been able to prove he was born in America while we get deeper into the Trump presidency, we learn more each day about how Obama politicized and compromised key government agencies, most prominently the FBI, the CIA, and the IRS, thus thoroughly shaking the public's confidence in the federal government to be fair and unbiased in its activities. He significantly set back race and other relations between Americans by stoking black grievances and pushing radical identity politics and racism. He instilled Obama supporters in all levels of federal government that are still there today presenting problems for the Trump administration. Obama's open support for the Iranian mullahs and his apologetic "lead from behind" foreign policy seriously weakened America abroad. His blatant attempt to interfere in Israel's election trying to unseat Netanyahu is one of the most shameful things ever done by an American president.

1). John Kerry—Some readers will likely say Kerry does not deserve to be number one on this list. He is here because he is regarded as the most despicable American who ever lived. After his three faked Purple Hearts during his cowardly service in Vietnam, he was able to leave the US Navy early. As a reserve naval officer and in clear violation of the Uniform Code of Military Justice, he traveled to Paris and met privately with the NVA and the Viet Cong. He returned to the United States parroting the Soviet Party line about the war and testified before Congress, comparing American soldiers to the hordes of Genghis Khan and atrocities. It was a clear case of treason, giving aid and comfort to the enemy in a time of war. We got a second bite of the bitter Kerry apple, when as Obama's Secretary of State, he fell into bed with the Iranian (Death to America) mullahs giving them the ultimate green light to develop nuclear weapons along with billions of dollars that further supported their terrorist activities. He along with Obama, secretly in the dead of night, delivered billions in cash to the Islamic Regime. Only the heroic Swift Vets saved us from a Manchurian Candidate Kerry presidency. Ultimately, we got Obama.

(Excerpted from Frank Hawkins, who is a former army intelligence officer, Associate Press foreign correspondent, international businessman, senior newspaper company executive, founder and owner of several marketing companies, and published novelist. He's currently retired in North Carolina.)

CHAPTER 52

Solutions to Save America

Thomas Jefferson in 1870, after the creation of the federal government after the US Constitution was written, remarked that a revolution may be necessary every twenty years. In fact, he so distrusted the formation of a central government that he stated, "God forbid we should ever be twenty years without such a rebellion. The people cannot be all and always well-informed. The path which is wrong will be discontented in proportion to the importance and the facts they misconceive. If they remain quiet under such misconception. It is lethargy, the forerunner of death to the public liberty.

"And what country can preserve its liberties, if its rulers are not warned from time to time that this people reserve the spirit of resistance. Let them take arms. The remedy is to set them right as to the facts, pardon and pacify them. What signify a few lives lost in a century or two.

"The tree of liberty must be refreshed from time to time with the blood of patriots and tyrants. It is its natural manure."

—Thomas Jefferson
November 13, 1787 letter to Wm S. Smith

Jefferson was not encouraging bloody revolution, but he was recognizing the potential tranny of government and the possible need for bloody revolution in order to neutralize the rise of tyranny.

Hence the reasoning behind the insertion of the Second Amendment into the US Constitution via the Bill of Rights.

Undoubtedly, the primary reason for the existence of the 2nd Amendment is to enable the populace to take up arms against the government if necessary.

Imagine how different history would be if the Germans had taken up arms against Hitler before he confiscated their arms.

So we may be into one of Jefferson's perceived revolutions so get ready to take up arms to save our great country and therefore the world (girded by the armor of God).

How many times was there war in the Bible?

It seems it is the same fight taking place in most of the Western world now. The leftists against the more conservatives (the Right).

The elitist powers that be are determined to control he country and thus the world. Brexit is an example. Aided and abetted by the liberal media—an arm of the Democratic Party. (They carry the water for Democrats.)

It is not news at all but a constant barrage of how bad Trump is—get Trump—we loathe him. So let's say the same things about him every day. Now every day, it's use the word "impeach" over and over. The word *d'jour*. He's guilty of collusion! Collusion! Collusion!" until the Mueller's report came out saying no collusion with the Russian interference with the election in 2016. (Something we knew all along.)

Actually, it's a ton of projection. Projection is more of the Marxist socialist agenda. Put onto others what you do yourself. The leftists constantly use projection to deflect the blame from themselves. The Russian collusion was a projection to deflect from Hillary and Obama collusion to spy on the Trump campaign.

CHAPTER 53

Canadian Health Care: It's Not What's So Good

Often, you hear Democrats say we should have socialism as Canada has and they have universal government-funded health care. And socialism works good there. But it is far different. Canada is not a socialist country—say as China, Russia, or Venezuela. They would be called a semi-socialist country.

Private health expenditure accounts for 30 percent of health care financing. The Canada Health Act does not cover prescription drugs, home care, or long-term care or dental.

My friends in British Canada told me this recently if you need surgery, one usually has to wait for a very long time, thus many go into the States for surgery or needed care. And if they went into the States as snow birds, as that was where we met them in BC and they traveled for several winters to Arizona and Southern California, then they said, that they used to spend three or four months in warmer Arizona and Southern California, but their government started limiting how long they could be gone and have any health coverage—so they've had to give up leaving for the winter, as they face the cold Canadian winters at home.

Most plans here cover prescription drugs (some with a co-pay) at a lower price, but no long-term care or dental unless you buy special coverage for this or only if you qualify for Medicaid, then you get prescriptions paid for.

Some of Canadian health care is free, but if you want better quality, there's a two-tier system for those who can pay for better care or faster treatment. Most countries, like in Europe, have public or privately funded health care—depends on how it's managed.

In Canada, about 70 percent is the public system and the rest is from private funding.

Hospitals there can charge patients for additional room charges not covered by public health insurance.

CHAPTER 54

What the Brexit Vote Means to England and to Us

The Brexit vote in England to exit the European Union was significant to the whole world. It came as a surprise. They are now working on the process of completely divesting from the European Union, which takes time. It no doubt will set the example for other countries to exit. Most of the liberals here thought we should be in the European Union or have one like it. They thought it was ideal. But as we see when Greece fell, all of the European Union countries were mandated to bail them out. So being in the union makes countries responsible for those who may not take care of their economy. And each county in it loses their autonomy and becomes a parasite of the whole order of the European Union. They lose their sovereignty. It is the same reason people went for Trump in the primaries and for Bernie. People are plain tired of the elite running everything, tired of Washington, tired of rich bankers running it all, tired of Brussels running the whole European Union. Are you tired of the establishment and status quo and the rich and elite? The people are rising up all over the world and saying, "Stop!"

President Obama hired forty or more czars that only answered to him. Most recent presidents had only one or two czars. These czars are not approved or vetted by Congress. They are to carry out his mandates. They had additional offices and staff, thus costing the taxpayers much more. President Obama had about seventy persons under his management control who answered directly to the president. His wife had many aides working for her. Far more than any other first lady ever had. In the business world, the unwritten rule is that "managers usually only have twelve persons directly responsible to him/her to manage," according to McGary in his book. Even Jesus, the greatest CEO of all time, only had twelve apostles. Could that tell us something?

There has never been so much executive power taken by any president than Obama did. Rather than working with Congress as most presidents have done and as successful presidents like Reagan did, our past president bypassed them and made his own mandates. He did not even talk to most of them. Our past President Obama traveled more than any other president, taking lavish family vacations paid for by our tax dollars and taking far more than any other president ever has. He stopped our drilling on public lands and offshore, so the only oil drilling is done on private land now. Gas is $5 per gallon in some areas of the country, and yet we have plenty of oil and natural gas to last for a long time now. He had rather we buy it at huge costs from Saudi Arabia and Iran. He purposefully brought the price of gas down just before the election so he would have something more to crow about. He is all for manipulation politically, with little actual concern for the people evidently.

A recent report is that our last president had given away islands off Alaska to the Russians, so that they can then drill in the oil rich waters off their shores. If we need oil, then we would have to lease back that area we want to drill in. If true, and we believe it could be, then how can he do this without Congress or a vote of the people?

The plans for solar and wind will not put gas in our cars. Alternative energy has its place, but it will be a long time before it will fuel our transportation without oil, natural gas, or other fuel means. Besides, it takes fuel to run an electric power plant that these impractical climate "oil free" characters forget about.

His Obamacare, the federal control of health care, which was estimated to cut over 474 billion cuts to senior and Medicare, according to the *Examiner*. *The Wall Street Journal* reports that Obamacare will gut Medicare. We have states rebelling against Obamacare, according to *Forbes* magazine. And *Bloomberg News* says that Obamacare only looks worse upon further review, which was developed in secret in the dark of the night, <u>with no Republican votes</u>.

Our captain of our ship then seemed oblivious to the effects on our economy, or did he want it to fail? He said the economy was recovering, but it did not, as unemployment was still high with reported by the administration to be 8.2 percent. The real rate of unemployment is closer to 12 percent as this administration did not count the ones who have quit looking for jobs or have had to go to part-time employment. He seemed determined to steer us into that iceberg. Our GDP was still way down to 2 percent.

It is not just that president, but the secretive strong forces behind, which were pulling his strings. As we have examined, since the early 1900s, these forces have worked to take over our country, with the League of Nations supplanted then with the United Nations as a world government force to swallow up all the major countries in the world, working through liberal governments, courts, and presidents.

Our President Trump won in 2016, a new captain of our ship. He is steering it in a far better course. And he has been able to appoint two justices to the Supreme Court. Due to advanced age, one or two more may resign before long. Now Trump, when he wins in 2020, and the chances are excellent that he will, he may have a chance to appoint one or two more to the Supreme Court. This could determine the balance of the Supreme Court for many years to come and drastically change the course of this country.

While Judges and Justices are not supposed to vote their political persuasions, many of them usually do, especially the liberal leaning ones. He has also appointed constitutionalist judges to the circuit courts. That is what our votes can do. We vote for a more conservative president, then we get more conservative-type constitutionalist judges.

Should the liberal/socialists get the vote their way with a Democrat president, House, and Senate in 2020 or beyond, they plan to pack the court and advance term limits for it, as they say "way too long we have had too many conservative judges?"

Well, folks, the liberals have actually ruled the courts for most of the twentieth and twenty-first centuries. Franklin Roosevelt tried to get thirteen judges appointed to pack the court and he almost got his way. The Congress at the time would not approve of it to start the process. It was only in Reagan's time, and with one each for the Bush's, and in now Trump's time that a little more conservative constitutionalist judges have been appointed. It would take a Constitutional Amendment approved first by 2/3 of Congress, then a constitutional convention held and then ratified by legislatures of ¾ of the states. A long drawn-out process. Our founders did not want to make it easy for the Constitution to be amended.

CHAPTER 55

There's a War Going On: On Faith, the Family, and Your Freedom of the First Amendment to the Constitution That Guarantees Freedom of Worship

They're trying to frighten you, they're trying to scare you, and if we don't stand up, then that's exactly what they're going to do. If we don't start standing up for our Constitution and for our rights, our beliefs, there's going to be nothing to stand up for.

—Barronelle Stutzman

[P]ortions of this are excerpted from the book *You Will Be Made to Care, The War on Faith, Family, and Your Freedom to Believe* by Erick Erickson and Bill Blankschaen].

Freedoms of speech, religion, and even thought has never been more threatened in our country than they are today, which should make you realize we have to resist. How can we resist? Do you believe in the First Amendment? The downright guarantee of freedom of conscience and freedom of religion, and if we don't resist, those freedoms will be gone.

The Leftists that seek to take away our freedom of conscience and religion think they are compassionate, but they are really "compassionate" bullies.

Under the guise of compassion and caring, the Left attacks a helpless grandmother, trying to force her to approve of that which she cannot in good conscience endorse. All the while it claims it is acting in the best interest of society, for not bowing at the altar of the sexual sin by refusing to bake and decorate a wedding cake for a homosexual couple. The couple had other alternatives with several bakeries around, but they sued her for her refusal, thus losing her business. She said she would still bake any other kind of cake for her friend. She was told she had to act against all of her beliefs in order to comply with the Left's PC rules.

These radicals want to look like they care as they force their views on others. It's what bullies do. That way, others will think better of them and they sleep better at night, assuaging any guilt they may feel for giving nightmares to normally law-abiding people. Their motto is "We scare because we care." Shades of the coronavirus. Sow seeds of scare. They will try to force you to care about their beliefs.

They believe they can become as their own gods redefining good and evil, for themselves and for the rest of us who lacked their alleged enlightenment and education.

The Progressives will not burn your home, but they will take the homes, businesses, and life savings of any who defy them. They will use the tools of the state and mob action, as we've seen recently seen in the protests and rioting going on in large cities and the destroying of private property—or sow fear and intimidation—to make it happen.

Apart from a vigorous defense of our first freedom, our freedom to believe—all other freedoms will not live long. That's why the Left, a relatively small but very vocal group wishes to shift culture outside of millennia of accepted norms, which shift really bloomed during the '60s, and they will silence those who disagree, but at the same time compel them to approve. It's amazing how many are accepted norms now even among a lot of Christians. We go to gender-neutral bathrooms now and accept their rules for quarantines for the pandemic.

The Left can be compared to the jihadist: they will not cut your head off, but they will destroy your reputation so that you will not show your face in public.

Like so many tyrants in history, first they will come for your faith. It not like they do not desire a society that has no faith. The Progressives just want you to embrace THEIR beliefs instead and to worship at the altar of a different higher power, one more compatible with their own religion, their secular beliefs, and the Kingdom of Man, not the Kingdom of God.

The Leftist Progressives will viciously attack those who disagree with them because they are tired of the debate, which they never really wanted. They do not wish to defend their beliefs. They only know victory, and to get it is to silence, isolate, and destroy anyone that gets in their way.

Take college campuses. Many drive Christian or Republican groups off campus, yet the Muslims can have their group activities and that's okay. Many campuses will try to destroy any conservative or Republican speaker that tries to speak on campus. Yet any Democrat or liberal speaker is welcome. Freedom of speech? Not at all.

Pastors and preachers used to be able to talk about morals and political happenings and beliefs and endorse certain candidates from the pulpit. The churches had a lot of influence in those days for centuries, but not anymore, as they are threatened that their tax-free nonprofit status will go away, if they speak out at all. Or they might be sued. Trump is trying to get this changed.

In many countries, just as the early Christians were forced to do, they have to meet underground in people's homes in order to worship.

Even during the recent coronavirus outbreak, then most Democrat governors declared churches as non-essential businesses and shut them down for months. While liquor stores, home depots, office depots, and grocery stores, Wal-Mart, and others were still open. Even one church in Mississippi had a drive-in service in their cars, but many drivers in cars were written up and cited for even being there, as supposedly the mayor in that town in Mississippi had a curfew. Parishioners were fined 500 dollars each for attending in their car the drive-in service. Now that was social distancing for sure, so what harm was that? In fact, the police barricaded the parking lot after that. That would appear to have been an anti-Christian mayor.

Churches are probably about the most essential business there is. They provide spiritual closeness and needs that nothing else can. Sure, we could watch a service and even join in with communion on YouTube, but it is not the same.

In most places, even pastors and priests were banned from death beds if anyone had the virus, especially in nursing homes. Therefore, many were dying alone as friends and family were not allowed in, and their priest or pastor could not be there to comfort them as they passed. They could dress as the nurses and caregivers dress in gear that would protect them and still be able to minister to the sick and dying.

At a time when all should be more compassionate and caring, there are these made-up rules by Progressives to thwart exercise of our first amendment rights.

CHAPTER 56

Why Trump Is Pleasing America Even with the Coronavirus Pandemic Going On

Plagues in the Bible lasted about four to five months and then played out. So if left alone, this one might only have lasted that long. That's called herd immunity. That's about how long now since we first knew about the coronavirus since January and what it was doing in China. And the first people brought it here. Maybe if no one stayed home and a few got the virus but the jobs went on and the economy went on, we might not be any worse off than we are today. In fact, maybe a lot better.

With a little research first, and not just a knee-jerk reaction, which the left is famous for, we could have quarantined the elderly, as that is where most cases came from, and left the rest of the country alone, not closed the schools, or closed down the businesses and restaurants, etc., so by June, the seniors could have had a graduation and senior proms, and people would not have had to stay home from work, so their pockets would be fuller and the economy going on the same. People quarantined in hospitals and nursing homes were dying alone as no one was allowed to be at their bedside. In fact, all residents of nursing homes or assisted care were locked down and could have no visitors or leave their rooms.

But there were a lot of left-wing political influences at work here, as they seem to actually want the economy to sink, some on media have even admitted they want the economy to tank, as well as the liberal Democrats deal in fear and the sky is falling in all the time. Look at the prediction the earth will end in 2012, and the fear that the oceans will rise very soon. One of the tenets of Liberalism, which is Marxism in wolf's clothing, is that to stir up chaos and fear is the way to control the people. Hitler was an expert on this. And so was Marx. Look how quickly we obeyed the lockdown, at first without even questioning, but as time went on, there were protests to unlock our state and counties. Indeed, Europe is reporting after lockdown unlocked, there is not a real problem of the pandemic returning. Sweden did not even lock down.

Excerpts from *The Post Editorial Board* March 26, 2020

As the coronavirus crisis unfolds, Scott Jennings notes at CNN.com, "President Trump's numbers are going up." Gallup, this week, recorded all time high approval for the president: 49 percent against 45 percent disapproval. Why? For one thing, centrists think the press, along with Democratic politicians have gone overboard "criticizing him" during the national emergency. Plus, "The Democratic rush to call the president racist over his terming the Chinese virus backfired"; to most Americans, he's just describing reality.

So with a little research, finding out the virus hits mainly older people, then quarantine the older people and let the younger ones go to work and schools remain open. But no, it was a knee-jerk reaction which the Left is famous for. Close everything down, scare the people to death, and hurt the economy.

Then there was the nonsense Dems (Pelosi) tried to stuff into the rescue bill, and the fact that people give wide latitude to the commander-in-chief during crisis. Still, it's up to Trump to "get this right" and it seems "an increasing share of the American people may believe he is on his way to doing just that. This came out of nowhere and blindsided everyone. Possibly no president could have done any better given the circumstances and the first time anything ever happened like this before. Of course, there's a lot of second-guessers out there, saying, if them, it would have been different. Like even coming from Joe Biden and the news media. But would it really?

CHAPTER 57

The Worldwide Lockdown May Be the Greatest Mistake in History

According to Dennis Praeger, radio host and political consultant, on May 5, 2020, "The idea that the worldwide lockdown of virtually every country other than Sweden may have been an enormous mistake strikes many—including world leaders; most scientists, especially health officials, doctors and epidemiologists, those who work in major news media, opinion writers in those media, and the hundreds of millions, if not billions of people who put their faith in these people—as so preposterous, as to be immoral." Timothy Egan of the *New York Times* described Republicans who wish to enable their states to open up as "the party of death."

As the elites are practically running the whole world now, they have become deceitful, cowardly, and immature and dominate most all supposedly free societies.

Here is why the lockdown may not only be a mistake but also possibly the worst mistake the world has ever made. The lockdown is a mistake. The holocaust, slavery, communism, fascism were evil. Massive mistakes are made by fools whose arrogance has no bounds, massive evils are committed by evil people.

What has led to our worst economy since the Great Depression has led people into believing they must do what politicians deem essential. It is sheer panic and hysteria, not the virus, that created this possible catastrophe. What is worse, the consequences may be even worse in much of the world than in America. We went into this with a very strong economy so it might be easier to bring it back. This also may lead to famine in quite a few countries. Most of the world will suffer from this.

And more people could potentially die from the economic impact of COVID-19 than from the virus itself.

That would be enough to classify this worldwide lockdown as a huge error. If global GDP declines even by 5 percent another 14 million people could be plunged into extreme poverty. It is already predicted that in 2020 it could decrease by 3 percent, making the biggest downturn since the Great Depression.

The collapse of the global food supply systems and widespread human starvation would be the outcome of the lockdown. But do the global elites and the far leftists care? Or do they care about the citizens of Oregon, whose governor had just announced the state will remain locked down until July 6. Or

California governor announcing it will open up in small phases, lasting for a while longer. And schools won't start until August. With a total of 109 deaths of the coronavirus in Oregon. Now let's see that's a total population of about 4.25 million. Do your math. That's about .00025 deaths. That the biggest problem. None of those so-called experts are doing the math. They throw out the deaths so everyone gets scared but not the percentage. And what about other causes of death of natural causes for example? The regular flu and pneumonia cause far more deaths, especially in the elderly.

Instead of a "knee jerk reaction," which the Liberals are so good at, a little study of who is more likely to contract the virus and to just lock down or rather quarantine those, and stop proclaiming as some doctors even reported they were told to state on death certificates that deaths were caused by the virus whether they were or not. That made the so-called count of coronavirus deaths a lot higher.

Second-Guessing the President on Dealing with the Coronavirus

David Limbaugh, a converted liberal to conservative commentator, tells us on May 8, 2020, that Trump's critics can't have it both ways. The left's position, or at least today's position, as it changes almost daily, on the nation's proper response to the pandemic, though shrouded in the language of their usual compassion, is completely not understandable and morally repugnant virtue signaling. Many of our national leaders, and of course, the left-wing media and the many never-Trumpers have been much more interested in making a case against President Donald Trump than in trying to help the problems caused by the virus.

As usual, they want it both ways so they can gleefully second-guess. Democratic Presidential candidate Joe Biden has been second-guessing Trump all the way, with his basement prologues that one can barely understand. It is so apparent that Sleepy Joe is suffering from memory loss and confusion, which could well be from the onslaught of dementia. Since my mother had dementia, then it led to full-blown Alzheimer's, I know the progression of the disease and how the person with it acts and how they talk.

How can the Democrats put up as their candidate, one that is too old and obviously confused, if not a lot more. Would it be because they can manipulate him, so he would just be a figurehead? Maybe that's why they are so concerned who he gets for his vice president nominee. Whomever that person is, they will probably be functioning as much more than a typical vice president, on the slight chance that he would win. And who knows, the Congress could use the 35th Amendment to declare the president is unfit to continue in his office due to his mental instability, so that therefore they would need to remove him and his vice president would automatically become the president? The polls, after the main part of the virus had slowed down, are reported that Biden is ahead in the polls. Well, as we know from Hillary's run and Trump's win, the polls are hardly ever right.

Before the outbreak, numerous Democrats were downplaying the virus and getting after Trump for being a racist for his China and Europe travel bans. Speaker Pelosi, indeed, was walking through Chinatown and hugging people there as if to say see nothing to it. She later ate ice cream out of her $24,000 freezer to show the old adage, let them eat bread.

But later, they blamed Trump for not taking the virus more seriously, when in fact, they were taking it less seriously than he was. But as Limbaugh learned, having been a progressive, that they never have to say they are sorry—and that yesterday's inconsistent positions are deemed wiped from our collective memory.

While from the beginning, Trump and Vice President Pence, along with medical teams, were conducting daily briefings to inform an anxious nation about the virus and the efforts to slow it down, organizing and distributing medical equipment to hot spots and pushing legislation to provide relief for individuals and businesses devastated by the outbreak. Trump brought in hospital ships from the Navy to LA Harbor and to New York Harbor, which were hardly even needed. He helped New York rebuild the Javitt's Center outfitting it to assist in the care of coronavirus patients. It was hardly used, making it all look overstated, the huge outbreak of the virus was going to overflow all hospitals. Trump distributed masks and respirators to hospitals, like in New York, where it seemed the outbreak was worse, but not near all were even used.

But instead the typical media used those briefings to try to humiliate Trump rather than try to inform viewers. That was more fun. Editorial after editorial crucified Trump for every sin imaginable and of course tried to hold him accountable for every death. Unfortunately, the media views everything through a partisan-looking glass, and no crisis is too severe to be exploited for their political gain.

And wrongfully, they said Trump was only interested in manipulating the crisis to enhance his re-election efforts. And had it not been an election year they would have used it in some other way to demean any efforts he may have made to help with the crisis. He's damned if he does and damned if he doesn't with the liberal media. The media and elite liberals claimed he was not listening to the medical experts when he jumped the gun wishing the country could open by Easter or that he was practicing medicine without a license. Well, as facts unfold, he may have been listening to the wrong medical experts as it's been reported by a fellow scientist, who used to work for Dr. Fauci, that he has personal invested interests in certain vaccines he's promoting and certain drugs that may or may not cure. Therefore, listening to the "experts" may have taken Trump down the primrose path as more and more of Fauci's model and other statements were possibly self-serving instead of being the real facts. Besides later on, Dr. Fauci changed his model and response several times.

Limbaugh goes on to say that "Considering themselves the sole exemplars of compassion, progressives insist that their views are the only morally acceptable ones, that all who oppose them are immoral and that so long as they have good intentions, neither their motives nor their policies can be questioned—even if they are inconsistent to cause major harm."

In Congress, Democratic leaders get away with anything and say stupid statements, often childishly shallow, and no one challenges them, as they are free from scrutiny from the liberal press.

Democratic Presidential nominee Joe Biden tweeted, "I've said it before and I'll say it again. No one is expandable. No life is worth losing to add one more point to the Dow." This may sound compassionate, but it was a cheap shot at Trump. Biden is expressing his party's position. You must choose between those at risk from the virus and reopening the economy. There are no competing interests to balance. There is no concern for those unemployed, devastated, isolated, depressed, and with other medical problems that are ignored because of the virus, which they deem legitimate.

To say nothing of the outright corruption Biden and his son and family were involved in with China and Ukraine, when he was vice president, leaving them all multi-millionaires to this day. The media does not even care to investigate any of this. Bidens, right after a trip to Ukraine by Biden and Ukraine was promised billions of dollars from our taxpayers money, his son, Hunter, was given a seat on the Board of Burisma an energy company, which he had no experience in at all, and he has made millions with this job. Where is the media on this? Why is this not well known?

To add one more point to the Dow, while he is personally raking it in from Ukraine, etc., that made him right. Biden is reducing the concern for those financially devastated to a class warfare soundbite. As if having a heart for the unemployed is promoting the rich. It does not have to make sense as long as it serves the narrative that Republicans are heartless. That is what the liberals say over and over about Republicans. That Republicans and Christians are mean-spirited and heartless. Matter of fact, Republicans give far more to charity, help the needy far more, and are the ones who freed the slaves, and voted for the civil rights, against the Democrats' wishes and women's rights, so who is heartless here? The Democrats fought all of that. And capitalism, which the Republicans embrace, has helped the whole world's economy. Those countries who practice capitalism are far richer and better off than those who promote socialism instead.

My opinion, having lived a long time and followed politics most of my life, is that no president or any country leader could have done any better than Trump has done with this completely unexpected pandemic. Sure, he may have made some mistakes, but anyone would as he does not have all the information available to deal with this out of the blue pandemic. And he's been told over and over to listen to the experts. But it now seems like it may have been a mistake to listen to Dr. Fauci as he appears to have a vested interest in the meds he recommends and in the potential vaccination. And he, as head of the infectious disease and NIAID (National Institute of Allergy and Infectious Diseases), along with Bill Gates gave 7.3 million to that virus lab in Wuhan, China. Connect the dots, folks!

Trump haters from both sides of the aisle have lost any semblance of fairness when their biases compel them to direct their energies toward destroying Donald Trump, rather than seeking solutions for our common problems. In this dire time we should all be working together, to reopen the economy while trying to prevent new flare-ups, which happens to be precisely what President Trump and his task force are doing. Talk is cheap and finger pointing is easy, but real world problems don't lend themselves to easy fixes. There are no perfect solutions here. We can only mitigate the death and financial destruction. And we can't avoid either.

It's apparently been in the interest of certain governors and law makers and certain Democrats to keep this thing going and keep people in fear and quarantined until after the election to try to prevent, in this way, Donald Trump from being re-elected. Just what do you think this whole thing was about anyway? Personally, I still believe it was intentional;

the manufacture of that virus in that lab in Wuhan, which incidentally was partly owned and funded by Bill Gates of Microsoft fame, the Democrat's best friend, and one of the richest guys in the world now and Dr. Fauci, Trump's so-called expert scientist, being a friend of Gates? Something's rotten in Denmark, as they used to say. And the model done by one of the Virginia University for Dr. Fauci to quote is one that is funded by the Bill and Melinda Gates Foundation? What a coincidence. Imagine that? Or if the virus was released accidentally, it was really taken advantage of to push socialism on us and to get a taste of the control that socialism could have on the scared public. And the timing? Well, what better timing than in the spring before the next election? Now that was NO coincidence.

And this is not only the problem in America, but in most of the western world now. The socialist/leftists versus the more conservatives in each country. The push is for one-world dominance, the statists or the elites have done, the one world order elites. Some of the richest in the world belong. They tried it with the League of Nations after WWI and that did not work, then after WWII the United Nations, which takes billions from our country and does nothing but thumb their nose at us.

I hate to say this, but people like the Bushes and Obamas belong to this order. That's why they were so against Trump. David Rockefeller used to dominate the cause, but then the elder Rockefeller finally died in 2017, and the Rothschilds, richest in Europe, are big in the New World Order. Now Bill Gates and George Soros are taking over from Rockefeller. Two of the richest men in America. We, our tax money, funds some of George Soros Foundation help around the world. While he contributes too many prominent Democrat's campaigns.

What's needed is accountability—reasonable people who will hold their leaders to some standards. While people often look to government during times of crisis, we must understand that there's only so much that government can do and sometimes it can also get in the way. Like we've seen with some liberal governors exercising their tyrannical ways and becoming overlords. It's time that state governments show a little faith in the American people and respect their prerogative to return to their lives while still exercising responsible behavior to protect themselves and their neighbors.

This was socialism at work, folks. How do you like the government mandating your every move? You can't work, you have to stay home, you have to hibernate? Schools closed and most offices and stores. That's only the beginning. Next time, it will be worse and even more control.

You've just experienced the appetizer. The main course is yet to come with the next crisis.

The leftist liberals have had a taste of blood, to see if they could control the people and it worked like magic. It was not so much the COVID, but the fear that was fostered greatly by the liberal media, Democratic leaders, and social media. And so we just followed like sheep. Eventually, a few of the people protested to the governors in areas where there were beaches, and open-air activities, like hiking, golf, and biking. And churches were ready to open and going to open anyway by May 31.

Now it is rumored that they are planning a tattoo chip to put in one's arm or hand, on the pretext to show you've been vaccinated

But the real reason is so that we can be tracked or traced is the word they use. In fact, HB 666 bill introduced in early May was designed to test everyone, and if anyone was tested positive, they could be traced with whomever they had been in contact with by their phone. Then if anyone in their family had the virus or tested positive for, it they could be removed and quarantined. This sounds like children could even be removed from their families.

This has been planned for decades, folks, some kind of a chip to identify. The idea is that someday we won't be able to get on a plane or in a government building or do anything without this chip being scanned. Could this possibly be the prophesied Mark of the Beast, as in Revelation 13:16 we were warned against in the Bible? It was described as a mark put on the forehead of those who worshipped the Beast (devil).

Eventually, if not sooner, they will do away with paper money and coins, as now they are saying it's dirty and can contain the virus, have a cashless society, and then go to all digital. This way, they, the government, can track what we spend and buy. And control our money. That's been planned for a long time. So now that we are used to scanning in our credit or debit cards, we can just as well scan in our hand or arm or wherever the mark is. Expect a big backlash to this HR666 and to mandated vaccines.

All the time, you can be tested positive for the coronavirus even if you've had a flu shot.

How Plagues (Pandemics) Can Change Societies

All is not lost, however, as from some of the lowest times in our world society, plagues and wars have visited, such as one of the outbreaks of the great Plague in the 1600s, where 60 percent of Europe's people died of the plague, that some good can come out of a plague or a pandemic, so that society is never the same again. Although it's hard to see any good coming out of this one. It did give people a chance to slow down and to contemplate and to enjoy family more and what was worthwhile. But after?

Before the Great Plague, in the 1600s, the people lived their lives how the Catholic Church told them to. The church had always told the people what was right and wrong and gave them direction. People thought the plague was the wrath of God. Priests and bishops lost their credibility because they could not explain the plague or offer a cure. Quite a few priests died giving last rites to persons dying of the plague. As a result, the people began to stray from the church and question its teachings. The church lost tens of thousands of members from the plague and they lost faith in its authority. They realized the clergy were just ordinary men, as some refused to minister to some of the dying and many abandoned their posts. Many new priests, who took the place of so many who died, were not very educated, so the church's teachings weakened. Some people had left their wealth to the Catholic Church so it became rich. It's still the richest denomination in the world. There were several Great Plagues in Europe in its grip from the 1300s to the late seventeenth century.

A plague can change economics, social elevations, and bring on serious change. From out of that, one of the worst plagues in 1395, the workers were far less, as so many had died of the plague, therefore, those workers remaining were paid more and some given a piece of land. They made the most of their situation, and some became fairly rich, hiring help themselves, and some became wealthy enough to sponsor some of the greatest artists of that time, such as Da Vinci, and Van Dyke, the Flemish artist, Michelangelo, and Rembrandt. Therefore, the Renaissance was sprung, an era of great art and sculpture. I have seen some of these great paintings, including the Mona Lisa, and famous statues in the Louvre Museum in Paris.

Also, because so many priests became ill and many died after giving the last sacraments to those dying with the plague, then that made the Catholic Church not nearly as strong as it used to as it had pretty much ruled the world. And the priests could not explain the black plague and why it was visited on so many hundreds of thousands of people. Therefore, priests and clergy reputations declined. Thus, out of this came the Protestant Reformation, the rise again of Christianity, headed by Martin Luther, taking more of a mainstream course and different denominations were started then. Luther started the Lutheran Church. Today, the Lutheran Church is very progressive with PC and recognition of same sex marriage, etc., and very liberal. Without the results of the plague, lessening the hold of the Catholic Church, there probably never would have been a Protestant Reformation.

We wonder how this pandemic of early 2020 will change our society. Rest assured it will and horrible to think, but it might in some ways we would rather not want to hear. All of this protocol now, such as wearing of masks, distancing, etc., could become the new normal. Some good might come out of it, as its possible people will have had more time to reflect and to maybe change their ways. More family time was not all that bad as kids and parents stayed home during the pandemic wave. But also some things not so good has come out of it. Economic depravity, with so many out of work, and so many businesses closed. Parents were not prepared to home school their kids, and some people and even kids became depressed. Some turned to drink and drugs. And loneliness set in. There was more domestic abuse. We are a social society and we need other people. The cruelest punishment in the prisons is to isolate the misbehaving prisoners into the hold, with no contact with anyone else nor the outside.

The ironic thing of it all is that plagues usually last four to five months and then they run their course. Called herd immunity. So if left alone, and the elderly had been quarantined, who were finally determined to be the ones more apt to catch the virus, and anyone had researched who was more likely to have the virus, then the workers would still be working and schools not closed down. Knee-jerk reaction, which is a known reaction of the Leftists. It would have not taken long to get the pattern even from China and other countries.

So if you don't want these lockdowns to continue or go back into place again for "whatever" reasons, vote the extremist Congress persons, governors, and mayors out and look for patriotic people to run for office. Vote for the ones who actually love America and want to represent you, the people, as it should be. Ones that are constitutionally aware that have values, family and personal, and have accomplished something in life, not just because they are rich or will bring home the gravy.

Now do you see Why *Your Vote Matters*? We must get accountable people into office this November. It's a crucial time that we need a Republican Congress, both Houses and a Republican president in order to bring this economy back and keep America great. Republicans have a reputation of economic success with capitalism. It does work. We don't need a divided House, bent on destroying the president. We badly need to kick the present House Speaker, Pelosi, out, who has no more respect than to tear up our President's State of Union Speech after his speech, while panning for the cameras. That act was totally pre-planned by the way. What an example for our young. No respect for our president. That was totally infantile, like she was in the first grade. In all of history, there's never been a House Speaker who misbehaved in this way. She should never be elected again. "Do you hear me, San Francisco?"

CHAPTER 58

Five Trillion Down the Drain

[From the *Washington Examiner* March 24, 2020, excerpted from an article by Stephen Moore.]

Government is not the solution; government is the problem.

—*Ronald Reagan*

Everyone should read Robert Higgs's economic classic *Crisis and Leviathan*. The critical warning of this book is that government always uses a crisis—from the Civil War, to the Great Depression of the '30s, to World War II to expand their power, but what happens is it is not for just during the emergency that seems to set precedent for what happens after. Emergencies tend to grab the power and make it stronger of government permanently.

Our government is already the largest enterprise in the history of the world, spending short of 5 trillion a year in Washington and at least another

1 trillion at the state and local level. NO wonder our taxes are high.

We wonder how the health security system in America with 2 trillion of federal tax dollars spent was so unprepared and ill-equipped? And in spite of all of these trillions, our politicians will still be pedaling Medicare for All—and in spite of this present huge bailout. Is there anyone out there who now thinks we should expand the State's control of the medical care system after this debacle?

Why is it that Germany and Japan quickly developed diagnostic testing for the new virus and South Korea was soon testing large number so quickly? Here's the problems at the CDC (Center for Disease Control) as they are at the center of this calamity. It gets $10 billion funding, and they did not have a screen or easily administered test to find out if people had contracted the virus. These failures cost our nation some 1 trillion of lost output.

"Of course, Trump's adversaries blame him on his proposed cuts in funding at the National Institute of Health and the CDC. But those cuts never happened. It's doubtful more money would have made any difference in this particular crisis. The CDC was no doubt too preoccupied in looking into gun control, climate change, and gay and transgender issues," Moore declares.

Moore goes on to say, "Just how is it that in our advanced technological age, over 50 years after we had the capability of putting a man on the moon and we have cellphones for under $100 that have the computing power of all the computers used during the World War II era, that the government planners had no contingency plan to deal with a pandemic? So as a result, we have been struck with a communist-style shutdown of the entire American economy with curfews, food rationing, and the equivalent of martial law in major cities."

But the politicians now say to solve the destruction, we need more government authority and bigger budgets. More programs and more bureaucrats and more giveaways?

Estimates are now 2 trillion to 3 trillion of new government spending. Those types of stimulus plans have never worked. And they may cause long-term damage to the economy even more than this virus already has. Nancy Pelosi wants not just temporary, but permanently paid sick leave for workers, underwritten by financially strapped businesses. The liberal Dems see this crisis as something to not go to waste in advancing their liberal agenda. Talk about opportunists in a time like this.

If any good comes out of all of this, we will have more Americans who have learned that, as Ronald Reagan put it, *"Government is not the solution, government is the problem!"*

CHAPTER 59

America Finally Comes Back Together to Patriotically Fight the Virus

From bipartisan packages passed by Congress to medical personnel fighting selflessly on the front lines this plague, that some said would divide us further, has actually achieved a unity not seen since perhaps World War II. Workers have banded together to fight and to try to defeat this indivisible enemy.

President Trump said, "It's been really amazing to see these big strong powerful companies, and in some cases small companies, step up and make a lot of great products for what we are going through and what we will continue to be going through for a while."

Thread Internationals Day Old Company, manufacturer of backpacks, in Pittsburg had to lay off fifteen workers when the shutdown hit. Then they teamed up with several other companies to retool his operation to make a product: medical-grade face shields that medical personnel use. He had hired all fifteen workers back and had plans to hire a lot more. He said, "I felt like we are supplying the front lines in a war." Well, it is a war with an invisible enemy.

During World War II, I remember what really helped to win the war was the large airplane companies and others retooled up to make everything needed for the war effort. Douglas Aircraft, North American, and Northrup, to name a few, became huge aircraft factories geared for building war bombers and fighter airplanes, parachutes, and other needs related to the war effort. They worked round-the-clock shifts in order to get as many out as possible. That is when women joined the work force, due to so many men on the front lines fighting the war, as the symbol was Rosie the Riveter. Haven't been able to get women to stay in the home since.

Before the end of the war, the government sold war savings bonds to help offset the huge costs of the war. Might be a good idea now, and that I ventured to President Trump. To have celebrities in his corner to make commercials and sell them as was a good investment when they mature. This has been a war against an invisible enemy, so why not war bonds?

Ford and General Motors halted normal production lines and retooled to produce ventilators, working round the clock. A coalition of nine t-shirt and hoodie makers retooled to produce face masks. Honeywell, an aerospace manufacturer, hired five hundred more workers in their Rhode Island plant to make N95 medical face masks.

Ansheuser-Busch, Pernod Ricard USA, and Bacardi were among dozens of breweries that produced hand sanitizers.

Bloom Energy, a fuel cell maker, retrofitted hundreds of older models of ventilators in California.

ASO LLC, a medical supply manufacturer, produced 1.2 million medical gloves for healthcare workers.

The New Balance Sporting Apparel Company met experts at Harvard and MIT to see what was needed and altered its production to spinout protective masks. They put in twenty-hour days because the passion was there to fight the battle.

AAON in Oklahoma ramped up production of HVAC systems for overstressed hospitals that were expanding particularly for temporary hospitals.

American Leather Holdings in Dallas put a halt to making furniture and shifted to production of protective masks and gowns.

A Rhode Island sporting goods company, along with others teamed up with other sporting companies and was soon manufacturing 20,000 face shields a day. "We love to help people," he said. They worked twenty hours a day.

That is capitalism at work, meeting up with a renewal of patriotism in this country. There's a silver lining in almost everything.

CHAPTER 60

Has the Public Lost Patience With the Lockdown?

There is a growing concern, impatience, and grumbling with this never-ending lockdown. Patience is clearly wearing thin.

America has always been a country of doing. We have been defined as such, as that is and what new things we are doing.

We have been on the move ever since we were founded. A bunch of nomads if you will.

The population centers have changed with the westward movement. As the pioneers ventured west and then the gold prospectors ventured to California and Alaska, we found "there's gold in them thar' hills," not only in the gold nuggets found in creeks and rivers, but in the form of new land, new ventures, and a future not ever seen before.

We built hundreds of miles of railroad tracks so we could more easily travel back and forth across the country. It was a huge celebration in May of 1869 when the east and western part connected with the Union Pacific and the Central Pacific railroads finally met at Promontory Summit in Utah Territory. Then women could more easily travel alone, where generally they could not before.

All the major population centers, such as Philadelphia, New York, and Boston, were thriving centers of huge economic activity. The Southern aristocracy, which had dominated before the Civil War, lost out to the Northern capitalists. Commerce and industry were the main modes of economic life.

We have a market society, with interaction, socialization, and chance-taking is in our genes. This rugged individualism, in fact, breeds an intense interdependence.

The destruction of the market economy is justified by the fact that it makes us more prosperous over time, and that is what we really want. For an overwhelming majority of Americans, any form of socialism used to idle our days, just seems like a bad prospect.

There's been an argument of what businesses are essential and nonessential. In the long run, the notion of essential industries does not make much sense. We are all interconnected to everyone else in the US. Shut down the restaurants and they default on their loans, putting pressure on the banks which increases a strain on credit for other businesses, then they have to lay off employees, as they close their doors. For a short time, the government can shut its doors and shut us down, and we rely on federal stimulus and easy access to money from the Federal Reserve, to take care of us in the meantime, but eventually, the money runs out and we are going to collapse, which will bring others down in turn.

This is not new. This story has been around several times in our history. In 1872, there was financial panic in New York City. But the country was not so integrated then, so it did not make a lot of difference. But starting in 1819, several panics have washed across the country every few years, starting with certain industries, then spreading near and far. We had a Great Recession downturn under Obama in 2008–2010 where 8.7 million private-sector jobs were lost. Unemployment was high. Partly due to overregulation and mismanagement of the funds. He also blamed Bush for years for his inheriting Bush's so-called mess. Many companies moved out of the US due to heavy regulation and taxes, taking a large chunk of taxes with them. Then Trump came along and got rid of a lot of the over regulation measures and was business friendly, so that the economy started to take off again, until this sudden, out of nowhere, coronavirus shutdown literally destroyed the economy overnight.

That's what's going to happen if this shutdown lasts much longer. You are destroying every kind of business and then everything else will fall apart in time. Every industry and economic activity depends on every other industry. Our fate is determined by economics. The only way I can do new and interesting things is if you get to do them too. That is not happening now.

We always want more. And we can't have more if we are all sitting at home watching Netflix. The key to our prosperity was a US-diversified economy with commerce and industry proliferating across the country.

The upshot of all of this is that our children and grandchildren are going to have to pay through the nose for all of these stimulus bailouts. Much of which billions are added by liberal Speaker Pelosi as goodies to fit her agenda to further the cause of the liberal/leftists, thus spending billions more on those added benefits, like Planned Parenthood bailouts, *Cannabis*, and illegal immigration, the Kennedy Center for the Arts, PBS, and she also wants all states to have votes by absentee only (a great way to ballot harvest by the way, which brings on much voter fraud).

We need to get back to work. We are a nation of workers and always have been. We need to be productive. Working at home, if we are lucky, and home-schooling our kids if we can, does not take the place of participation at our work, nor of kids in school. Depression is setting in with so many out of work and out of income, causing a rise in suicides and other maladies. Medical needs are not being met. We don't even know for sure if masks (some experts tell us that masks, breathing in our own bacteria and CO_2 is not healthy either) and social distancing really helps or not or even washing our hands twenty times a day. Heard of herd immunity? If left alone, that builds antibodies, that give us immunity. That is what vaccines do.

We do know we are tired of the government (governors and mayors) telling us what to do with our very personal lives. Maybe we have had a taste of socialism, where the government tells you what to do. And it does not feel all that good. Our Constitution is set up so that we, the people, are to tell the government what to do. Not the other way around.

One thing for sure, this country will not stand still for a second shutdown. Do you think?

If there's anything to gain through all of this, it might be that it's given us a chance to step back and look at the scheme of things, to look at ourselves, to enjoy family and friends more, to maybe change our goals, and to perhaps search for something more meaningful in our lives. We need the spiritual contact that our churches give us, as governors deem churches as nonessential businesses.

Interaction, socialization, and taking of chances is who we are. While we appreciate that people have died from the Covid-19, so have many more died from the regular flu and overdose and other natural causes. We did not shut down for them. So why now? We are all essential workers, none are nonessential. We need our interdependence and our individualism. That's who we are as a country and as individuals. So let us get back to work and to school and get on with our lives as we have known them. Enough is enough!

CHAPTER 61

Civil Unrest: The Protests and Rioting Over a Case of Police Brutality

When asked by a bystander as he left Independence Hall, "What type of government did you form? *"A Republic if we can keep it."*
—Benjamin Franklin.

Barbarism is never finally defeated; given propitious circumstances, men and women who seem quite orderly will commit every conceivable atrocity.
—Writing in the dark days of 1939, Evelyn Waugh noted

Oh! Oh! Our ship hits the perfect storm—rocking to and fro—back and forth

If the market crashes, COVID comes back, cities burn, police are defunded, and murdering hornets sting me in the ass, I'm still voting Trump!

Organized Chaos

We were not even over the coronavirus scare and lockdown, and we were just starting to steer our Ship of State to head for a more even keel with smoother waters, when on May 25, 2020, a Minneapolis policeman held a black man, Mr. George Floyd, down, after arresting him and kept his knee on his neck until he expired while other officers stood around. Now it is reported that Mr. Floyd had a record of several arrests and was in prison, is a very huge man, and had given police problems before.

Now there is no excuse for what happened, as people were asking this policeman to stop, so he is being charged with manslaughter, and we grieve for his life and his family. Of course, there were videos of it all so that went viral. Protests broke out immediately. First in Minneapolis, but then extended to all major cities. While we can all extend our sympathy and understanding on the reason for this, and there was no excuse for that, what happened after was intruders/rioters from all over joined in and started looting, rioting, and burning in many major cities all over the country. Starting in Minneapolis, moving to New York, Atlanta, and Los Angeles, Chicago, etc. Such places as Macy's in downtown New York City (of *Miracle on Thirty-Fourth Street* fame) and St. John's Church in Washington, DC, and CNN's building in Atlanta were burned.

Organized groups, reportedly funded by George Soros and other Marxist elites, joined in and all were dressed the same and carried the same signs and used the same weapons on the police. Appearing to be well prepared, they would carry ammo and water bottles in a car which they would park along the protestor's parade route and have them ready as they ran out of ammo. Such groups as *Black Lives Matter* and *Antifa* were among the outsiders. President Trump and Attorney General Barr want to consider the Antifa as an anti-terrorist organization.

To prove the Antifa protestors and rioters are funded, here's an ad on the internet in about first week of so of June 2020.

Protestors Needed (Dtown)

"We are Antifa and we're willing to pay up to 1,000 people $25 an hour for protestors in Lincoln, NE, and Omaha, NE. Basically, we want to cause as much chaos and destruction as possible. We have a bail fund and legal counsel set up. This will take place every night through the BLM protest on June 13. You will be paid nightly and can come and go as you please. We want chaos to help further our agenda."

What was NOT reported and no sympathy for David Dorn, a retired BLACK police captain, that was killed by the rioters, as he tried to protect his friend's pawnshop business. Why were there not protests over that? No protests over that. Black on black killing is not protested, only white on black. I thought Black Lives Matter?

What This Is Really All About

Hold your hats, folks! What you're watching is the ancient battle between those who have a stake in society and would like to preserve it and those who don't and seek to destroy it. Tucker Carlson, host of *Tucker Carlson Tonight* on Fox News, went on to say, "The ideologues will tell you that the problem is race relations or capitalism or police brutality or global warming. The real cause is deeper than that and it's far darker. What you are watching is the ancient battle between those who have a stake in society and would like to preserve it, and those who don't and seek to destroy it."

What is not complicated is the snarling criminality of those smashing storefronts, setting fires to cars and police stations, and sending innocent passersby to the hospital or the morgue.

While most of the country is locked down by the say so of the health police, enforced by power-mad governors and those aspiring to power in city councils and mayor's offices throughout the country, abetted by virtue-signaling sheep who scream at their neighbors if they get within six feet of them or appear in public without a mask, while thousands of vicious criminals are given leave to loot and burn and pillage while the rules about social distancing are suspended so long as people are bent not upon making their living but destroying the livings of others.

Another outcome of the rioting and looting causing the police to act more pro-actively and the leaders to invoke curfews, causing the anti-police sector to start chanting and carrying signs that say Defund the Police. While this may sound great to some, have they ever thought about what they would do if they were being robbed or some other crime against them or need police to help them when they have an accident, direct traffic, call the ambulance, etc.? And make a report to be used by the insurance company. Sure, the Hollywood and other elites are all for it as they live behind gated communities and walls and have security at the gate, as well as many have their own security bodyguards carrying guns, which they try to get rid of for others. Regardless of our Second Amendment Rights.

Speaker Pelosi Outed

(Two photos here of Pelosi and her black caucus kneeling.)

During the rioting in DC, Speaker Pelosi had a fit over President Trump carrying a Bible and going to the church close by that was burned and with photos of him in front of the church, and she called it a photo-op for his re-election. She accused him of pandering to his Republican base. Then a few days later, she and fellow congressmen in the Black Caucus dressed in African garb, with African Kente cloth stoles draped over their shoulders, knelt in silent prayer for 8 ½ minutes, the length of time Floyd was under that policeman's knee. This was an Akan royal and sacred cloth worn only in times of extreme importance and was the cloth of kings—and it comes from Ghana. People from Ghana were affronted. This Kente cloth is not a US political prop.

Could that have been a photo-op? Was she possibly pandering to *her* base? She's more than a hypocrite. It was over the top, as it was carefully choreographed for the cameras. Pelosi owes an apology to Ghana. Never in all of my years has a speaker done so many outlandish things, to get photo-ops. She made a mockery of the seriousness of the actions that brought this incident to light.

Coach Anthony Dungy, former professional football player and coach in the National Football League, tweeted, "Those of us who call ourselves Christian must demonstrate the qualities of the One we claim to follow, Jesus Christ."

He goes on to say that "America is in a very sad place today. We have seen a man die senselessly, at the hands of the very people who are supposed to be protecting our citizens. We have seen people protest this death by destroying property and dreams of people in their own community, the very people they are protesting for. We have anger and bitterness winning out over logic and reason.

"Justice needs to be served, but in seeking justice, we can't fall into the trap of prejudging every police officer we see. Peaceful protest should never end with arson and looting. We do not have license to perform criminal acts because we are angry.

"What is the answer? We can no longer be silent. As Dr. King said many years ago, 'Injustice anywhere is a threat to justice everywhere.' But we can't go forward with judgmental bitter spirits. We need to be proactive but do it in the spirit of trying to help make things better. It has to be ALL churches taking a stand and saying, 'We are going to be on the forefront of meaningful dialogue and meaningful change. We have to speak the truth. We are fighting against Satan and his kingdom of 'spiritual darkness.'"

In the words of the Apostle Paul, "Do not be overcome by evil, but overcome evil with good" (Romans 12:21 NIV).

Coach Dougey shares a prayer for our nation.

- *I agree that our nation is in deep trouble and that we are in desperate need of God's help. You can count on me. I am praying for our nation.*
- *I am praying for healing against the sickness of sin that has divided our country.*
- *I am praying for wisdom and direction for President Trump, Vice President Pence, for governors, mayors, and officials in cities experiencing destruction and civil unrest. I am praying that they will rely upon God in every situation and for the decisions they make.*
- *I am praying for comfort for George Floyd's family members.*

- *I am praying for God to pour out His Holy Spirit across our land and touch the hearts of people with peace and love for one another.*
- *I am praying that God will forgive our sins and heal our land.*
- *I am praying that God will change hearts and heal this divide in our nation.*

CHAPTER 62

From the Left: The Democrats Aren't in Love with Biden!

How the heck could this be? What an excuse for a candidate. What on earth are they thinking of pushing him in the forefront of the race? He denounces what is going on while at the same time he was a senator for thirty-six years and vice president for eight years, so I would venture he had a lot to say about past laws, activities, and what was done. Yet he is second-guessing the president and stating what he had done better. At the same time, Trump had already done in most cases what Biden is saying he would do if he were president. Biden blames Trump for all the problems of the country. How soon we forget who is really responsible here.

Hiding for months in his basement studio, where his every word is monitored and edited out, then it's time for him to come out and hold rallies. I seriously doubt his health and stamina would stand up to very many rallies at this time The Democrats on his team wants him to stay in the basement, as they can control what he says there. They realize that he might not hold up too well with Trump in debates. And a lot may depend on who he picks for his vice president. He has said it would be a woman so as of this writing in June 2020, there are six women on his short list. Elizabeth Warren, Kamala Harris, Susan Rice, Atlanta Mayor, Keisha Bottoms, a black Florida Rep. Val Demings, a black woman, New Mexico Gov. Michelle Lujan Grisham, a Latina. Whomever he chooses, should he win, the VP will be very important and no doubt would end up having to take over—either officially or unofficially as Biden remained a figurehead.

The top presidential debates will be crucial this year, and it would be a good idea if the Republicans requested six debates instead of three. We will see how well Biden holds up in debates with Trump.

CHAPTER 63

Patriotism Is Not Dead

Lincoln spoke of a "great task remaining before us" after the historic battle in Gettysburg, Pennsylvania.

"*That from these honored devotion to that cause for which they gave the last full measure of devotion—that we here highly resolve that these dead shall not have died in vain—that this nation, under God, shall have a new birth of freedom—and that government of the people, by the people, shall not perish from the earth.*"

As we approach July 4, 2020, as the day we celebrate our independence, it is time to pause and remember from whence we came and why we are here. It is time to reflect on just how we have been able to maintain our freedom and independence even these many years, but with hope, we can keep our freedom many more years for the sake of our children and grandchildren.

It is a time for parades; however, many may have been cancelled due to the pandemic or by governors. But we can still fly our flags and sing songs to our great nation: "Mine Eyes Have Seen the Glory and America" and "God Bless America." And meet with our family and close friends in the backyard barbecues. As we listen and see the fireworks coming from different directions.

What has made this the greatest nation of all time? The natural urge to remain free and to maintain this government—by the people and for the people. Unshackled by government by over-regulation or control. And because we were formed a more perfect union under God. Our founders were believers in freedom and faith and were so far-sighted to develop the Constitution—no doubt with God's help—that still remains our standard for laws, and the most perfect and successful country in the whole world. No wonder so many have wanted to come to this free nation.

But our freedoms may be stretched and forces prevail to tighten the screws of our very fiber, to take over our country, and to make it into something we may not recognize. This must never happen, and this we must fight for our freedoms, just as have so many fought in the trenches, in the air, to protect, and in the streets to peacefully protest and to save our great country. We owe such a debt of gratitude for those with the guts to fight for our great country.

Many have come back in coffins or so many wounded and dismembered that we owe a debt of gratitude for their endurance.

Long Live America, May She Stand as a Living Tribute to the World! And God Bless America! Long May She Live!

CHAPTER 64

Where Does our Voyage Go from Here? Vote!

Hickory dickory dock,
our country is on the clock,
the clock strikes one
we owe a ton,
hickory dickory dock

I s our clock running out? Are we concerned about our voyage from here now? We well could find that we have one last chance to vote to seriously keep on our course, before we hit that iceberg. That is the election of November 2020. It may well be the most crucial election of our time, and maybe of all time in the history of our country. It's the taking over of the Socialists versus the conservatives/capitalists=Freedom.

This is serious business now, folks. We look through our periscope and see there are icebergs in our ocean almost in our sights. Are we going to keep on sailing right into a gigantic one, with no escape, and end up in Davy Jones' Locker? Or are we going to keep on course now and go in a similar direction that Trump has led us and the country voted for in 2016 in—a far better direction away from these icy dangers?

Our vote is so important that we can write history with it.

It may be our last chance to control the course of our country. With more and more government control, higher taxes, poor economy, an even greater movement toward socialism versus freedom, is what we can expect if the socialists win and control our country. All of your freedoms will vanish overnight, to include property rights, right to worship, right to carry a gun, and all your God-given Constitutional Rights, down the drain.

Getting rid of capitalism and no balanced budget, we are reminded of this accounting of the stages each society goes through until its demise:

* *From bondage to spiritual faith;*
* *From abundance to complacency;*
* *From spiritual faith to great courage;*
* *From complacency to apathy;*
* *From courage to liberty;*
* *From apathy to dependence;*
* *From liberty to abundance;*
* *From dependence back into bondage.*

At what stage do you think we may be in now?

The average age of the world's greatest civilizations from the beginning of history has been about two hundred years. Our country is now one of the longest-lived societies of its kind in history. Could it be because much thought was given by our Founders to establish a Republic (not a democracy)? Could they have realized that human behavior never changes, so based much of the Constitution on that concept? They had a great deal of faith and were men of strong convictions and faith in God. And huge insight. They were intelligent persons, who loved their new country and went through the Revolutionary War to walk away from a tyrannical government, high taxes, and lack of freedom of religion, to establish their new country in a different freer manner. They would probably roll over in their graves now if they knew what is happening to their specially planned country, they fought so hard for independence.

A democracy is always temporary in nature; it simply cannot exist as a permanent form of government. It will continue to exist until the time that voters discover that they can vote themselves generous gifts from the public treasury. From then on, the majority always votes for the candidates who promise the most benefits from the public treasury, with the result that <u>every democracy</u> will finally collapse due to loose fiscal policy, which is <u>always followed by a dictatorship.</u>

When the time ever comes when we shall go to pieces
It will be from inward corruption
From the DISREGARD OF RIGHT PRINCIPLES
From losing sight of the fact that
RIGHTEOUS EXALTETH A NATION!
—Francis Grunke

The liberal element apparently in charge now in our society honestly seems to believe socialism will work for our country. Never mind that it has been tried in many other countries in the form of Socialism, Marxism, Communism, and Fascism and other similar forms which have been tried for thousands of years, but <u>all</u> have failed.

Socialist types of governance have never worked. They have failed miserably over and over. The powers that want this so desperately mistakenly seem to believe that <u>they</u> would do it differently, while the forces behind this movement believe they would benefit greatly with much more power, money, and control. But only a few will profit, and the rest will find out they are left out.

When history is overlooked and we are doing the same thing over and over, it is insanity. Albert Einstein's definition of insanity is *"doing the same thing—in our case, making the same mistakes—over and over again, and expecting different results."* "Things, such as increased taxation, schemes with expanded government management and control, have been tried many times and have been proven unsuccessful," says McGary in his book *Instantity.*

If we vote to allow this creeping decline and tyrannical rule that is when we hit the iceberg, with few lifeboats. Or are we going to vote for a free society, with a brake on spending, as President Reagan faced in 1981 and again in 1994 when the Republicans took over Congress for the first time in many long years, with their Contract with America. President Clinton, a Democrat, wisely with advice from his political adviser, Dick Morris (who is a Republican now and adviser for FOX News) corrected course toward the middle in 1994 and worked with his new Republican Congress, as they voted to cut down on welfare and working to balance the budget. We ended the twentieth century with a surplus, yet.

By 2006, when the Democrats once again took over Congress, the housing meltdown had occurred, after years of regulations for the banks, invoked by a Democrat-controlled committee, headed by Barney Frank, mandating that banks must provide loans for houses even for sometimes questionable borrowers. "Everyone should own a home," they said. When the housing crises came, the stock market went down, and unemployment started to escalate. The same problems of economic meltdown are occurring all over the world now, due to lack of fiscal responsibility, along with too many social programs. Europe is in serious trouble, for much of the same reasons. How America goes, goes the rest of the world.

Change WE can believe in?

In reaction and because "change" sounded good to many, we voted for our first (not even half) African American, who is actually as much Arab than African American for president. His name is even Arabic. He promised change. But has it been the change we thought he was talking about? In fact, he has kept few of the promises he made when he was campaigning. As Kevin McGary in his book, *Instantity*, pointed out, we voted for probably the least experienced person for president, as our CEO, in all of our history. Our captain of our ship has never nor has any of his staff or czars ever even run a lemonade stand. They are mostly academics or lawyers, with absolutely no business or management experience. Our Ship of State is a huge business and our president, the CEO, McGary states in his brilliant book, "While we, the voters, are the Board of Directors who hired a completely inexperienced CEO." Would most owners of large ships hire a captain with little or no experience? Would you go as a passenger on that ship?

Therefore, we, as the Board of Directors, with our votes, can fire any incompetent CEO captain and crew and start all over on our voyage with someone with more business experience who is not bent on changing our country into something we cannot recognize.

Some say it would be going backward, but to change course we must stop and sometimes go backwards or in a different direction in order to correct course and head in a safe course for our Ship of State. We have to insist to our representatives that they correct course or leave office.

A president who then appoints Justices in his or her own ideology, and then instead of interpreting the Constitution, as most Supremes have done since our inception, they vote ideologically on all issues, this is not according to the Constitution. So no surprise to find a 5 to 4 vote in most cases. Along ideological lines.

He has drastically cut spending to our military to 1919 level or less and would likely turn them over to the UN. We are far less secure now. What our votes did!

What kind of world would that be for our Ship of State? Were we in danger of losing our sovereignty? Or could we still lose it later on?

Along comes Trump and our ship is righted again.

When have been our most successful periods of economic security?

In studying our history, since the 1900s, it appears that the period of times when we have had more prosperity and we grew were when we had either a Republican President and Congress or at least a Republican Senate and President/and or both. That is because more conservative representatives are more apt to vote for individual rights, for balanced budgets, are pro-business growth, and to cut spending.

The more conservative representatives believe in individual freedom with the unalienable rights in this country that anyone can make it good, can rise above any difficulties or lack of money to make something of their selves. The liberal elements in our country seem to push toward more dependency with more and more social programs and generous spending, with no faith in that individuals can make it without the government paying it all.

Many people of faith did not vote. When people of faith (records show that 80 percent of the country say that they believe in God) do not vote, it contributes to the downfall of our country. Even if you are not real happy with the candidate, would he be a man or woman of faith, as our Founders were? Does he really love America? Does he have experience in economics, business, or administration? Or just plain common sense? Does he believe in our values of family and in our freedoms? Is he a real leader? Is he more fiscally conservative? Surely, he would do better in most areas.

What if China refused to lend more and called our loan? They are starting to have fiscal problems, there, also, so they may need the money.

We also must have a Congress that listens to the people and is not just concerned about their next election, becoming rich, to what lobbyists they are beholden to, and who will be fiscally responsible in order to cut down on spending. We must have a mandate in Congress, not just for 2020, but for a period of time in order to get our Ship of State on even keel again. Our vote is what will make the difference.

We have changed course in this country several times and we can do it again. It took votes of those who believed in those changes to change course. In Newt Gingrich's recent book *Change,* he points out several times in the history of our country when we have changed course rather drastically and instrumented profound changes, heading our ship in a different direction.

Will this election save us from extinction? God only knows! But He has shown us over and over that if his children of faith—and our country was founded upon faith in Him—choose to change, ask for forgiveness, and go back in a direction of faith and determination that he can forgive, as he did over and over with the children of Israel, we could rebound. Unless we vote and try and let our voices be heard, we will never know. It is a sin against God and against our country to not vote and let our voices be heard at all levels. We can, by voting, conquer the forces that would destroy our country. This may be our last chance, and Lord willing, we have another chance. Eight years of a socialist/liberal/progressive leaning president has almost been the end of our way of life, of our freedoms, or our ability to succeed and even might have been the end of a two-party system. But thankfully, Trump came along and turned our ship in a new direction, trying to undo the harm done and to straighten out its course.

You can contact all you know to remind them to vote. You can go on e-mail, Facebook, or Twitter with reminders, the weeks before the election. You can help register people, even at your churches after services. (Yes, that is allowed.) Get off your turf and do something. We can all contribute something. The Democrats are registering a lot more voters than the Republicans are. Call your state party office to obtain registration forms.

You can be sure all of the young turning eighteen are registered to vote and let them know what is really going on, especially with the coronavirus shut down and the state and county government's trying to control our every breath, as that's socialism. Tell them that's just a small part of what they can expect under Socialist control by government.

Let them know sincerely what dire straits our Ship of State is in if we don't vote conservative and we just let the socialists run the country. The world may be far different than they have ever known. And they will be the ones paying for all of this. Little history is taught in the schools so the young may not even know what is going on nor have anything with which to compare. They do not watch the news or read the newspapers. History repeats itself, so it is vital to know something about our past history. And real history has not been taught in the schools for a long time.

Think of how our brave military, young men, and now young women, for all the history of our country, have been willing to give their lives for our freedom, and if we don't vote, then they will have died in vain. How sad! How utterly sad!

FREEDOM IS NOT FREE! It has been paid for by the blood of those who gave their lives or their bodies maimed for life for our great country.

We have to keep on voting in now in 2020 and onward and at all levels. Not only for President but for a more conservative reasonable Congress. We must educate our young in a far different manner, if we are able to change our course. They must learn history—as it repeats itself. We may not realize just how much in danger the future of our country is in. The way our debt is growing now, our children will have to pay off this enormous debt for most of their lives and their children's lives, even if this country survives for them. Do they realize this? What are we leaving our children?

Are we headed for the worst "Perfect Storm" that we have ever sailed into? Wake up, America! Before it is too late and change the course of our Ship of State before it hits that iceberg, crashes and sinks.

Can America Survive?

What we have to ask ourselves when we vote is can America survive to 2025? It will take all of us working together, speaking out, one person at a time, to millions literally rolling up our sleeves and pushing on the rudder, hitting reverse and literally swinging our Ship of State bodily around to a renewed course—full steam ahead—to make it the greatest nation in the world once again, with renewed energy and purpose to meet the challenges of the twenty-first century. To fight the "swamp" which is trying to sink us. As we did in 2016, turning the ship around with our vote. We have a Captain now who is steering our ship in the right direction for a change. We have a chance now to pursue freedom, independence, and the values our founders envisioned for this great one of a kind country.

Thank goodness for our new Captain Trump for turning our ship around as it is in smoother waters now. He has added to the military and to our ships around the globe and let the world know we are back now as a leader in the world. He says we will never be a Socialist country. As long as he is in charge, we will not be a socialist country, but what about 2024?

Our ship will not sink now, and it is sailing to smoother waters.

So full steam ahead now, and steer our ship straight to freedom and the greatest port of all. *America*!

DEFINITION OF
A VETERAN

A veteran—whether active duty, retired, national guard, or reserve—is someone who, at one point in his or her life, wrote a blank check made payable to the United States of America for an amount of "up to and including his life."

Silence is not an option! Take back, America! Let's roll!

OUR VOTE IS POWERFUL! WE ARE THE MASTER OF OUR FATE! WE CAN STEER OUR SHIP! WE CAN CHANGE COURSE! VOTE GOD 2020!

Submitted by Twila Le Page-Hughes
3535 W. 187th St.
Torrance, CA 90504
Cell 310-433-9472
E-mail twllcc09@gmail.com

Writing credits: Articles and regular columns in newspapers in two states, and as editor/publisher of *Solar Living* and *The SMART Traveler*, articles for the *Christian Bee* and regular contributor/writer to Western Journalism.com and two Republican newsletters. Author of *Our Ship of State, Don't Hit the Iceberg! VOTE!*

Bibliography

World History and Atlas, 2nd Edition, 2005

US History, Wikipedia

Wikipedia, Google

Reader's Digest.com

Instantity by Kevin McGary, Stephen Douglas
    Foundation

Western Journalism.com

From the trenches.worldreport.com

WND News Blog

FOX News

Good News Christian Ministry 5/4/12

Fellowshipofourminds.com, Dr. May 2012

The Weekly Standard, article by Jonathan V. Last,
    American Narcissus

WND worldnetdaily.com reports

The Economist, May 26, 2012

Millercenter.org/academic/American   President
    Clinton essays/biog

Canada Free Press.com, Douglas Hagen 5/16/12

Bloomberg News

Hannity Times Forum, 5/9/21

K Glass@Townhall.com

GrassfireNation.com

Fox News.com, Hannity, Laura Ingraham, Mark Levin

Rush Limbaugh on radio, The Patriot

The Wall Street Journal, April 2012

The Whistleblower, May 2012 David Kupelain

Dennis Praeger

EyeWitness to History.com

Askheritage.org

thomaswyatte.org/landmark Supreme Court Cases

Bloomberg news

Emmett Tyrell Jr. The Death of Liberalism

Jonathan Haidt: Righteous Mind

Ctjreportsform clk.org

General Web Resource in US History, Dr. Qunitard Taylor, Jr.

Scott Peck

Los Angeles Times, 2015–2020

David Limbaugh, *The Great Destroyer*

Bruce Herschensohn, *Obama's Globe*

Titanicinfomercfras.com

Cnn.com

Reader's Digest.com

TeaPartyNation.com

Press Democrat, Sonoma County, CA

Best Quotations for all Occasions, Lewis C. Henry

Hope of the Wicked by Ted Flynn

Change by Newt Gingrich

www.questia.com/library   supreme-court   appointments.jsp

www.wichovia.com/white/wscourt schools

Dr. Charles Krauthammer, MD, Columnist, Fox News Commentator

Barack Obama News

Real Clear Politics

Gary Byrne book *Crises of Character* about Hillary Clinton

Daily Mail

The LA Times

Hillary: The Other Woman, by Dolly Kyle (Clinton's Mistress)

Armageddon, by Dick Morris

Dennis Praeger, commentary on Trump and conservatism, Meaning of Life and The Worldwide Web

Lockdown May Be Greatest Mistake in History

Lou Holtz on Two Americas

Washington Post Editorial Board 3/26/20

Epoch Times

Washington Examiner

Newsmax TV and Magazine

What Women Really Want with Anne Marie Murrell, Morgan Brittany, Dr. Gian Loudon

50 Shades of Politics, Dick Morris

The Great Hoax, Greg Jarrett

Freedom Outpost on Google

Unfreedom of the Press-Mark Levin

The Worst President in History by Matt Margolis and Mark Noonan

Trumps America by Bill O'Reilly

Rogue Spooks by Dick Morris

Emmet Tyrell Is Liberalism Dead? 5-7-2012

World Net daily
Hillsdale College
Washington Post Editorial Board
Washington Examiner
The Whistleblower
Westernjournalism.com
Rightwing.org
Faith and Freedom Outpost on Google
Trending Politics Publication
Kimberly Strassell
Citizens Journal, an online newspaper
You Will Be Made to Care: The War on Faith, Family,
    and Your Freedom to Believe by Eerick Erickson
    and Bill Blankshaen
Frank Hawkins, former Intelligence Army Officer